Passage qui
communique aux deux
portiques

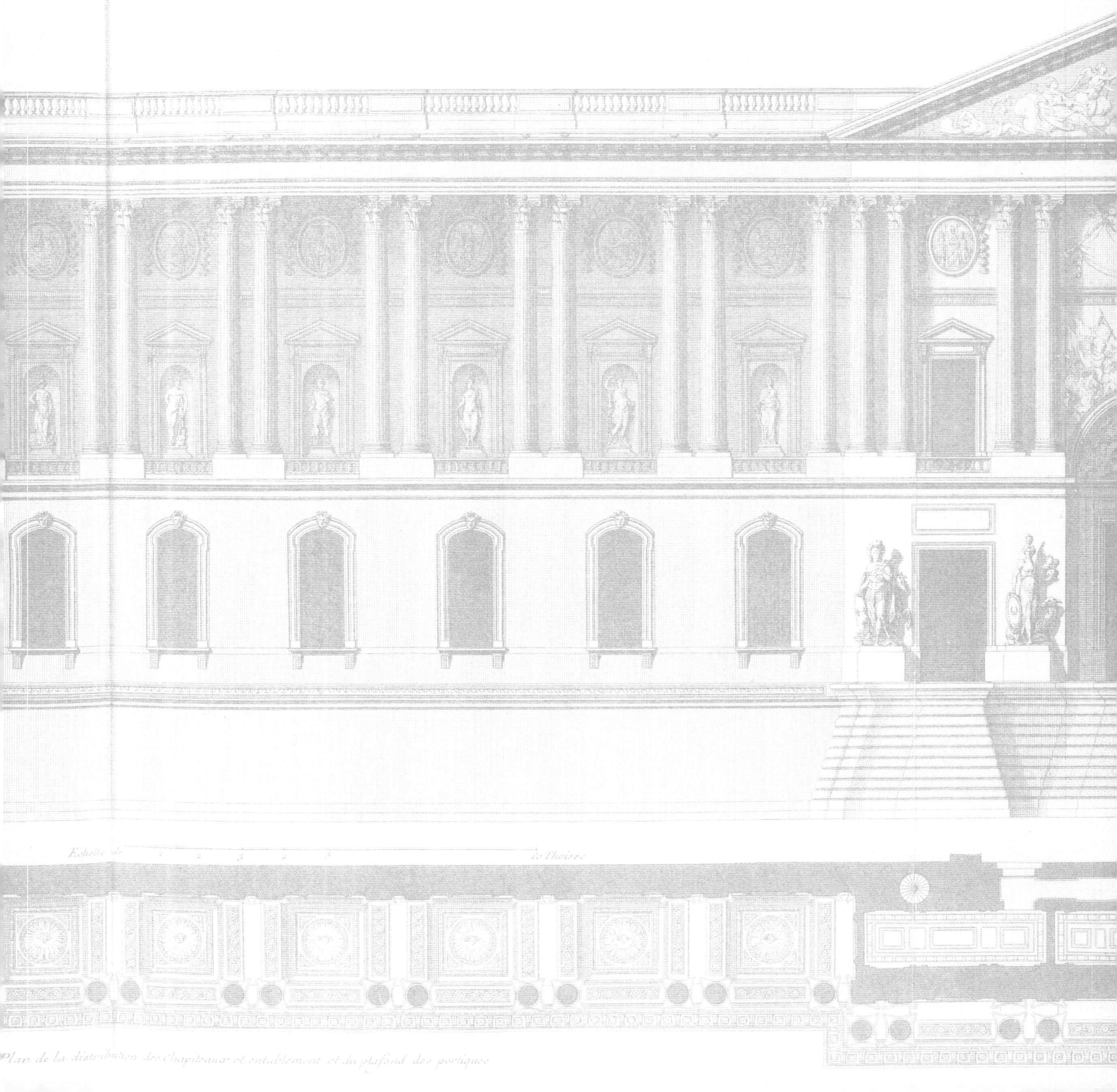

...pale façade du Louvre du côté de saint Germain l'Auxerrois, bâtie sous le reg...
Echelle de   1   2   3   4   5   10 Toises
Plan de la distribution des Chapiteaux et entablement et du plafond des portiques

Royalists to Romantics

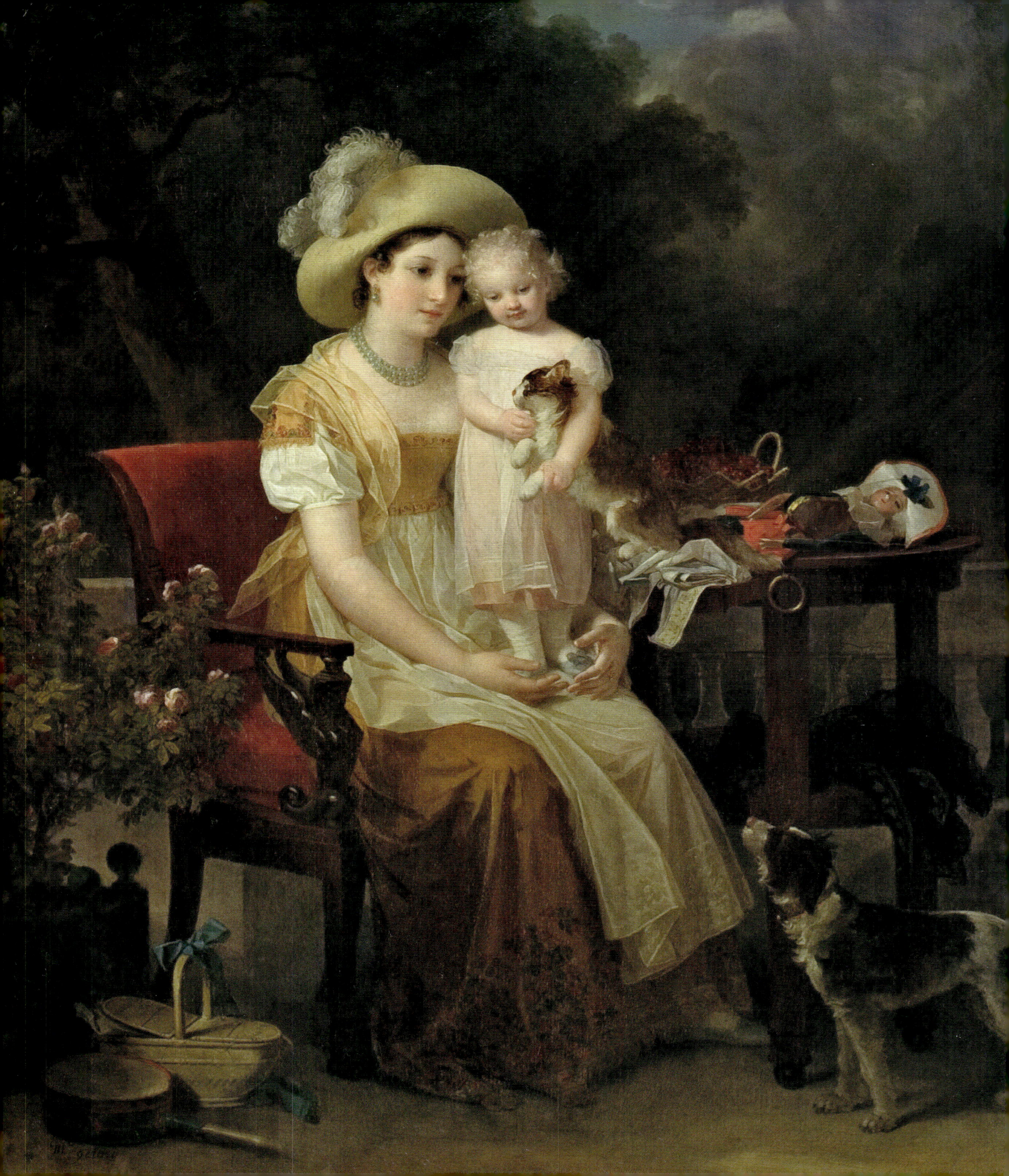

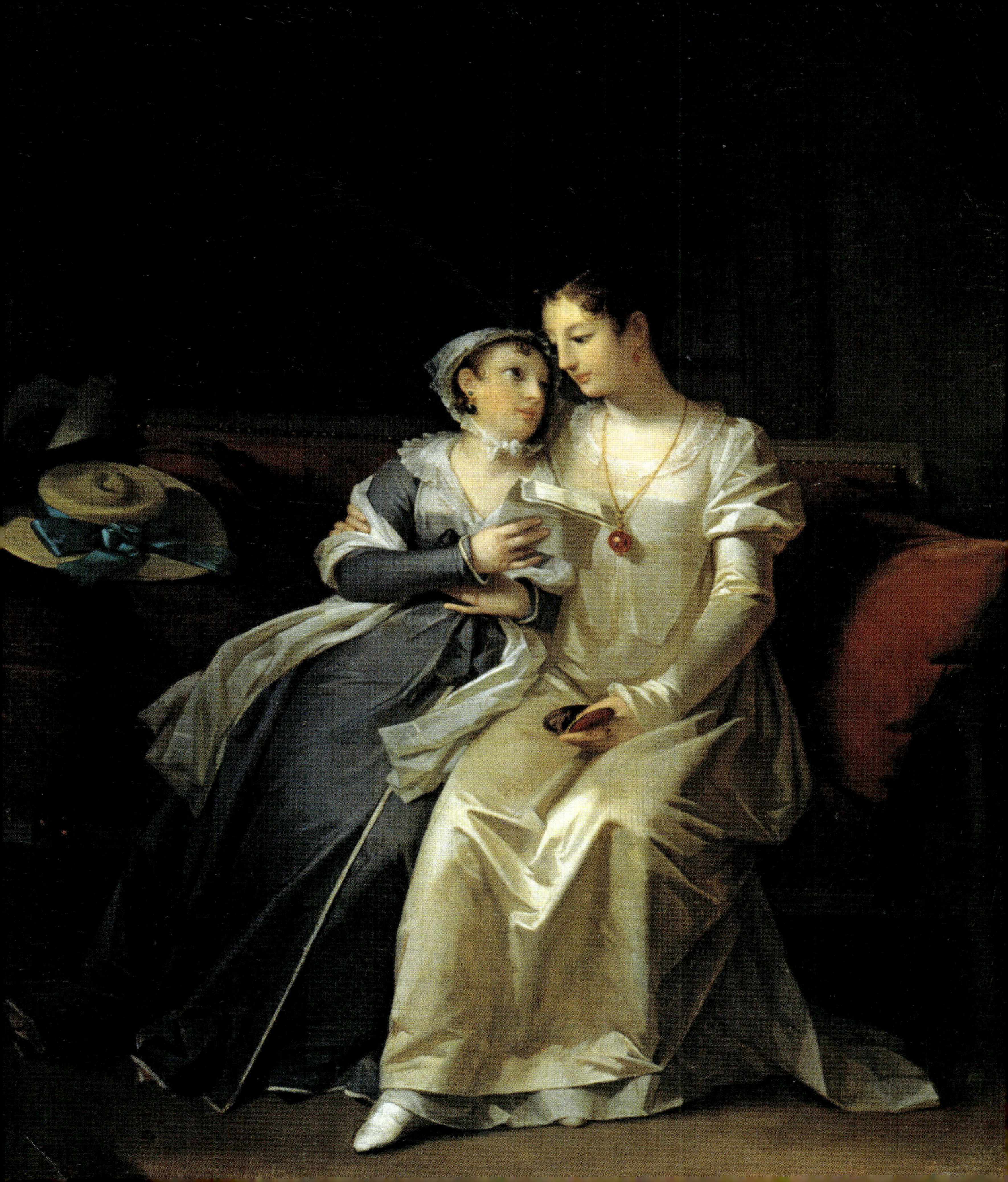

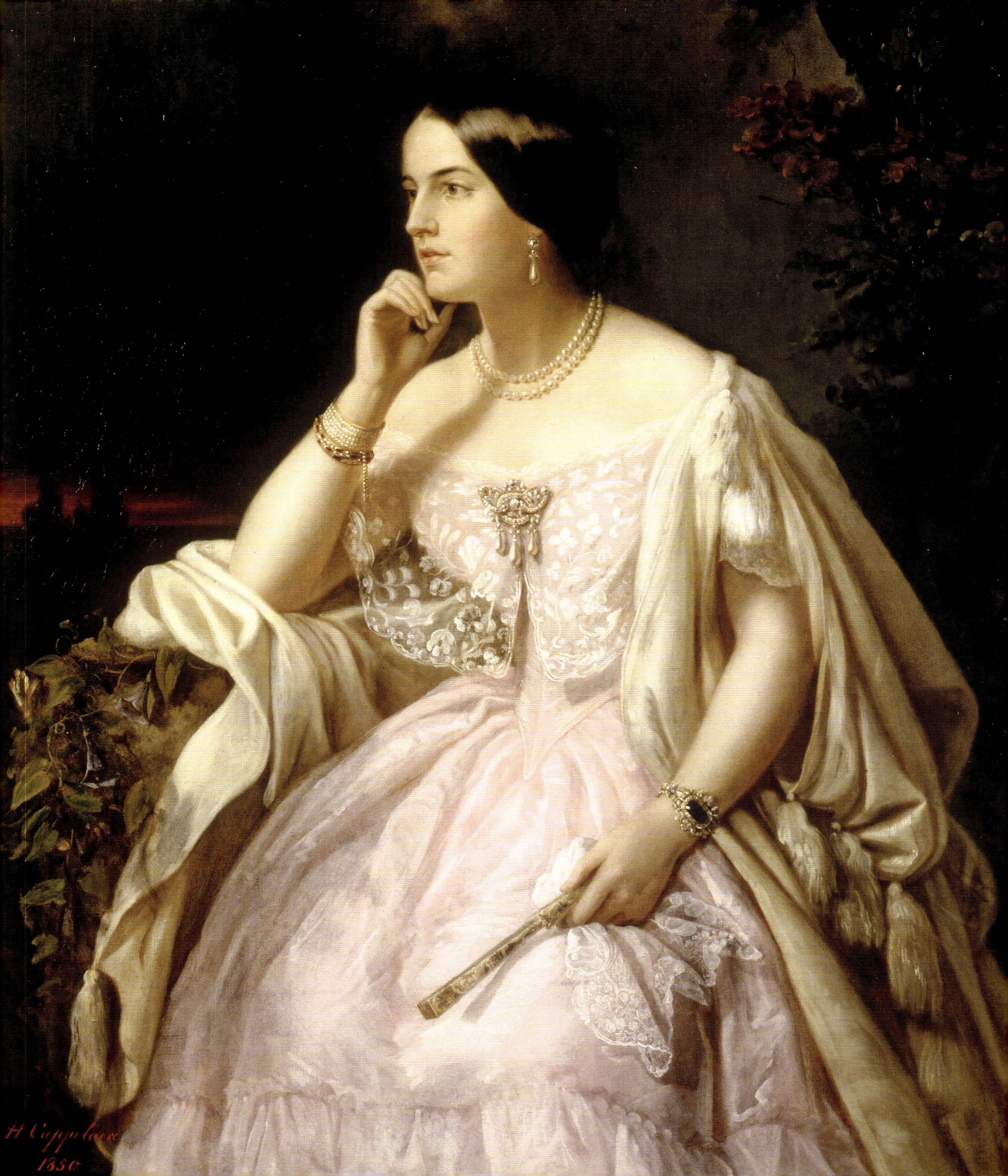
H Cappelen
1850

Royalists to Romantics

*Women Artists from the Louvre, Versailles,
and Other French National Collections*

NATIONAL MUSEUM OF
WOMEN IN THE ARTS
WASHINGTON, D.C.

IN ASSOCIATION WITH
SCALA PUBLISHERS LIMITED
LONDON

SCALA

Royalists to Romantics: Women Artists from the Louvre, Versailles, and Other French National Collections

National Museum of Women in the Arts
Washington, D.C.
February 24 – May 27, 2012

This exhibition has been organized by the National Museum of Women in the Arts (NMWA), Washington, D.C., with the logistical support of sVo Art, Versailles.

Critical funding has been provided by Hermès, Teresa L. and Joe R. Long, Jacqueline Badger Mars, and an anonymous donor. We also wish to express our thanks to the Annenberg Foundation, the Florence Gould Foundation, and the National Endowment for the Arts for their generous support, and to acknowledge the Robert Lehman Foundation and the Samuel H. Kress Foundation.

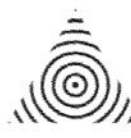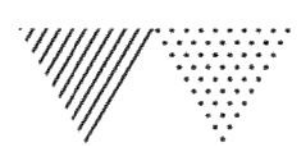

ART WORKS.
arts.gov

Exhibition Curator
Jordana Pomeroy, Chief Curator

Exhibition Advisers
Laura Auricchio
sVo Art

Catalogue Contributors
Laura Auricchio
Melissa Lee Hyde
Mary D. Sheriff

Biography Contributors
Laura Auricchio
Yuriko Anne Jackall (Marie Geneviève Bouliar; Jeanne Philiberte Ledoux)

Cover: Eulalie Morin (1765 – 1837), *Portrait of Madame Récamier (1777 – 1849)*, 4th quarter of 18th century (detail). Musée national des châteaux de Versailles et de Trianon

Back: Antoine Cécile Hortense Haudebourt-Lescot (1784 – 1845), *Self-Portrait*, 1825. Musée du Louvre, Département des peintures, Paris

Frontispiece: Henriette Jacotte Cappelaere (act. 1846 – 59), *Portrait of Elisabeth-Ann Haryett, Called Miss Harriet Howard, Wife of Trelawny, comtesse de Beauregard*, 1850 (detail). Musée national du château de Compiègne

All measurements are in inches and centimeters; height precedes width

Publication coordinated by Amy Pastan
Edited by Jane Bobko
Designed by Inglis Design, Galesville, Maryland
Typeset in Fournier by Duke & Company, Devon, Pennsylvania
Produced by Scala Publishers Limited, London

First published in 2012 by
Scala Publishers Limited
Northburgh House
10 Northburgh Street
London EC1V 0AT
United Kingdom
www.scalapublishers.com

In association with the National Museum of Women in the Arts

ISBN 978-1-85759-743-1
Printed in China
10 9 8 7 6 5 4 3 2 1

Contents

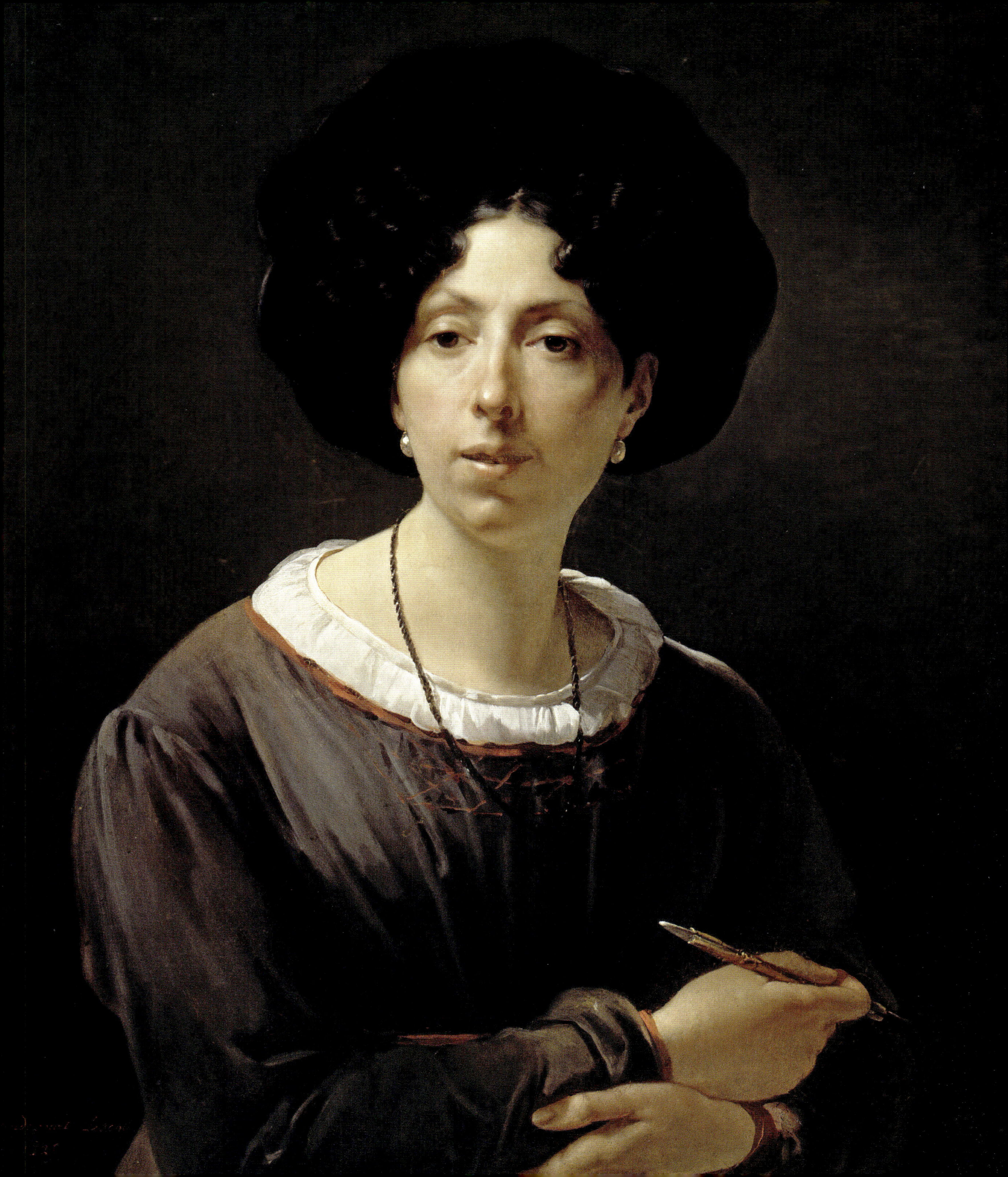

Foreword

In celebration of the National Museum of Women in the Arts' twenty-fifth anniversary, we are delighted to present *Royalists to Romantics: Women Artists from the Louvre, Versailles, and Other French National Collections*. This is the first exhibition to reveal the extraordinary breadth and depth of women's artistic practice in France from 1750 to 1848. Like other important historical surveys NMWA has organized, including *An Imperial Collection: Women Artists from the State Hermitage Museum, St. Petersburg* and *Italian Women Artists: From Renaissance to Baroque*, the exhibition *Royalists to Romantics* demonstrates our museum's continued commitment to articulating issues that resonate for women artists over the centuries, including their education and professionalization, the prospects and constraints they faced, and how they reconciled ideals and definitions of womanhood with the practice of their livelihood.

The years between 1750 and 1848 encompass the waning of the ancien régime, the tumult of the French Revolution, the emergence of the Empire, and, finally, the Restoration. In the arts in France, this century of political upheavals naturally affected academic instruction, patronage, and subject matter. The changing political climate provides a vivid background against which to examine women artists' production. Indeed, during this time women were so integrated into the fabric of the aristocratic world, the Revolution, Napoléon's rise, and the return of the monarchy that women artists' absence heretofore from scholarly discussion of the era throws into question assumptions that reach far beyond the particulars of individual careers.

A spotlight on the thirty-five exceptional women featured in the exhibition illustrates the means by which they navigated the hierarchical system of the artistic and social worlds of their day. Although most women artists were excluded from the Académie royale, prejudice did not prevent them from becoming well-trained, thriving, and even wealthy artists. The patrons of women artists came from royalty, the aristocracy, and the merchant class. *Royalists to Romantics* examines the relationships between patron and artist, including the ways in which women marketed their reputations and their cultural positions in France's social hierarchy. By focusing on this cross section of art history, we enrich our understanding of the layers and complexities that make this a culturally as well as politically captivating era.

Foremost in our thanks is Wilhelmina Cole Holladay, Chair of the Board of Trustees of the National Museum of Women in the Arts, who as a collector and admirer of eighteenth-century French women artists championed the idea of this exhibition from the beginning of our discussions with French art institutions and authorities.

Cat. 1. Antoine Cécile Hortense Haudebourt-Lescot (1784–1845), *Self-Portrait*, 1825 (detail). Oil on canvas. Musée du Louvre, Département des peintures, Paris

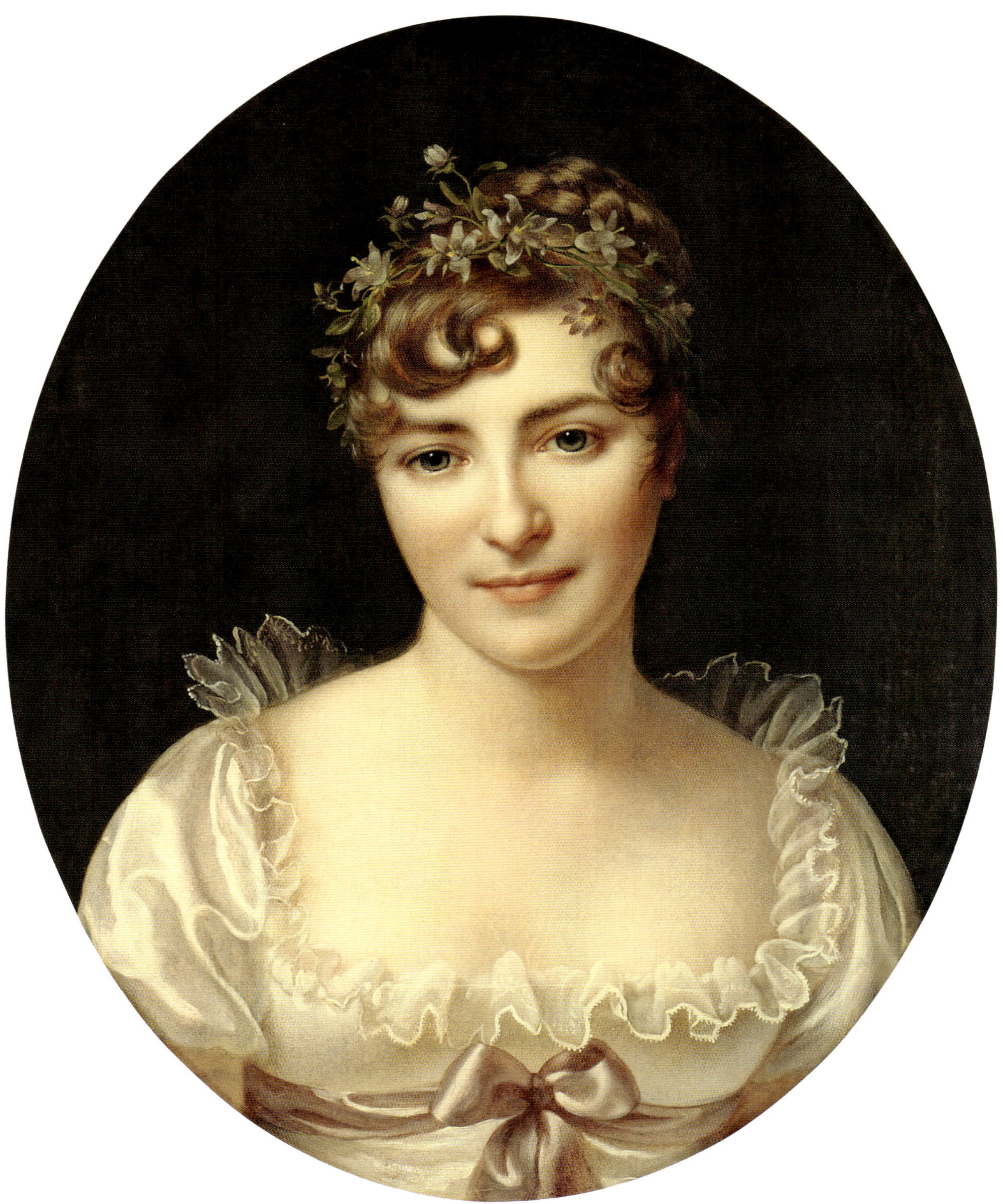

CAT. 2. HENRIETTE LORIMIER (1775–1854), *Portrait of Madame de Marjolin, née Duval*, 2nd quarter of 19th century.
Oil on canvas. Musée des beaux-arts, Grenoble

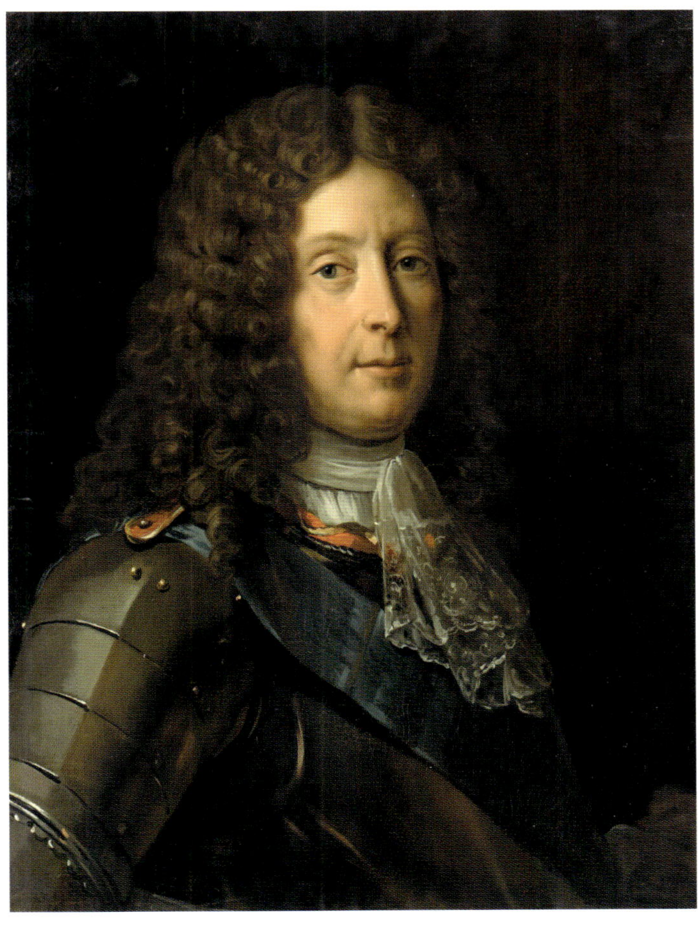

We also gratefully acknowledge the museum's Board of Trustees for their enthusiasm, as well as Les Amis du NMWA, the museum's Paris-based committee that promotes our mission in France. From the founding committee chair, Ondine Langford, to the current president, Tara Whitbeck, Les Amis du NMWA has offered singular support for the exhibition and is integral to our success.

Further, we are especially grateful for the patronage of the Ambassador of France to the United States, François Delattre, and wish to acknowledge the assistance of Cultural Counselor Roland Celette, Embassy of France, Washington, D.C., as well as our program partnership with the Maison Française of Washington. We also thank the Ambassador of the United States to France and Monaco, Charles H. Rivkin, and Susan Tolson for hosting NMWA's exhibition-announcement event in Paris.

It is our good fortune to have worked closely with some of the foremost specialists in the United States on the history of French women artists; they have served as advisers in the development of the exhibition and as authors of the catalogue. We are grateful to Laura Auricchio, Chair of Humanities and Associate Professor of Art History at The New School, New York; Mary D. Sheriff, W. R. Kenan, Jr. Distinguished Professor of Art History and Department Chair, University of North Carolina at Chapel Hill; Melissa Lee Hyde, Associate Professor of Art History, University of Florida, Gainesville; and Yuriko Anne Jackall, Assistant Curator of French Paintings, National Gallery of Art, Washington, D.C. Their scholarship restoring women artists to their rightful place has helped to shape a new narrative for the field of eighteenth-century art history. We extend our deepest thanks as well to our organizing partners, Sylvestre Verger and Ariane de Guernon of sVo Art, Versailles, whose expertise, insights, and advice were instrumental in negotiating loans with French institutions and bringing the exhibition to fruition.

Among the generous lenders are, of course, the French national museums, without whose generosity we would not have been able to consider organizing this exhibition. Our thanks go to Sabine Cazenave, Diretor, Musée de Picardie, Amiens; Patrick Le Nouene, Director, Musée des beaux-arts, Angers; Jacky Guindet, Curator, Musée des beaux-arts, Arras; Guillaume Ambroise, Director, Musée des beaux-arts, Bordeaux; Patrick Ramate, Director, Musée des beaux-arts, Caen; Marie-Noëlle Maynard, Chief Curator, Musée des beaux-arts, Carcassonne; Christiane Sinnig-Haas, Director and Chief Curator, Musée Jean de La Fontaine, Château-Thierry; Emmanuel Starcky, Director, Domaines nationaux de Compiègne et Blérancourt; Pierre Ickowicz, Chief Curator, Château-Musée de Dieppe; Sophie Jugie, Director and Chief Curator, Musée des beaux-arts, Palais des ducs et des états de Bourgogne, Dijon; Xavier Salmon, Director of Collections and Patrimony, Musée national du château de

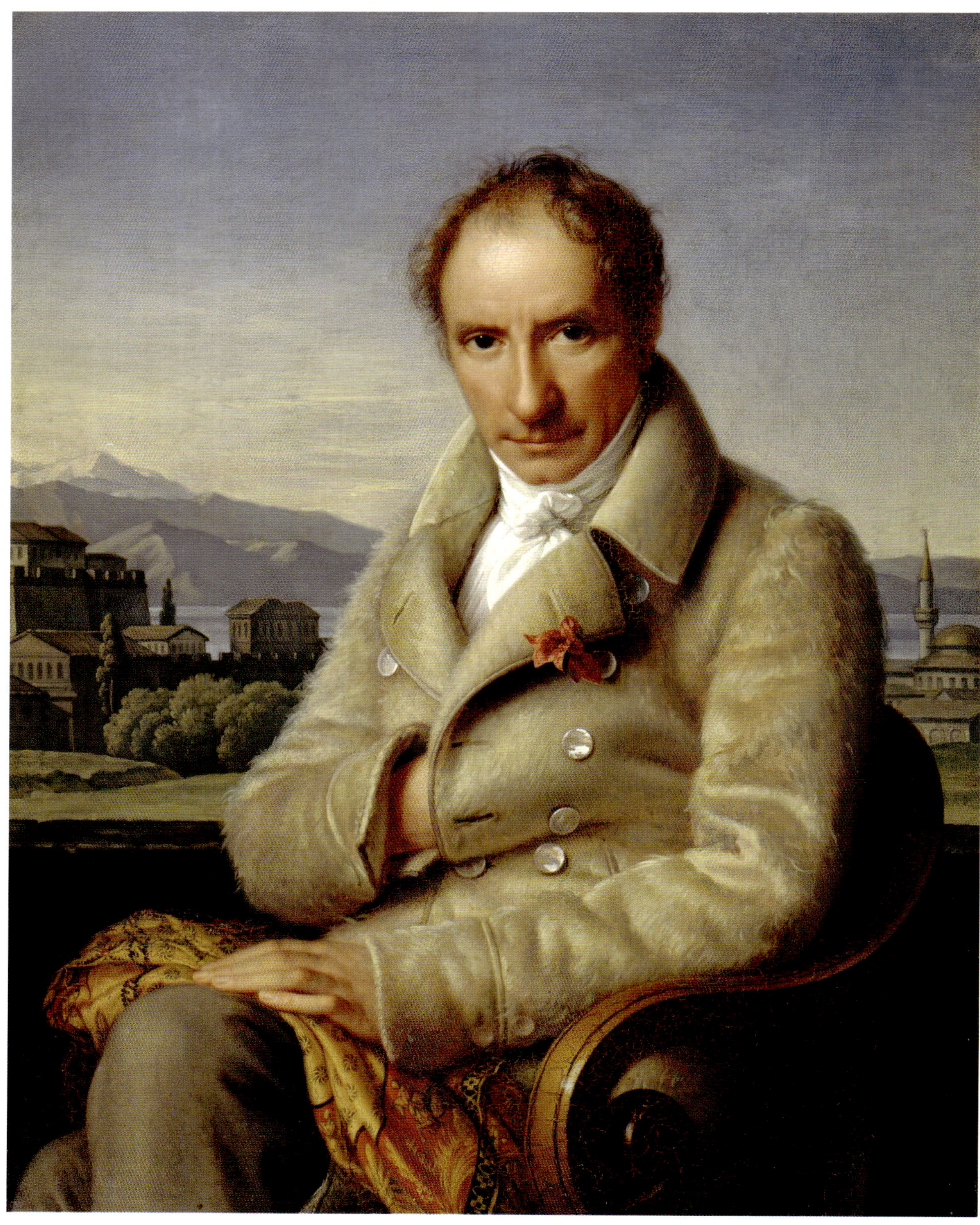

Cat. 4. Henriette Lorimier (1775–1854), *Portrait of François-Charles-Hugues-Laurent Pouqueville (1770–1838)*, 1830.
Oil on canvas. Musée national des châteaux de Versailles et de Trianon

Fontainebleau; Hélène Barbiero, Head of Collections, Musée Jean-Honoré Fragonard, Grasse; Guy Tosatto, Director, Musée des beaux-arts, Grenoble; Roger Lecoq, Director, Musée de Tessé, Ville du Mans; Alain Papié, Director, Palais des beaux-arts, Lille; Michel Natier, Director, Musée de Louviers; Sylvie Ramond, Director and Chief Curator, Musée des beaux-arts, Lyon; Blandine Chavanne, Director and Chief Curator, Musée des beaux-arts, Nantes; Isabelle Klinka, Chief Curator, Musée des beaux-arts, Orléans; Bruno Racine, President, Bibliothèque nationale de France, Paris; Jean Marc Léri, Director, Musée Carnavalet—Histoire de Paris; Vincent Pomarède, Curator of Paintings, Musée du Louvre, Paris; Jacques Taddei, Director, Musée Marmottan Monet, Paris; Muriel Mayette, General Administrator, Bibliothèque-Musée de la Comédie-Française, Paris; Olivier Py, Director, Théâtre national de l'Odéon, Paris; Eric De Visscher, Director, Musée de la musique, Paris; Thomas Grenon, Director, Muséum national d'histoire naturelle, Bibliothèque centrale, Paris; José de Los Llanos, Director and Chief Curator of Patrimony, Musée Cognacq-Jay, Paris; Dominique Vazquez, Curator, Musée des beaux-arts, Pau; André Cariou, Director, Musée des beaux-arts, Quimper; Diederik Bakhuÿs, Interim Director and Curator, Musée des beaux-arts, Rouen; Bertrand Maratier, Director of Museums, Musée du Présidial, Saintes; Axel Henery, Director, Musée des Augustins, Toulouse; Emmanuelle Delapierre, Director, Musée des beaux-arts, Valenciennes; Frédéric Lacaille, Curator of Nineteenth-Century Paintings, Musée national du château de Versailles; Juliette Trey, Curator of Eighteenth-Century Paintings, Musée national du château de Versailles.

We would like to especially recognize Henri Loyrette, President of the Musée du Louvre, Paris, and Jean-Jacques Aillagon, Director of the Musée national des châteaux de Versailles et de Trianon at the time this exhibition was organized, who lent a total of twenty-one works, including paintings, drawings, and sculpture.

We are delighted to augment the scientific and natural-history section of this exhibition with loans from two Washington, D.C., institutions. The Library of Congress has lent illustrated treatises; the Dumbarton Oaks Research Library and Collection has offered a stunning watercolor drawing by Camille de Chantereine, a student of Pierre-Joseph Redouté.

For the organization and development of this important international exhibition, special acknowledgment is given to NMWA Chief Curator Jordana Pomeroy. Dr. Pomeroy, working in close cooperation with sVo Art and the catalogue's contributors, selected works for the exhibition and shaped the Washington presentation. Essential assistance on the catalogue was provided by two of the museum's curatorial assistants, Raphael Fitzgerald and Rebecca Price. Delphine Galloy, a graduate student at the École du Louvre, contributed to the early stages of the catalogue. For the publication we are grateful to Scala Publishers, where we relied on the guidance of Jennifer Norman, Amy Pastan, and Patty Inglis, and to Jane Bobko for her editorial expertise.

An exhibition of this scale can be realized only with significant financial support from many generous sources. Major funding for this groundbreaking twenty-fifth-anniversary exhibition has been provided by Hermès, Teresa L. and Joe R. Long, Jacqueline Badger Mars, and an anonymous donor. We also wish to express our thanks to the Annenberg Foundation, the Florence Gould Foundation, and the National Endowment for the Arts for their generous support, and to acknowledge the Robert Lehman Foundation and the Samuel H. Kress Foundation.

We are extremely proud that the exhibition and the catalogue for *Royalists to Romantics: Women Artists from the Louvre, Versailles, and Other French National Collections* will help to banish the obscurity that has veiled the legacy of many eighteenth-century French women artists. They were renowned during their lifetimes. We now return luster to their reputations by introducing them to a public that will once again know of and value their remarkable accomplishments.

Susan Fisher Sterling
Director, National Museum of Women in the Arts

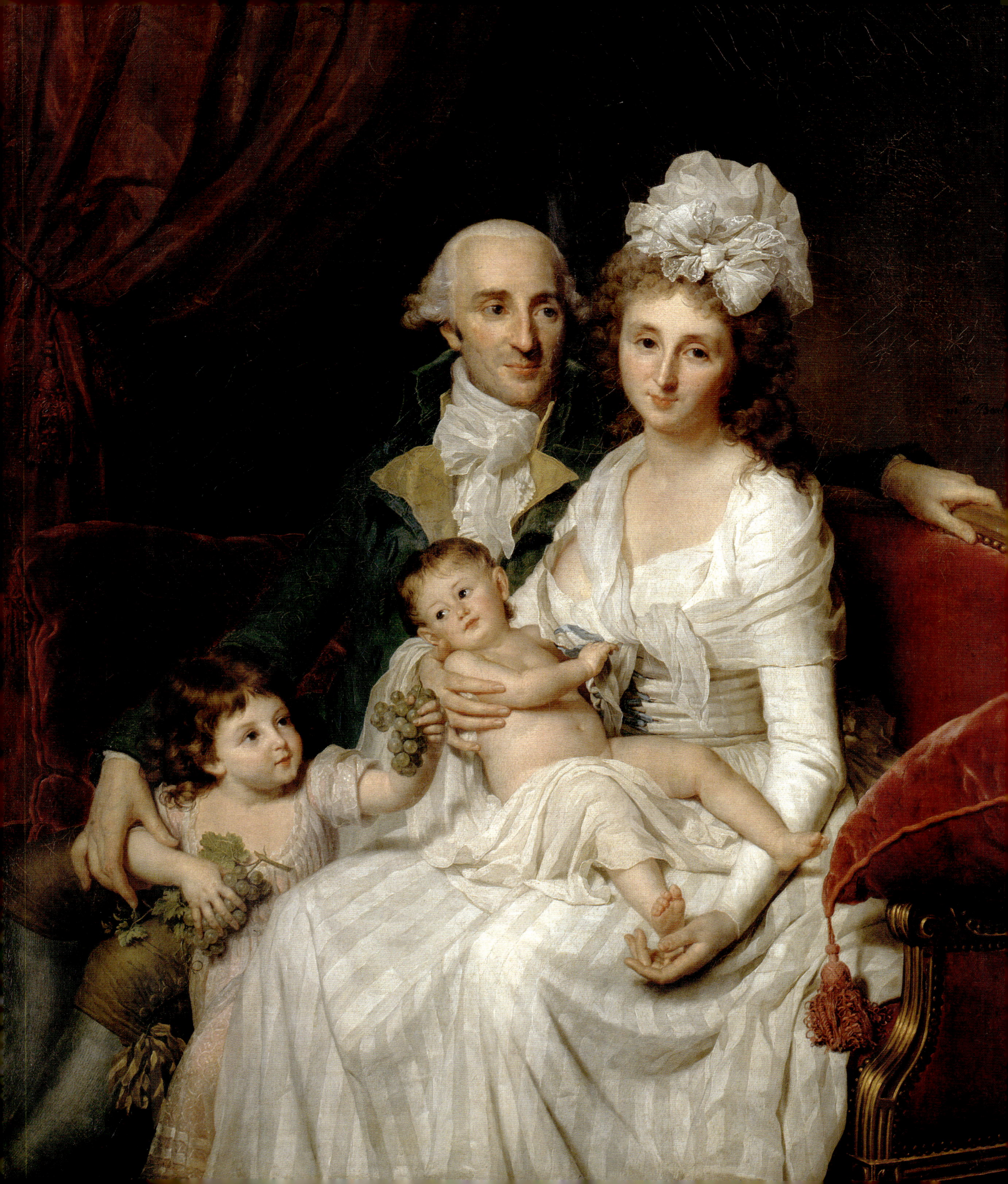

Introduction | *Jordana Pomeroy*

Seen through the lens of history, the late eighteenth century in France has become both a democratic model and a cautionary tale. In less than five years, French society was transformed from a centuries-old aristocracy to a republic governed by popular will, before once again succumbing to despotism. During this age of uncertainty and contradiction, the situation of women artists in France was equally precarious. It was a moment when, in certain regards, the arts accorded women more respect and more freedom than they had ever experienced. The pinnacle of this trend was perhaps in 1783, when the number of female members in the French Académie royale de peinture et de sculpture reached four—the full quota of women allowed entrance. But just as artists like Élisabeth Louise Vigée-LeBrun and Adélaïde Labille-Guiard began to make their mark, politics pushed back. A new republican government effectively disbanded the Académie. From that point, the opportunity for women to gain entrée into the art world and attain the fame and fortune of a Vigée-LeBrun vanished. For eighteenth-century women artists, the personal was deeply political, as affairs of state both drove careers and destroyed them.

The story of women artists around the time of the Revolution typically ends there, briefly told and consigned to the more detailed texts of art history. Too much scholarship has hewed to a worn-out narrative of the eighteenth-century artistic experience. The exhibition *Royalists to Romantics: Women Artists from the Louvre, Versailles, and Other French National Collections* shows, however, that though Vigée-LeBrun and Labille-Guiard may be the only two French women artists of the time to secure a place in most history books, they were by no means the sole female standard-bearers. Nor were women artists, as many might suspect, relegated to the least prestigious forms of art. *Royalists to Romantics* features thirty-five artists and numerous genres and media, from history paintings by Antoine Cécile Hortense Haudebourt-Lescot and landscapes by Louise Joséphine Sarazin de Belmont to portraits of distinguished artistic and cultural leaders and members of the royal court. Although women were primarily engaged in painting, Julie Charpentier and Félicie de Fauveau worked in stone and metal, producing sculpture busts, stone and bronze reliefs, and decorative metal objects. Even if they were a minority among artists, women formed a vibrant community within the art world, one far more prolific and more varied than popularly portrayed.

Nonetheless, the lives of women artists in Revolutionary France were far from easy. Practitioners of pseudo-science declared that though women possessed the *sensibilité* essential to the production of art, that very perception and responsiveness to the external world also made them aloof and temperamental, incapable of the discipline

Cat. 5. Marie Geneviève Bouliar (1763–1825), *Portrait of Monsieur Olive,* *Treasurer of the Legislative Assembly of Brittany, with His Family,* 1791/1792. Oil on canvas. Musée des beaux-arts, Nantes

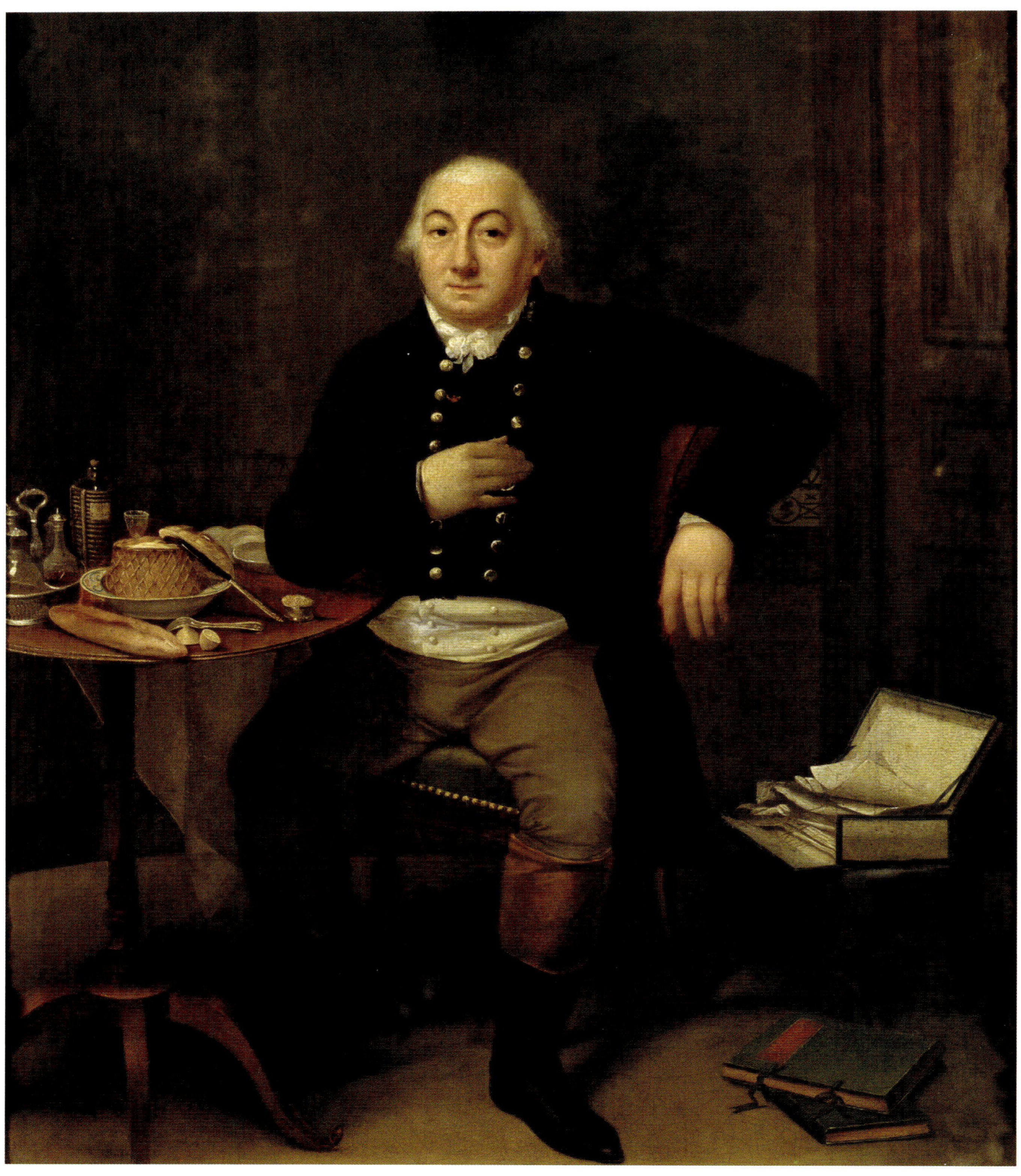

CAT. 6. ADÈLE ROMANY (1769–1846), *Portrait of the Artist's Father*, 4th quarter of 18th century. Oil on canvas. Musée national des châteaux de Versailles et de Trianon

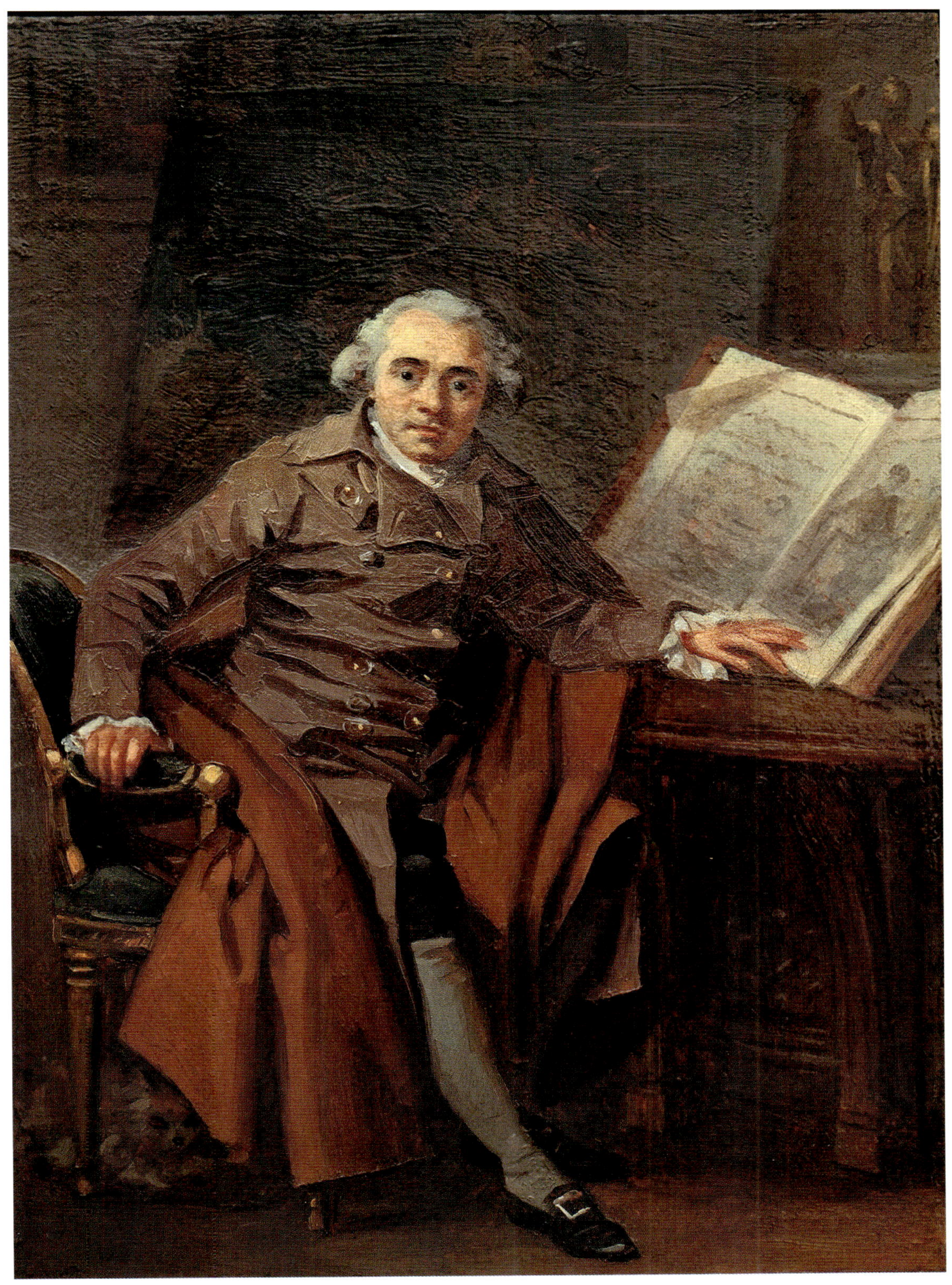

Cat. 7. Marguerite Gérard (1761–1837), *Presumed Portrait of Jean-Jacques Lagrenée*, ca. 1787.
Oil on zinc. Musée Cognacq-Jay, Paris

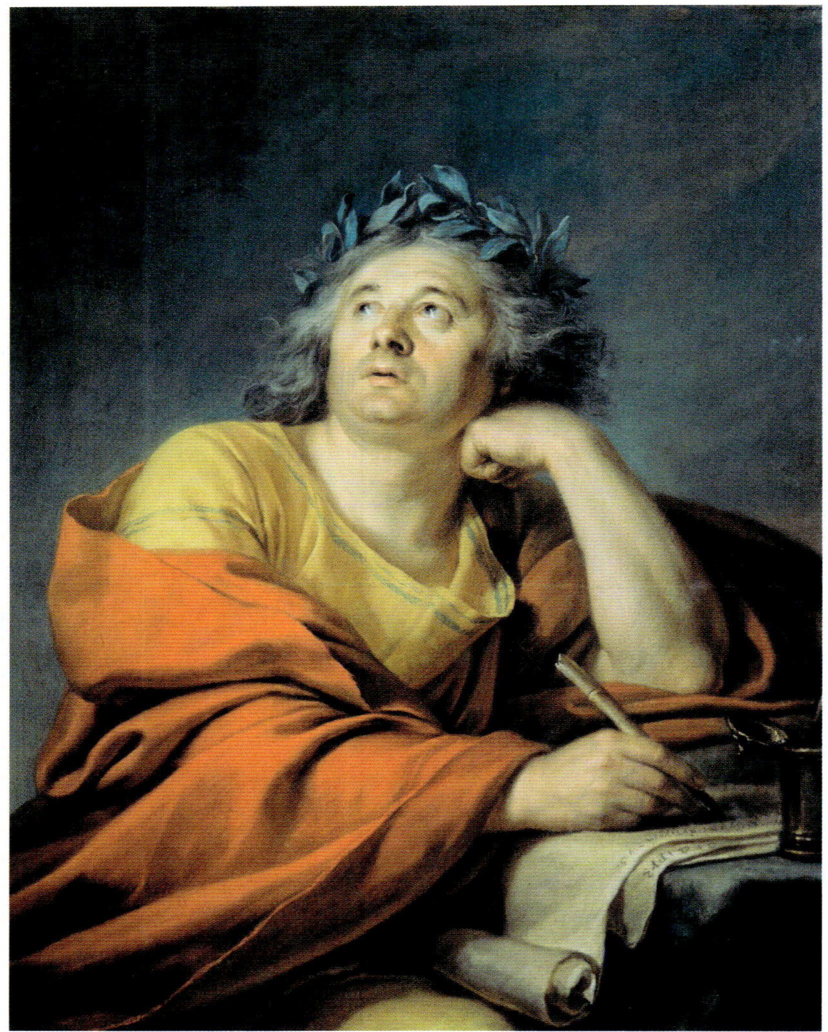

necessary to great artists. Other critics simply resorted to slander, baselessly claiming that male painters had helped complete women's works. The most blatant opposition to women came, not unexpectedly, from bureaucrats within and without the Académie. Despite a progressive streak in the Académie's policy toward women artists in the 1780s and early 1790s — besides increasing the number of women in its ranks from two to four in 1783, the Académie allowed an open Salon in 1791 (albeit forced by legislation passed through the National Assembly) — overall government policy throughout the period was regressive. Prior to the Revolution, most officials had sought to ban women from the Académie and deny them its exhibition privileges. The fall of the Bastille did little to halt this effort. Indeed, it gave women's critics new ideological ammunition, as the Académie and its acceptance of women now symbolized monarchical decadence. There was ample incentive to strip the Académie of its power. In July 1793 the Commune générale des arts effectively replaced it, and though initially accepting of women artists, the Commune's members passed a bylaw forbidding them a mere five months later.

It is this inconsistency of society's attitude toward women artists that makes the Revolutionary era such a complex period for feminist historians, too. Yet the French government's waffling, which surely caused women anguish and pain, arguably shaped the evolution of art by women more than any other factor. Although it was certainly not the intention of the bureaucrats of the era, a fine balance had been struck with regard to official policy toward women artists. On the one hand, enough support for their work existed both within the Académie and in the private sector such that women who otherwise only *might* have become artists did, in fact, produce art. On the other hand, the lack of full recognition and acceptance isolated women from the rest of the artistic community. Forbidden from completely integrating with men on a professional level, women artists were forced to define themselves by what made them different — their gender. Although women had been involved in producing art since well before the Renaissance, never before had this self-concept of a *woman artist* been so precise, and it dominated women's art production in the Revolutionary period. It should come as no surprise, then, that the self-portrait, rarely utilized before by women, became their favored form of expression, most famously in Vigée-LeBrun's *Self-Portrait in a Straw Hat* (1782, National Gallery, London) and Labille-Guiard's *Self-Portrait with Two Pupils, Marie Gabrielle Capet (1761–1818) and Marie Marguerite Carreaux de Rosemond (died 1788)* (1785, Metropolitan Museum of Art, New York). By choosing to

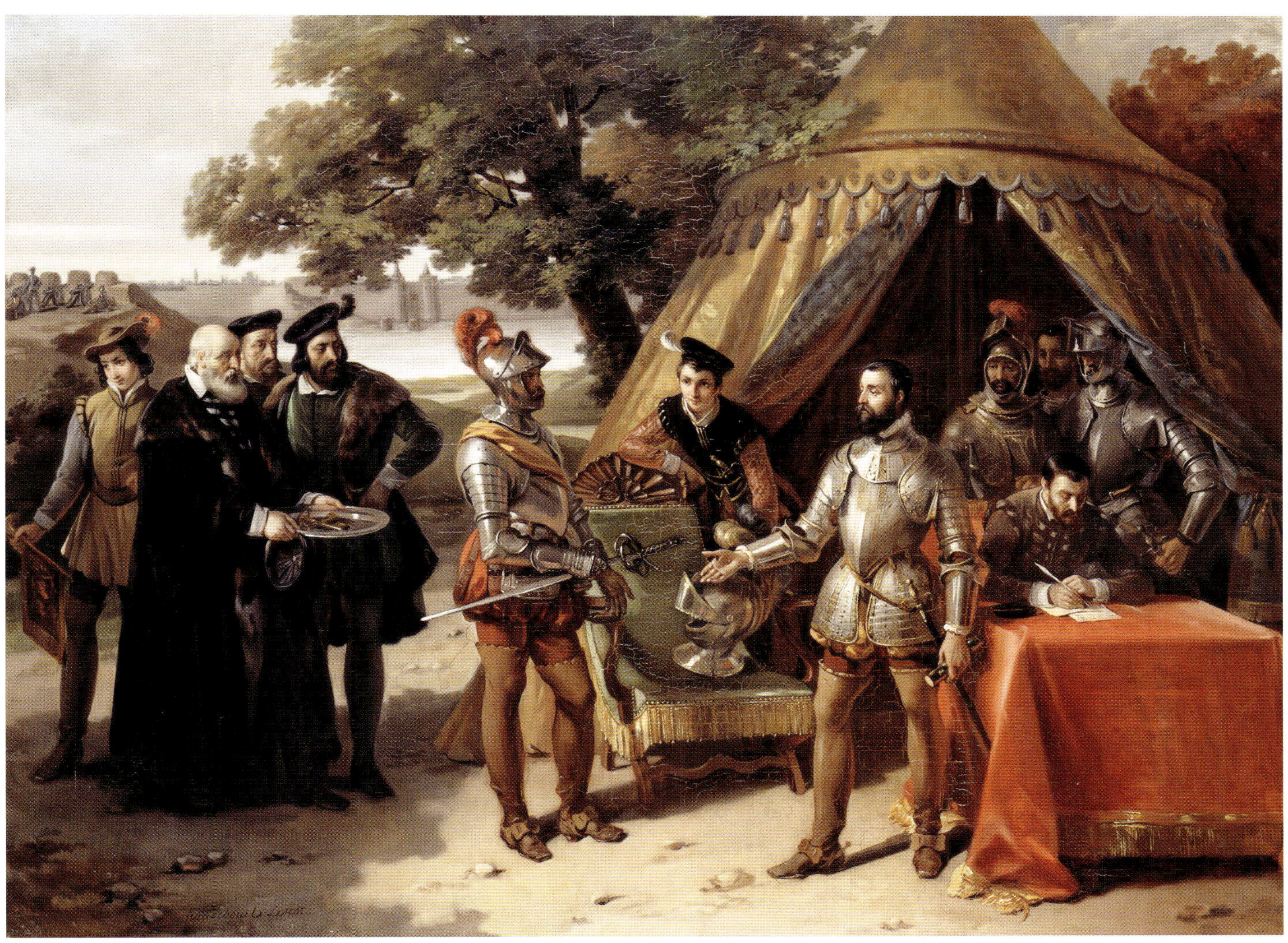

Cat. 9. Antoine Cécile Hortense Haudebourt-Lescot (1784–1845), *The Capture of Thionville*, 1837.
Oil on canvas. Musée national des châteaux de Versailles et de Trianon

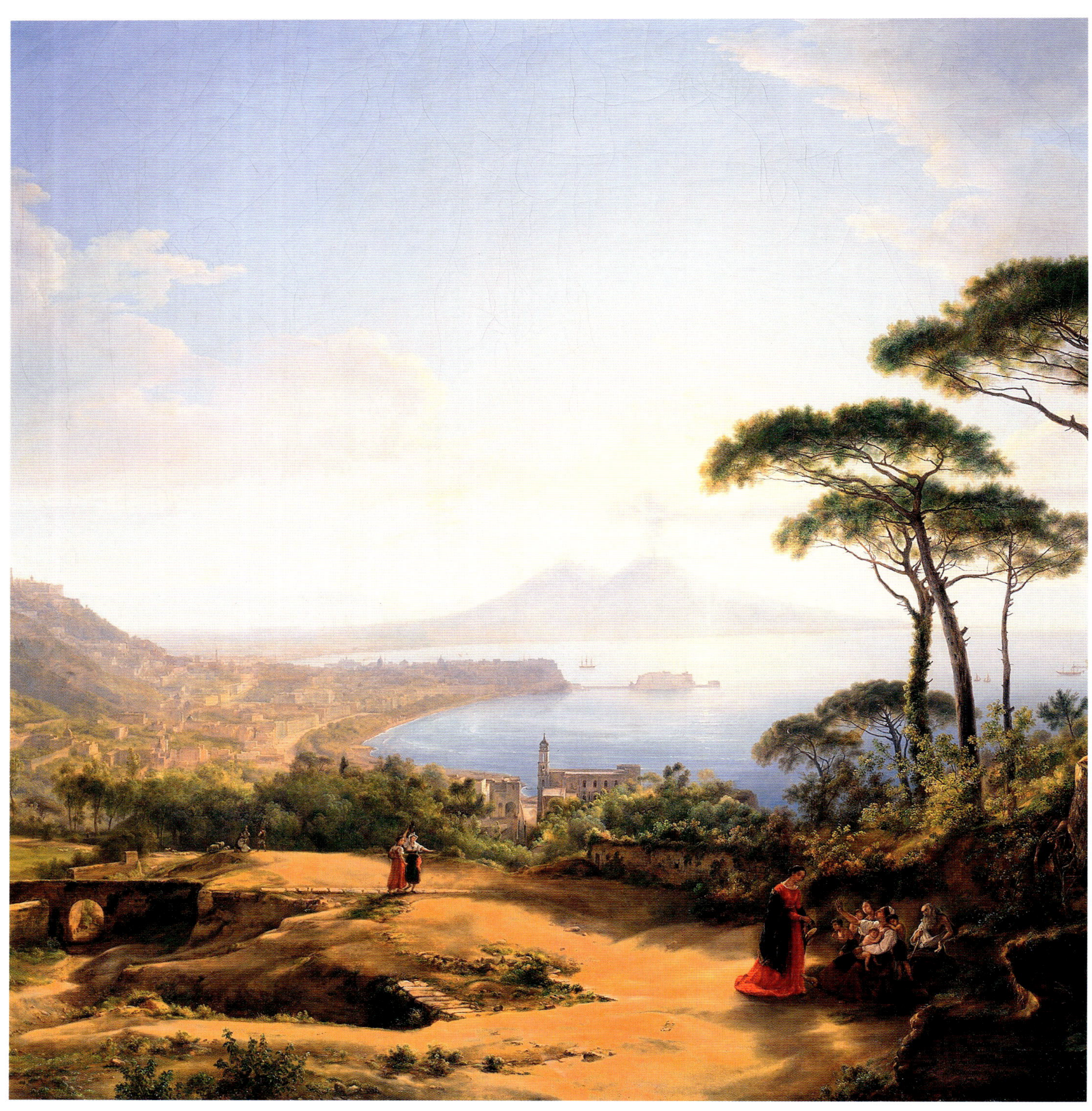

CAT. 10. LOUISE JOSÉPHINE SARAZIN DE BELMONT (1790–1870), *Naples, View from Posilipo*, 1842–59.
Oil on canvas. Musée des Augustins, Toulouse

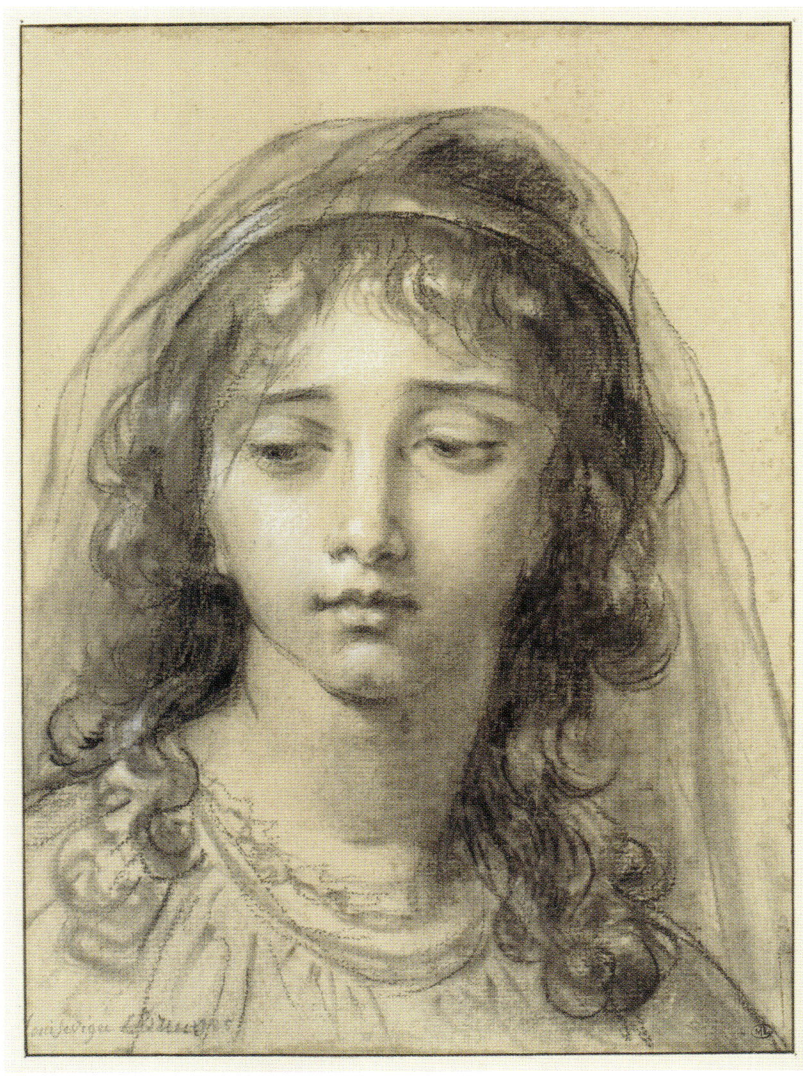

depict themselves in the role of painters, Vigée-LeBrun and Labille-Guiard establish a notion of authorship of their art formerly reserved for male artists. Women artists in Revolutionary France asserted their role as creators, not mere conduits, of art.

Recognition of women as representatives of an independent artistic movement was not limited to the artists themselves, as female patrons coalesced around the burgeoning community of women artists. Patronage was not restricted to one social class or political system; rather, it extended all the way from fellow artists and architects to Marie-Antoinette herself, whose recommendation was instrumental in assuring Vigée-LeBrun's admission to the Académie, albeit for only a few years before Louis XVI was deposed. The existence of such a network of women patrons supporting women artists underscores the emerging concept of a woman artist as one who does not merely follow in the tradition of her male peers but, rather, seeks to represent the perspective of her sex.

Support of women artists defied not only a gendered tradition but also a broader artistic one, for in sponsoring a woman, a patron chose to promote an artist who had of necessity developed her talents outside of the Académie's strict curriculum. The network of women that developed in late-eighteenth-century France not only skirted male-dominated academic and exhibition venues; it also gave more weight to genres of painting that had been assigned to women artists because of their operation outside the academic artistic hierarchy. In this sense, we see in these women the first glimmers of a fundamental shift toward a modern relationship between artists and patrons. To commission a portrait was to proclaim that artistic excellence and desirability lay in the eye of the beholder. No official imprimatur was needed. This notion, unusual at the time, underlies art production and the art market today. Art is *personal:* the careers of women artists in late-eighteenth-century France suggest that there existed many paths to a solid reputation and financial success that did not require an academic pedigree or a pass to an officially sanctioned venue. For all of the republican government's embedded misogyny, the cause of *liberté*, *égalité*, and *fraternité* began a new narrative for women, who by the end of the nineteenth century would be painting in the Louvre's corridors alongside their male colleagues.

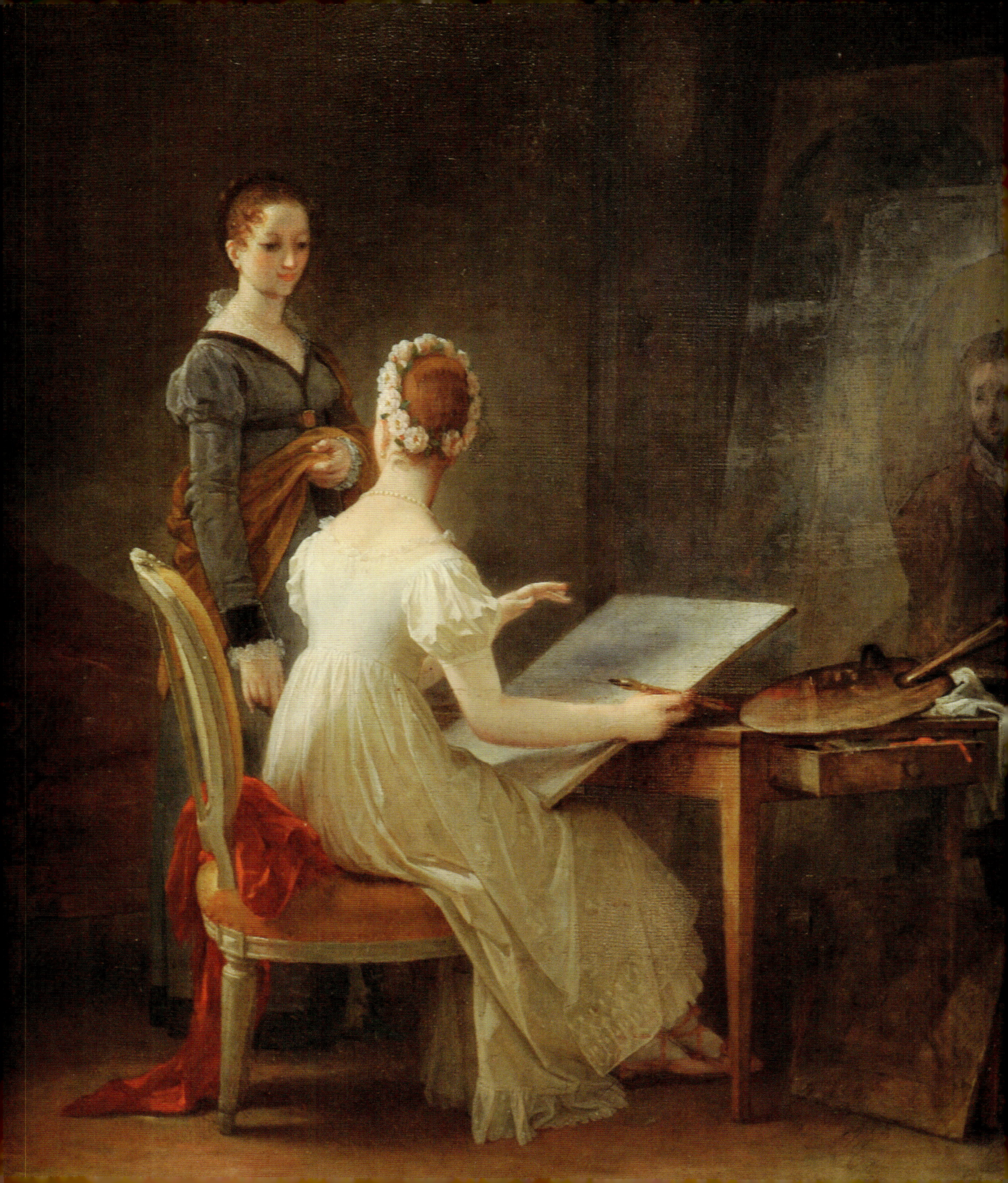

Revolutionary Paradoxes: 1789–94 | *Laura Auricchio*

THE REVOLUTIONARY YEARS WERE PARADOXICAL AT BEST for France's female artists.[1] When the nation's institutions first embarked on a thorny path of reassessment and reform, it seemed that women might win equal access to Paris's most prestigious art associations and exhibitions. In 1791, for instance, the doors to the biennial Salon exhibitions were opened to all artists, permitting an unprecedented number of women to display their work in the Palais du Louvre. But other opportunities vanished. Whereas the Académie royale de peinture et de sculpture had established a quota of four female members, the Revolutionary-era art institutions ultimately barred all women on the grounds that professional art making was incompatible with virtuous republican femininity.

Institutional Upheavals

The months following the fall of the Bastille held great promise for women artists. A proposal to admit unlimited numbers of women to the Académie royale appeared as early as November 20, 1789, when an academician, the engraver Simon Charles Miger (1738–1820), launched a published assault on the status quo.[2] Specifying eight problems in need of correction, Miger admonished the Académie to set its house in order lest it be dismantled by the National Assembly, France's new legislative body. Surprisingly, perhaps, the first item on Miger's list concerned female artists. "It is an abuse," Miger began, that regulations "fix the number of women academicians at three or four: either none must be received, or else, since some are received, all those women with true talents have legitimate rights [to admission]." "The Académie," he continued, "must be like a church open to all the faithful." Nodding to moral concerns, Miger allowed that the ethics of female aspirants should be closely scrutinized.[3] Nonetheless, he concluded that "any honest woman who is truly an artist is a man for the Académie."

In arguing for the reform, but not the abolition, of the Académie royale, Miger gave voice to the beliefs of a group of academicians who came to call themselves the Académie centrale. On September 23, 1790, the faction's most controversial member, the portraitist Adélaïde Labille-Guiard (1749–1803; see cats. 8, 13, 17, 45), reiterated Miger's argument for the unrestricted admission of women. In addition, while conceding that a "woman, whatever talent she might possess, could nonetheless never aspire to be a professor in the schools, nor to have any governing

CAT. 12. MARGUERITE GÉRARD (1761–1837), *The Drawing Lesson, or The Studio*, ca. 1820.
Oil on canvas. Collections Musée Jean-Honoré Fragonard, Grasse

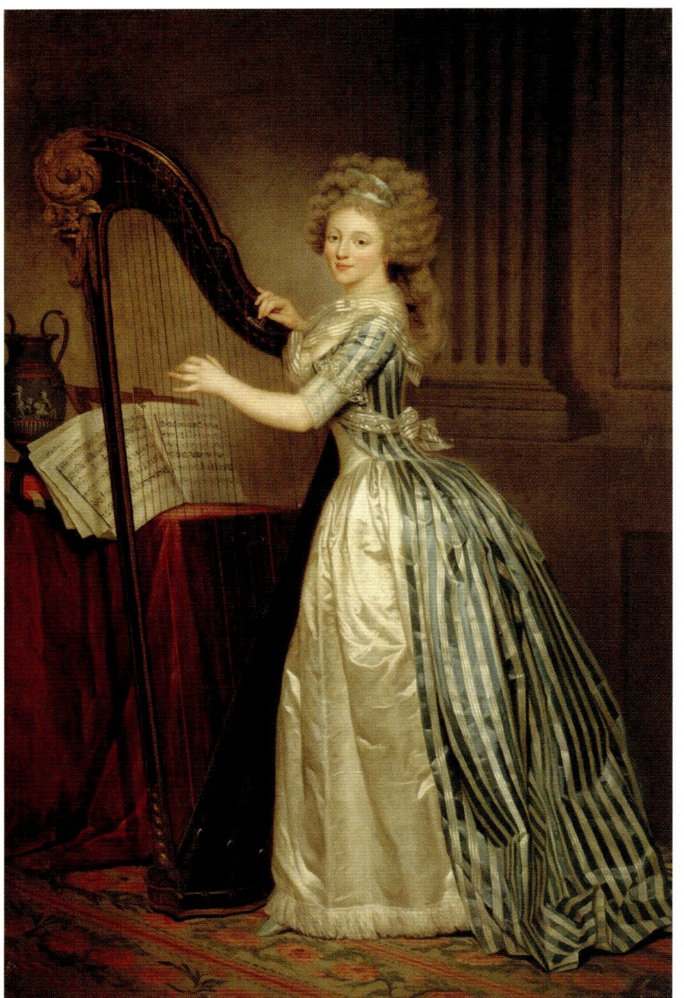

role whatsoever in the Académie," Labille-Guiard suggested that certain women, "for good and valid reasons, be compensated by a distinction that would be only academic, honorific, and that they would have no other distinction than to be admitted among the number of counselors."[4] Proposed statutes drafted by the Académie centrale included one other concession to gender difference: whereas male applicants would be required to submit full figure studies copied from classical sculpture and from life, women would present only "drawings of heads, feet, and hands from life," with entire figures copied from the antique.[5] Unfortunately, the Académie centrale never came to power, and these opportunities never materialized.

Women did, however, receive a significant boon on August 21, 1791, when the National Assembly opened the Salon to all artists.[6] More than 180 artists, including 21 women, sent approximately eight hundred works to the Louvre exhibition that year. In fact, as Margaret A. Oppenheimer has observed, an astonishing 207 women ranked among the thousands of artists who exhibited at the open Salons held between 1791 and 1815. To select just one example, Rose Adélaïde Ducreux (1761–1802; see cat. 36), daughter of the portraitist Joseph Ducreux (1735–1802), was a painter of the highest caliber who had,

nonetheless, been unable to breach the walls of the Académie. In 1791 she exhibited the stunning *Self-Portrait with a Harp* (fig. 1.1), a work that demonstrates such a command of drawing and perspective and such confident handling that scholars attributed it to various academicians until 1988, when Joseph Baillio identified it as one of Ducreux's Salon submissions.[7]

Yet, even as female artists were exhibiting in droves, France's reborn art institutions struggled to decide whether to admit any women at all. Initially, the Commune générale des arts de peinture, sculpture, architecture et gravure, which effectively replaced the Académie as the nation's governing artistic body on July 18, 1793, welcomed women.[8] In the Commune's first months, at least seventeen women presented themselves for admission.[9] By October, however, the acceptance of women was being cast as potentially antithetical to Revolutionary values. At a meeting of the Commune, an unidentified speaker insisted that "among republicans, women must absolutely renounce tasks destined for men." Although he acknowledged that a talented woman who practices art for her own satisfaction might be a pleasant companion, he warned that artistic skills should not be used to contravene the "laws

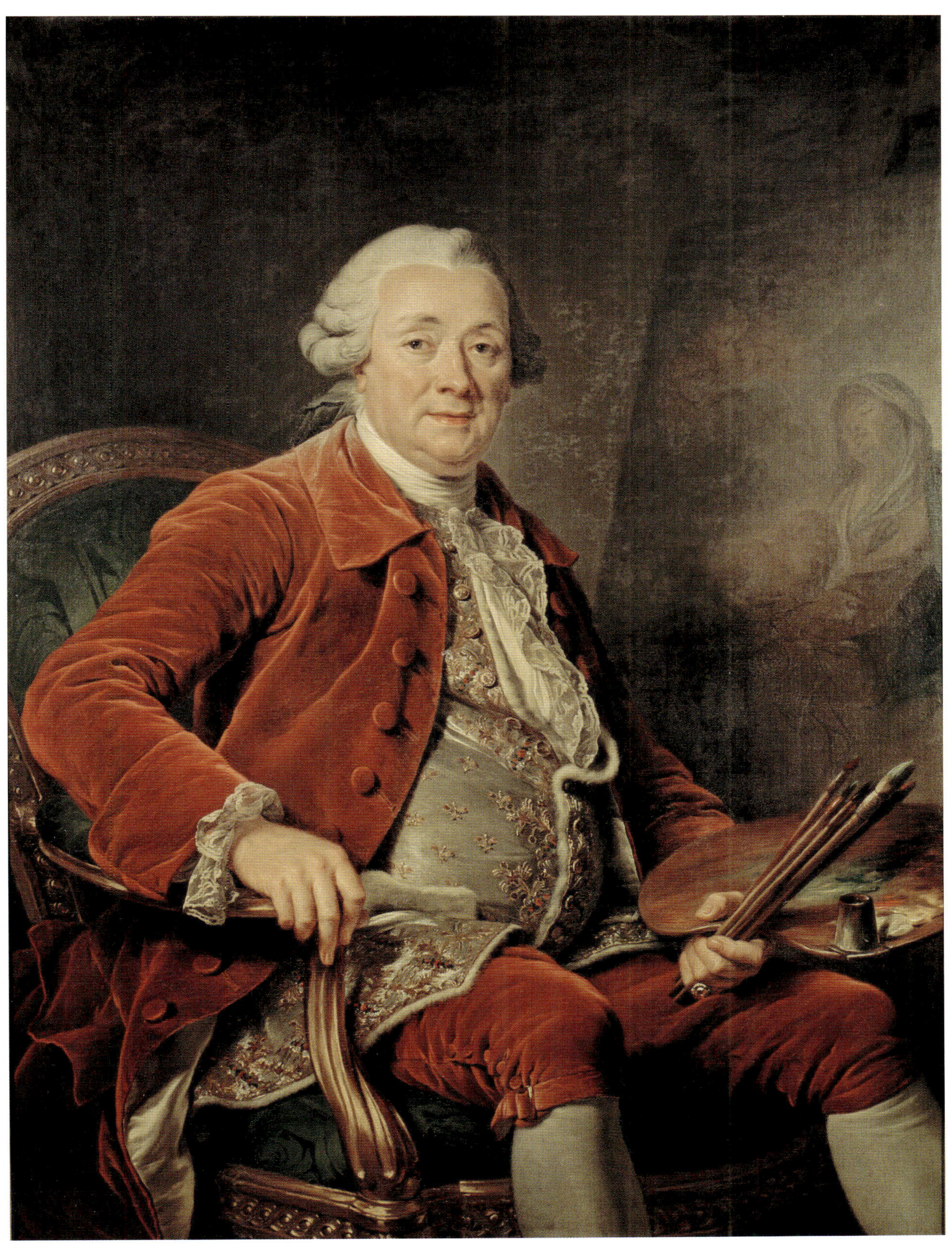

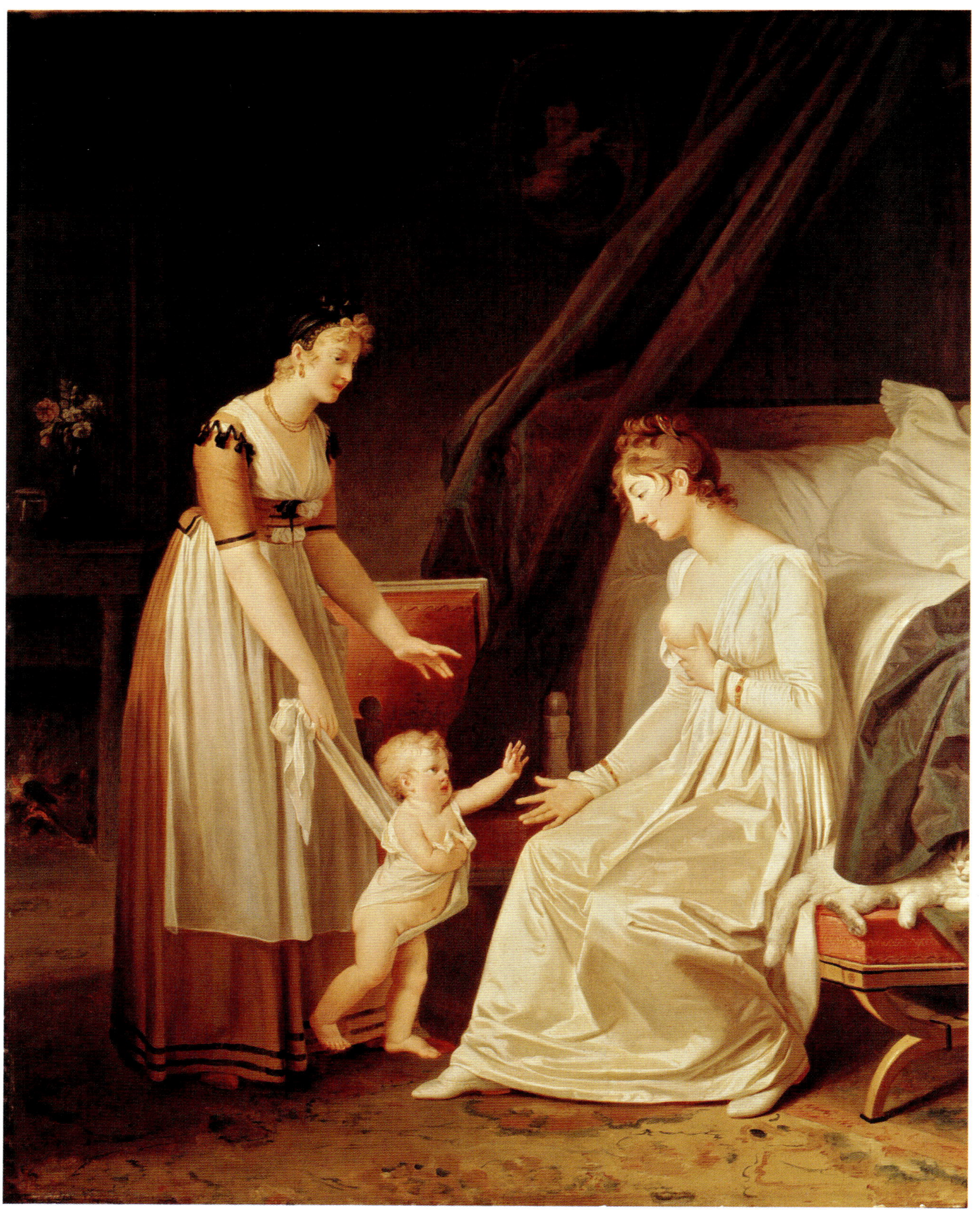

of nature." Moreover, he viewed the very notion of female artists as potentially counter-Revolutionary, arguing that the example of the royalist academician Élisabeth Louise Vigée-LeBrun (1775–1842; see cats. 11, 23, 63) had led a "host" of women "to take up painting when they should have been doing nothing but embroidering uniform belts and hats for the police."[10] Although some members of the Commune dissented and another proposed admitting women of proven moral probity, the discussion ended with a decision to permit no women, "purely and simply." The verdict was reaffirmed on December 23, 1793, in keeping with a national law prohibiting women "from assembling and from deliberating on any subject."[11]

Productive Destruction

If painting could be inimical to the virtues of republican women, might a royal portrait created by a woman endanger the nation itself? A dramatic episode involving a work by Vigée-LeBrun seems to have rested on such logic.

Following the nationalization of royal properties, a Commission temporaire des arts was established to record, classify, and describe all monuments, objects of scientific interest, and works of art found in properties confiscated from the royal family, émigrés, and other enemies of the Revolution. The Commission's mission statement, adopted on March 5, 1794, also charged the group with overseeing the transportation of these objects and ensuring their preservation in appropriate storehouses.[12] But on June 13, 1794, the Commission turned its attention from conservation to destruction.

The story began while Jean-Michel Picault, of the Commission's painting division, and Casimir Varon, representing the division of medals and antiquities, were inventorying the royal château at Saint-Cloud.[13] There they happened upon a portrait of the dauphin painted by Vigée-LeBrun, which, according to their report, they set aside for shipment to a warehouse.[14] Later that day, a commissioner identified only as LeBrun — either the art dealer Jean Baptiste Pierre Le Brun (Vigée-LeBrun's ex-husband) or his brother, Joseph-Alexandre LeBrun — came across the portrait where Picault and Varon had left it. LeBrun declared the portrait's separation from the rest of the furnishings to be suspicious, and ordered the painting to be burned on the spot.

In the weeks that followed, an investigation into the incident yielded a sweeping decree ordering the destruction of all portraits of the royal family. The inquiry began as a jurisdictional matter, with the Commission attempting to ascertain what had happened, and seeking to regulate all future acts of destruction.[15] Picault and Varon gave depositions. Then, perhaps concerned that their republican credentials had been tarnished, the pair proposed "that all paintings and portraits representing individuals of Capet blood will be inventoried and brought together in the same storehouse, and that, according to the inventory, we will carry out their total and complete destruction, so that royalist superstition will never be able to gather them together again." One commissioner objected "that some of these paintings or portraits might contain elements of genius or originality that might be useful to preserve for instruction and for the arts." Nonetheless, "the Commission, firm in its patriotic principles, maintained the order discussed above." The motion passed and was "communicated to the Committee of Public Instruction in order to obtain its prompt and entire execution." On June 17, the Committee of Public Instruction approved the legislation.[16]

Cat. 14. Marguerite Gérard (1761–1837), *First Steps, or The Nursing Mother*, ca. 1804. Oil on panel.
Collections Musée Jean-Honoré Fragonard, Grasse

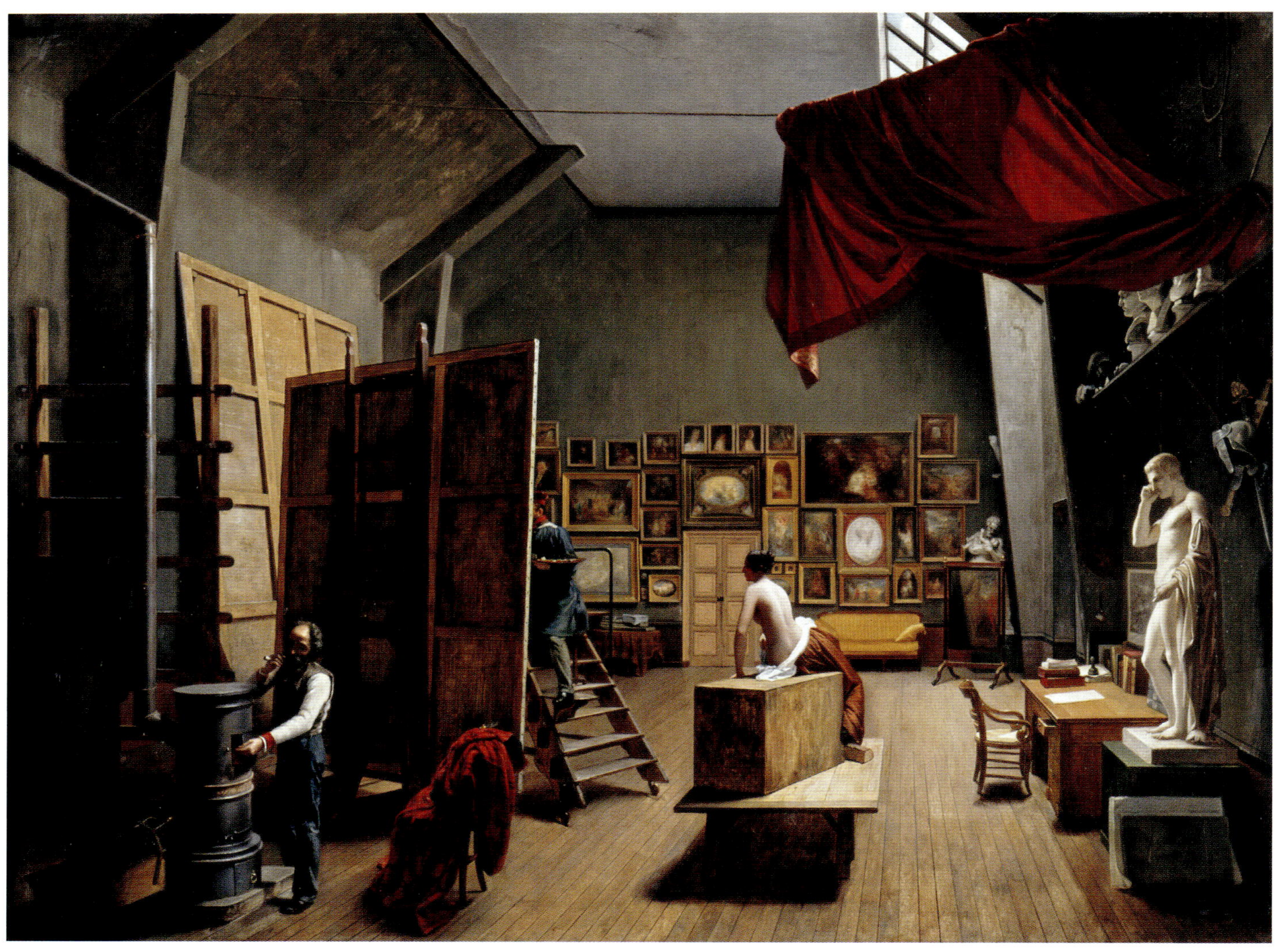

CAT. 15. ADRIENNE MARIE LOUISE GRANDPIERRE-DEVERZY (1798–1869), *The Studio of Abel de Pujol*, 1836.
Oil on canvas. Musée des beaux-arts, Valenciennes

We do not know how many works of art were lost in this wave of iconoclasm, but scattered records identify some of them. As it happens, the properties of the château de Bellevue, formerly the home of Labille-Guiard's most notorious patrons — Mesdames Adélaïde and Victoire, two of the aunts of Louis XVI — were being inventoried just as the purge was mandated. There, in the dining room of Madame Victoire's apartments in the pavilion of Brimborion, commissioners noted "a picture painted on canvas representing a portrait of a woman of the former royal family, by the Citoyenne Guiard, 4½ feet by 3½ feet in a gilt border."[17] In the same room were found three full-length portraits of Mesdames' ancestors, each measuring more than 7 feet high; in the Grand Salon at Brimborion, "an equestrian statue of Louis XVI in bronze by Pigalle," mounted on a marble pedestal and standing 25 inches high, was located. In the margins next to each of these entries, the simple words "to destroy" seal the works' fate.

The tale does not end here, however, for the story of Vigée-LeBrun's portrait also played a rhetorical role in the downfall of Robespierre.[18] On June 15, 1794 — some six weeks before Robespierre's demise — Marc-Guillaume Alexis Vadier, of the Committee of General Security, presented a fantastic report of a counter-Revolutionary conspiracy linking Robespierre and his religious ally Dom Gerle to the aged mystic Cathérine Théot.[19] Théot, also known as the Mother of God, had at one time been imprisoned in the Bastille on account of her rants and visions. More recently, she had won a small group of adherents to an eccentric theology which saw the Revolution in terms of apocalyptic prophecy and predicted the imminent arrival of the Messiah, soon to be made flesh through the word of Théot. According to Vadier's report, which ultimately sent five accused conspirators to the guillotine, these religious fanatics were plotting to "spoil the Revolutionary public spirit, to redirect minds from political opinions toward superstitious ideas."

Robespierre, with his suspicious devotion to the cult of the Supreme Being, was implicated in this scheme, which also involved Vigée-LeBrun's portrait. According to Vadier, the work had been found "mysteriously hidden behind a bed," having been "fraudulently removed from the inventory of the furnishings." Vadier alleged that the work painted by Vigée-LeBrun, "mistress of the traitor [discredited finance minister Charles Alexandre de] Calonne," had probably been set aside for future use by the Mother of God. The act of placing it in the Paris law school, near the Panthéon, "was to have been the prelude to the miraculous incarnation of the divine word and the fulfillment of her prophecies." In this masterfully fabricated piece of propaganda, Vadier binds together the Revolution's moral, gendered, and philosophical opposites, and figures them all in a royal portrait created by a licentious woman.

Was the French Revolution a hopeful era for women artists? Women who had been stifled by the Académie royale's limitations clearly received extraordinary benefits from the newly open Salons. But women who had risen to the top of the Old Regime art world suffered damage to their careers, their works, and their reputations.[20] And though more female artists received professional recognition in the early nineteenth century than ever before, decades would pass before another woman artist would attain the status and acclaim that Vigée-LeBrun and Labille-Guiard enjoyed before the fall of the Bastille.

Notes

1. Much of the material discussed below is also addressed in Laura Auricchio, *Adélaïde Labille-Guiard: Artist in the Age of Revolution* (Los Angeles, 2009), chaps. 3 and 4.

2. The debates on women in the Revolutionary-era Académie have been analyzed by Vivian P. Cameron, "Woman as Image and Image-Maker in Paris during the French Revolution" (PhD diss., Yale University, 1983), and Nicholas Mirzoeff, "Revolution, Representation, Equality: Gender, Genre, and Emulation in the Académie Royale de Peinture et Sculpture, 1785–93,"*Eighteenth-Century Studies* 31, no. 2 (1997–98), pp. 153–74. These authors directed me to many primary sources cited below. Quotations in this paragraph are from Simon-Charles Miger, *Lettre à Monsieur Vien* (Paris, 1789), Collection Deloynes, vol. 53, no. 1446, pp. 6–7: "C'est un abus qu'une loi qui fixe à trois ou quatre le nombre des dames académiciennes: ou il ne fallait pas en recevoir, ou, dès qu'on en a reçu, toutes celles qui ont un vrai talent ont des droites légitimes. L'accadémie [*sic*] doit être comme une église ouverte à tous les fidèles. Qu'on soit difficile sur le talent comme sur les mœurs, voilà la véritable loi; mais toute honnête femme, vraiment artiste, est un homme pour l'académie."

3. On moral, physical, and emotional problems attributed to female artists in eighteenth-century France, see Mary D. Sheriff, "The Woman-Artist Question," in this volume, as well as the far larger discussion in Mary D. Sheriff, *The Exceptional Woman: Elisabeth Vigée-Lebrun and the Cultural Politics of Art* (Chicago, 1996).

4. Georges Duplessis, *Mémoires et journal de J. G. Wille* (Paris, 1857), vol. 2, p. 268: "C'était que, comme aucune femme, quelque talent qu'elle pût avoir, ne pouvait cependant jamais parvenir à être professeur dans les écoles, ni avoir de gouvernement quelconque dans l'Académie, il serait cependant juste que telle ou telle, par de bonnes et valables raisons, fût récompensée par une distinction académique et honorifique seulement, et qu'il n'y en avait d'autres que celle d'être admise parmi et au nombre de conseillers."

5. *Adresse et projet de statuts et règlemens pour l'Académie centrale de peinture, sculpture, gravure et architecture, présentés à l'assemblée nationale par la majorité des membres de l'Académie royale de peinture et sculpture en assemblée délibérante* (Paris, 1790), Collection Deloynes, vol. 53, no. 1488, p. 59.

6. For a complete list of artists and works at the Revolutionary-era Salons, see Jean-François Heim, Claire Béraud, and Philippe Heim, *Les salons de peinture de la Révolution française, 1789–1799* (Paris, 1989). See also Udolpho van de Sandt, "Institutions et concours," in *Aux armes et aux arts!: Les arts de la Révolution 1789–1799*, ed. Philippe Bordes and Régis Michel, Librairie du bicentenaire de la Révolution française (Paris, 1988), pp. 138–65. On the women who exhibited at the open Salons, see Cameron, "Woman as Image and Image-Maker"; Margaret A. Oppenheimer, "'The Charming Spectacle of a Cadaver': Anatomical and Life Study by Women Artists in Paris, 1775–1815," *Nineteenth-Century Art Worldwide* (Spring 2007), http://19thc-artworldwide.org/spring_07/articles/oppe.shtml; and Margaret A. Oppenheimer, "Women Artists in Paris, 1791–1814" (PhD diss., New York University, 1996).

7. Joseph Baillio, "Une artiste méconnue, Rose Adélaïde Ducreux," *L'œil* 399 (October 1988), pp. 20–27.

8. The Académie was officially suppressed by decree of the National Convention on August 8, 1793. Henri Lapauze, ed., *Procès-verbaux de la Commune générale des arts de peinture, sculpture, architecture et gravure de la Société populaire et républicaine des arts* (Paris, 1903), p. xix. See also Archives Nationales (henceforth A.N.), Paris, F[17] 1310, and Collection Deloynes, vol. 53, nos. 1497, 1498.

9. Lapauze, *Procès-verbaux*, pp. 64, 73, 77, 81, 86, 121, 139, 146, 151, 156.

10. Ibid., p. 184: "Il pense que c'est par ce qu'une femme célèbre, la citoyenne Le Brun, a montré de grands talents dans la peinture, qu'une foule d'autres ont voulut s'occuper de la peinture tandis qu'elles ne devraient s'occuper qu'à broder des ceinturons et des bonnets de polices."

11. Ibid.: "Les femmes doivent être exclues de la Société attendu que la loi leur défend de s'assembler et de délibérer sur aucun objet."

12. *Instruction sur la manière d'inventorier et de conserver, dans toute l'étendue de la république, tous les objets qui peuvent servir aux arts, aux sciences et à l'enseignement* (Paris, Year 11), A.N., F[17A] 1045/1320.

13. M. Louis Tuetey, *Procès-verbaux de la Commission temporaire des arts* (Paris, 1912), vol. 1, pp. xxvii, xxxv, lvi, lxi.

14. Joseph Baillio tentatively identifies this painting as *The Dauphin Louis Charles Holding a Dog*, exhibited at the 1789 Salon. Joseph Baillio, *Elisabeth Louise Vigée Le Brun, 1755–1842*, exh. cat. (Fort Worth, 1982), p. 18.

15. All quotes are from A.N., F17*7, fol. 98, reprinted with invaluable footnotes in Tuetey, *Procès-verbaux*, vol. 1, pp. 225–26.

16. M. J. Guillaume, *Procès-verbaux du Comité d'instruction publique de la Convention nationale* (Paris, 1901), vol. 4, p. 657: "Ils proposent, et la Commission arrête, que tous les tableaux et portraits représentant des individus de la race Capet seront inventoriés et réunis dans un même dépôt, et que, conformément à l'inventaire on procédera à leur destruction totale et complète, afin que la superstition Royaliste ne puisse en recueillir aucun; que le présent arrêté sera communiqué au Comité d'instruction publique pour en obtenir la prompte et entière exécution. Malgré l'observation d'un membre que quelques-uns de ces tableaux ou portraits pourraient contenir des traits de génie ou d'originalité qu'il serait utile de conserver pour l'instruction et les arts, la Commission, ferme dans ses principes patriotiques, maintient son précédent arrêté."

17. Archives départementales des Yvelines et de l'ancienne Seine-et-Oise, 2 Q 74/11² Inventaire Brinborian an II, no. 85: "Un tableau peint sur toile représentant un portrait de femme de la ci devant famille, par la Cⁿᵉ Guiard de quatre pieds ½ sur trois pieds ½ dans la bordure d'orée, lequel nous avons fait à l'instant fait transporter où sont les autres portraits de la même famille, prisé trois cent livres."

18. Another version of the story presented to the National Convention linked the portrait to counter-Revolutionary uprisings in the Vendée. See *Moniteur universel* 269 (29 Prairial Year II [June 17, 1794]), pp. 739–43. For three different approaches to the role of the supposed Théot conspiracy in Robespierre's downfall, see Dominique Godineau, *The Women of Paris and Their French Revolution*, trans. Katherine Streip, Studies on the History of Society and Culture 26 (Berkeley, 1998), pp. 259–66; G. Lenotre, *Robespierre et la "mère de Dieu"* (Paris, 1926); and Albert Mathiez, *The Fall of Robespierre* (New York, 1927).

19. All quotes are from Marc-Guillaume Alexis Vadier, *Rapport et projet de décret, présenté à la Convention nationale, au nom des comités de sûreté générale et de salut public* (Paris, 27 Prairial an II [June 15, 1794]). On the rhetorical and political functions of counter-Revolutionary plots, see François Furet, *Interpreting the French Revolution*, trans. Elborg Forster (Cambridge, 1981), pp. 51–55.

20. For a more optimistic reading of the impact of the Revolution on the careers of women artists, see Gen Doy, *Women and Visual Culture in Nineteenth-Century France. 1800–1852* (London and New York, 1998).

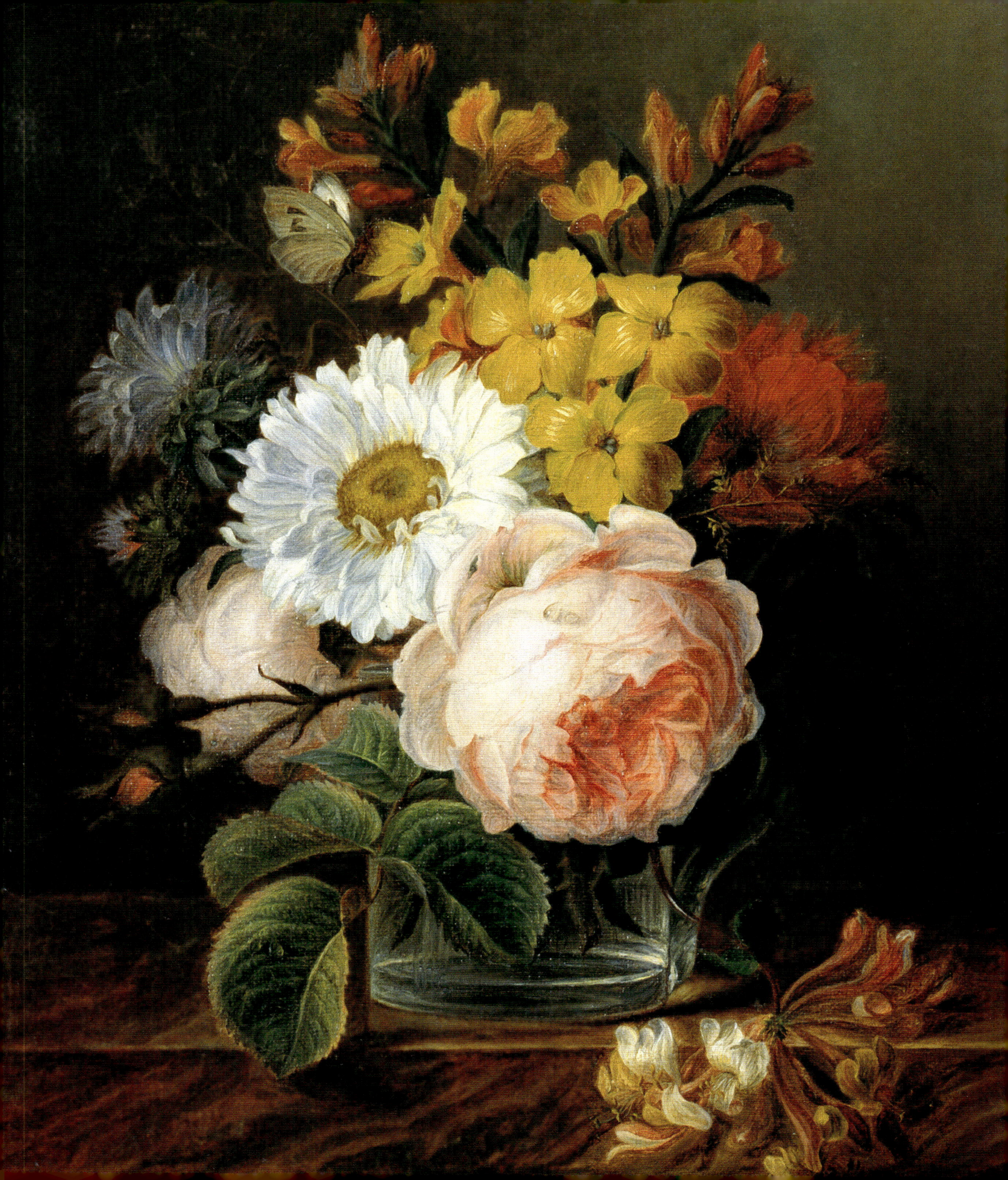

Looking Elsewhere: Women and the Parisian Art World in the Eighteenth Century | *Melissa Lee Hyde*

IN HER 1785 STUDY OF PROFESSIONS PRACTICED BY WOMEN in France, the feminist author Madame de Coicy (d. 1841) listed only two contemporary women as painters of note: Anne Vallayer-Coster (1744–1818; see cats. 16, 61) and Élisabeth Louise Vigée-LeBrun (1755–1842; see cats. 11, 23, 63).[1] If not exactly household names in Europe and the United States today, these two artists are the subjects of some of the best recent scholarship on eighteenth-century art, and they are regaining a portion of their former fame through monographic exhibitions in major museums.[2] This renewed interest in Vallayer-Coster and Vigée-LeBrun is entirely warranted. Both were spectacularly successful, in no small part because they were members of the Académie royale de peinture et de sculpture, in Paris. This afforded them the enviable privilege of showing their work at the greatest exhibition venue of the time in Europe: the biennial Salon, held in the Salon Carée of the Palais du Louvre. To belong to the Académie was a rare distinction for any artist, but it was especially so for women. In fact, Vallayer-Coster and Vigée-LeBrun made up half the quota of women allowed in that most prestigious of art institutions. Since one of the aims of Coicy's book is to lament the devaluation of women's work, it is impossible to imagine that her omission of the other two living *académiciennes*, Marie Thérèse Vien (1728–1805; see cat. 62) and Adélaïde Labille-Guiard (1749–1803; see cats. 8, 13, 17, 45), was a dismissal of their worth. Although Vien ceased to exhibit at the Salon after 1767, and may never be more than a footnote in art history, the younger Labille-Guiard was Vigée-LeBrun's nearest female contemporary in the Académie, and her equal in talent and success. (Perhaps she was not yet well known in 1785, when Coicy's book was published. In recent years, happily, Labille-Guiard has begun to receive her share of serious study.) In any case, Salon critics often thought of Vallayer-Coster, Vigée-LeBrun, and Labille-Guiard as a trio. More than one likened them to the three Graces.[3] Despite the near-celebrity status of these women in their own time, the picture of pre-Revolutionary French art that has emerged in most accounts of the period is of a man's world, defined by the Académie and the Salon, in which women figured rarely, and even then, mostly as marginalized exceptions. Coicy's omissions, ironically, prefigure the general pattern of women artists' steady disappearance from the histories of art written over the next two centuries.

CAT. 16. ANNE VALLAYER-COSTER (1744–1818), *Flowers in a Glass*, end of 18th century (detail). Oil on canvas. Musée des beaux-arts, Carcassonne

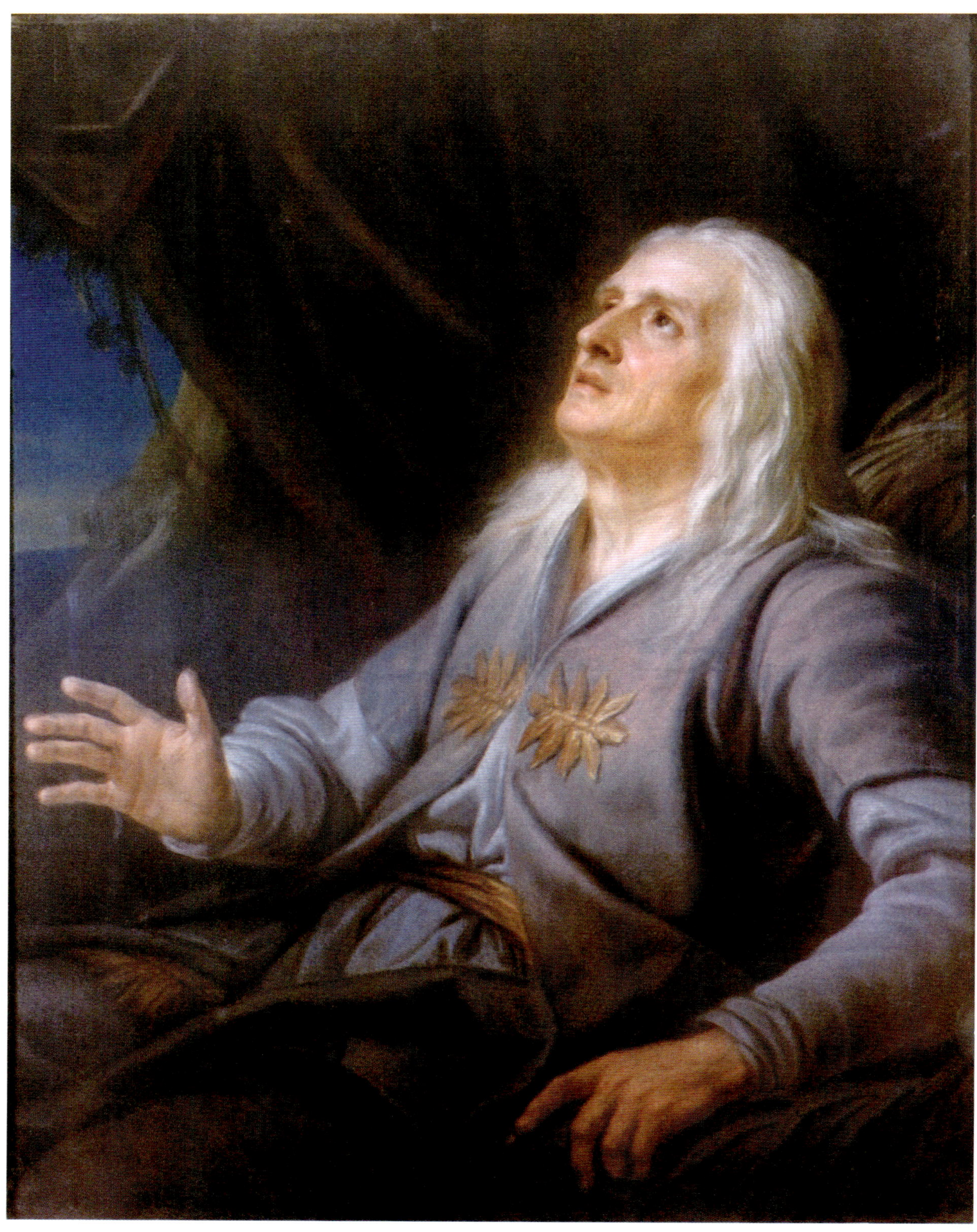

CAT. 17. ADÉLAÏDE LABILLE-GUIARD (1749–1803), *Portrait of the Actor Brizard in the Role of King Lear*, 1783.
Pastel on canvas. Collection Théâtre national de l'Odéon, Paris

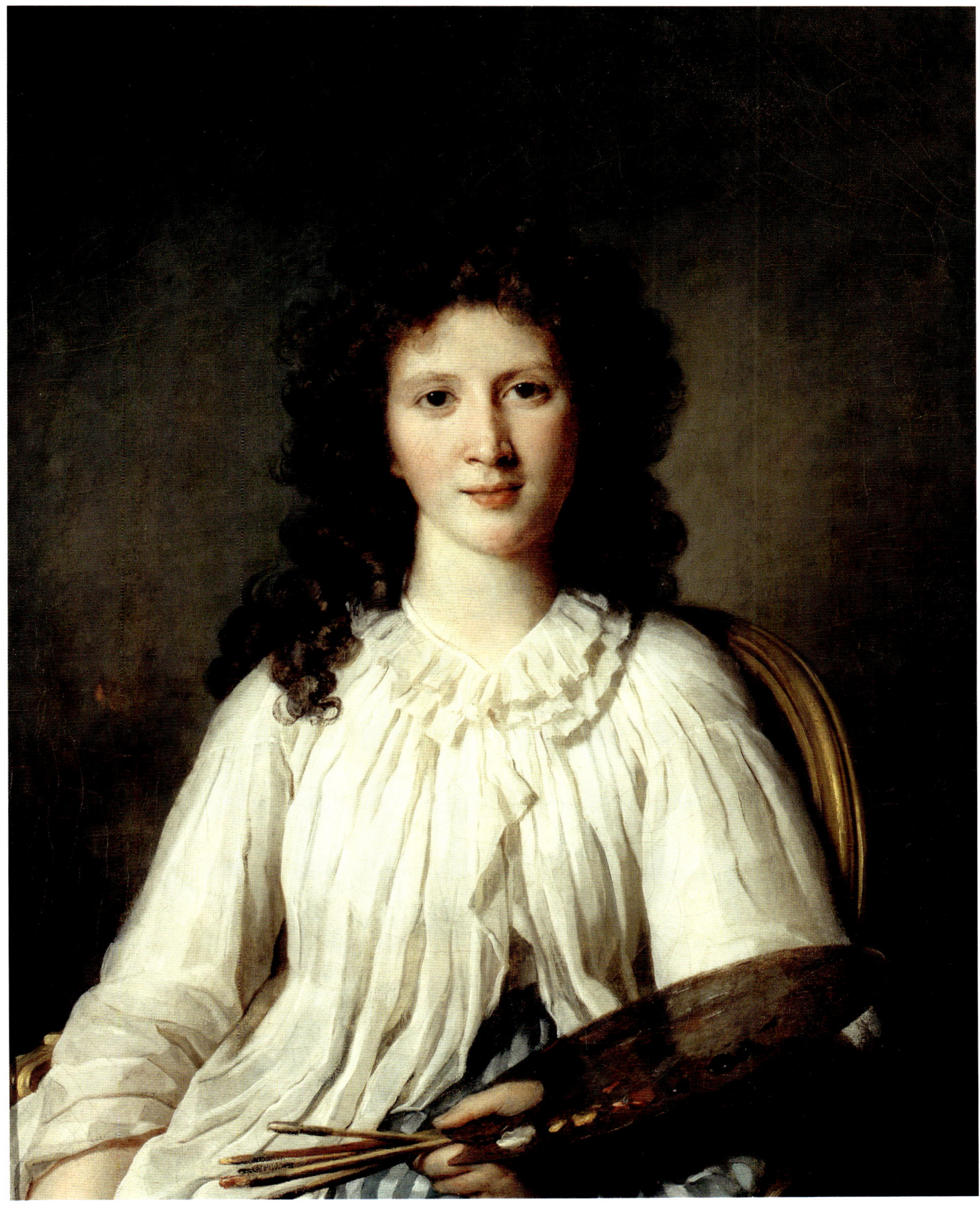

CAT. 18. MARIE GENEVIÈVE BOULIAR (1763–1825), *Portrait of Adélaïde Binard, Wife of Alexandre Lenoir*, ca. 1796. Oil on canvas. Musée Carnavalet – Histoire de Paris

Without wishing to diminish the importance of the French royal institutions, I will insist in this essay that histories focused on them offer a partial and skewed view. First, these institutions were but one part of a larger aesthetic culture in which women *were* a real presence. Although always a minority, women artists worked in their own right, for the open market or the court, or, more obscurely, in the studio of a husband or relative. Their presence became conspicuous after 1791, when the Revolution's liberalization of the Salon made it possible for artists to exhibit without being Académie members. However, as recent scholarship has begun to show, substantial numbers of women were active participants in the art world throughout the eighteenth century. (Marie Geneviève Bouliar [1763–1825; see cats. 5, 18, 29] and Marie Guilhelmine Benoist [1768–1826; see cats. 20, 27, 28] are examples of such artists.)[4] Like most professional male artists, who also had to operate outside the Académie, these women managed with little or no institutional support. Although some, like Charlotte Madeleine de Silvestre, née Le Bas (1700–1770), her relative Marie Maximilienne de Silvestre (1703–1797), and Vigée-LeBrun's girlhood friend Anne Rosalie Filleul (1752–1794; see cat. 38), were able to secure court appointments, these were outside the purview of the royal arts administration, known as the Bâtiments du roi.[5]

There is a second reason why traditional art histories, based on histories of the Académie and the Salon, do not tell the whole story about the art world. They describe the official business of the Académie, in which women like Madame de Pompadour and Marie-Antoinette did sometimes play a role (both intervened in behalf of favored artists, for example), but not its unofficial business, in which women were essential. As mothers, wives, sisters, daughters, and godmothers of academicians, women were critical links in the kinship networks that often affected the day-to-day affairs of the Académie — matters such as who studied with whom, or who sponsored whom for admission. Many of these para-academic women were artists themselves, so they also shaped the production of art, sometimes as engravers or copyists who helped to disseminate the works of their male relatives, sometimes by affecting the artistic practices of men in the family. For example, the portraitist Alexander Roslin (1718–1793) possibly left aside the making of pastel portraits in favor of oil painting because he married the pastelist Suzanne Giroust (1734–1772). In short, women were *always* players in the "manly" art world, though in ways not discernible from traditional art-historical sources — that is, from Salon criticism and from the official proceedings of the Académie, the correspondence among its royal administrators, and other archival records concerning it.

Women also played important roles as patrons of art — a matter I do not have room to discuss here. Even larger numbers were consumers of, or simply the audience for, art.[6] In the pages that follow I hope to add to the growing evidence that women in the eighteenth-century Parisian art world were not in every way excluded "others" but, rather, active agents.

Showing (up) in the Salon

Although prior to the Revolution non-academic women could not exhibit their work at the Salon, there were a few occasions before 1791 when they made a showing indirectly. Such was the case at the Salon of 1739, when Gilles Allou (1670–1751) displayed a portrait (untraced) of the artist Marie Maximilienne de Silvestre, daughter of the academician Louis de Silvestre (1675–1760). Mlle de Silvestre was the drawing instructor, reader, and lady-in-waiting to Marie-Josephe de Saxe, the mother of Louis XVI. Allou's portrait showed her holding a palette, thereby publicly advertising the sitter's identity as a practicing artist (rather than, say, as a reader) — an identity reinforced

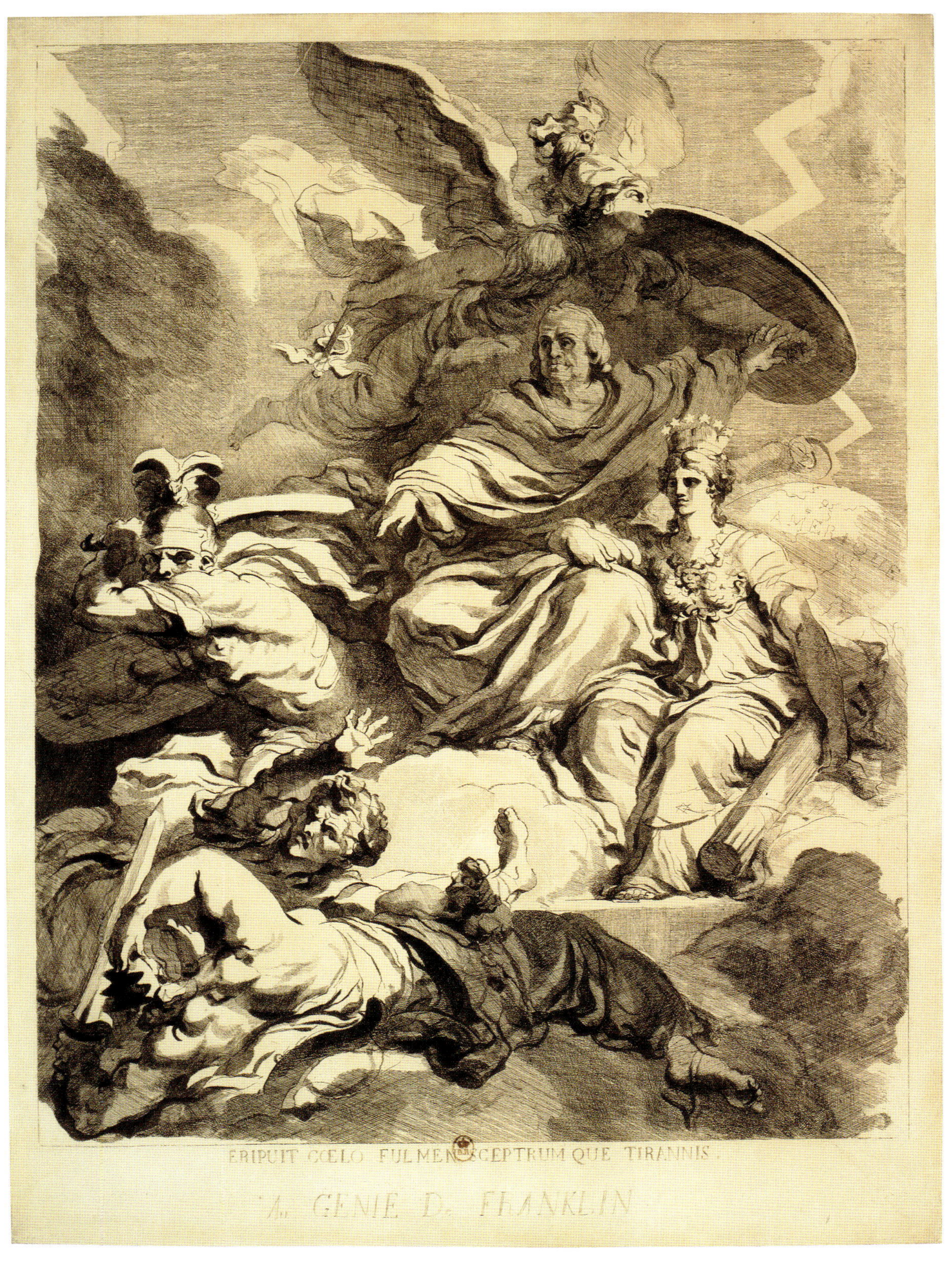

Cat. 19. Marguerite Gérard (1761–1837), *Honoring the Genius of Franklin*, 1778. Etching.
Cliché Biblicthèque nationale de France, Paris

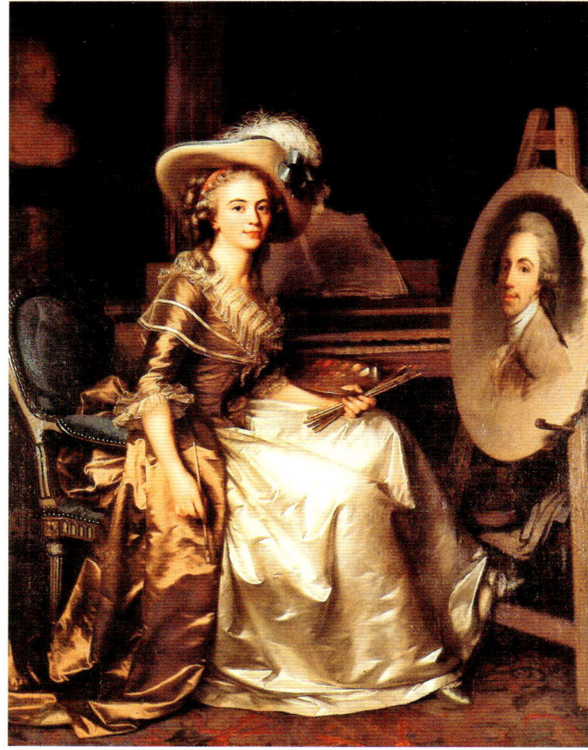

Figure 2.1. Antoine Vestier (1740–1824), *Full-Length Portrait of Mlle Vestier Painting the Portrait of Her Father*, 1785. Oil on canvas, 67¾ × 50¼ in. (172 × 127.5 cm). Private collection, Buenos Aires (artwork in public domain)

Figure 2.2. Marguerite Gérard (1761–1837), *Artist Painting a Portrait of a Musician*, before 1803. Oil on panel, 24 × 20¼ in. (61 × 51.5 cm). The State Hermitage Museum, Saint Petersburg

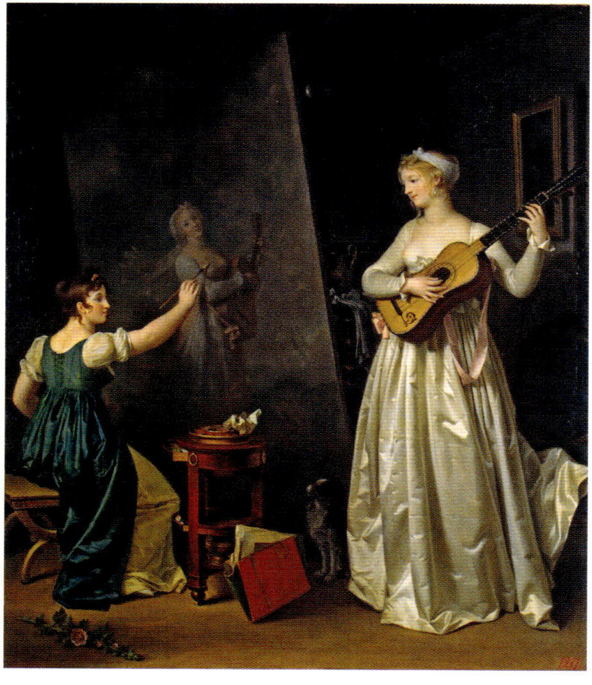

by Allou's portrait of Louis de Silvestre (untraced), which hung nearby at the same Salon. Previously, at the Salon of 1737, Allou had exhibited a portrait of his wife drawing an optical figure (untraced). Given how rarely the image of the woman as artist graced the walls of the Salon, these must have been eye-catching works.

By the 1770s and 1780s, the Parisian public was far more accustomed to seeing portraits and self-portraits of women artists. But it was still fairly unusual iconography at the Salon, which must be one of the reasons why the stunning *Full-Length Portrait of Mlle Vestier Painting the Portrait of Her Father* (fig. 2.1), by Antoine Vestier (1740–1824), attracted the attention of so many when it appeared at the Salon of 1785. A large-scale portrait that bears striking similarities to Labille-Guiard's magnificent *Self-Portrait with Two Pupils, Marie Gabrielle Capet (1761–1818) and Marie Marguerite Carreaux de Rosemond (died 1788)* (Metropolitan Museum of Art, New York),[7] also shown at the Salon that year, it emphasized Marie-Nicole Vestier's talent as a painter (as well as her musical ability). It did not just show her as a painter, however; it also vividly evoked the visual language of the eighteenth-century self-portrait—she is seated before an easel, palette in hand, and her steady outward gaze is that of the artist studying her own reflection—so that the impression is given that Marie-Nicole represented herself. Since Vestier (later Dumont) was barred from showing her own work at the Salon, this "self-representation" by proxy is as close as she could get to exhibiting there, until 1793, when her true self-portrait (*The Artist at Her Occupations*)[8] appeared along with eight other self-portraits by women. The 1785 portrait by her father advertised her artistic talent while masterfully demonstrating his own. Antoine Vestier was thus able to capitalize for both of them on the privileges of membership in the Académie.[9]

Lacking even Marie-Nicole Dumont's indirect entrée into the Salon, Marie Renée Geneviève Brossard de Beaulieu (1760–1835), a student of Jean-Baptiste Greuze (1725–1805), attempted at this same time to secure some of the other privileges of membership (such as official affiliation and lodging and a studio in the Louvre), but to no avail.[10] A bid for full membership had earlier been made for another woman, in 1769. At that time a Mme Durocher wrote to the marquis de Marigny, the director of the Bâtiments du roi, in behalf of the pastelist Mlle Allais (or Allet) (1759–1779), to plead for his intervention in getting her admitted.[11] He demurred, but the

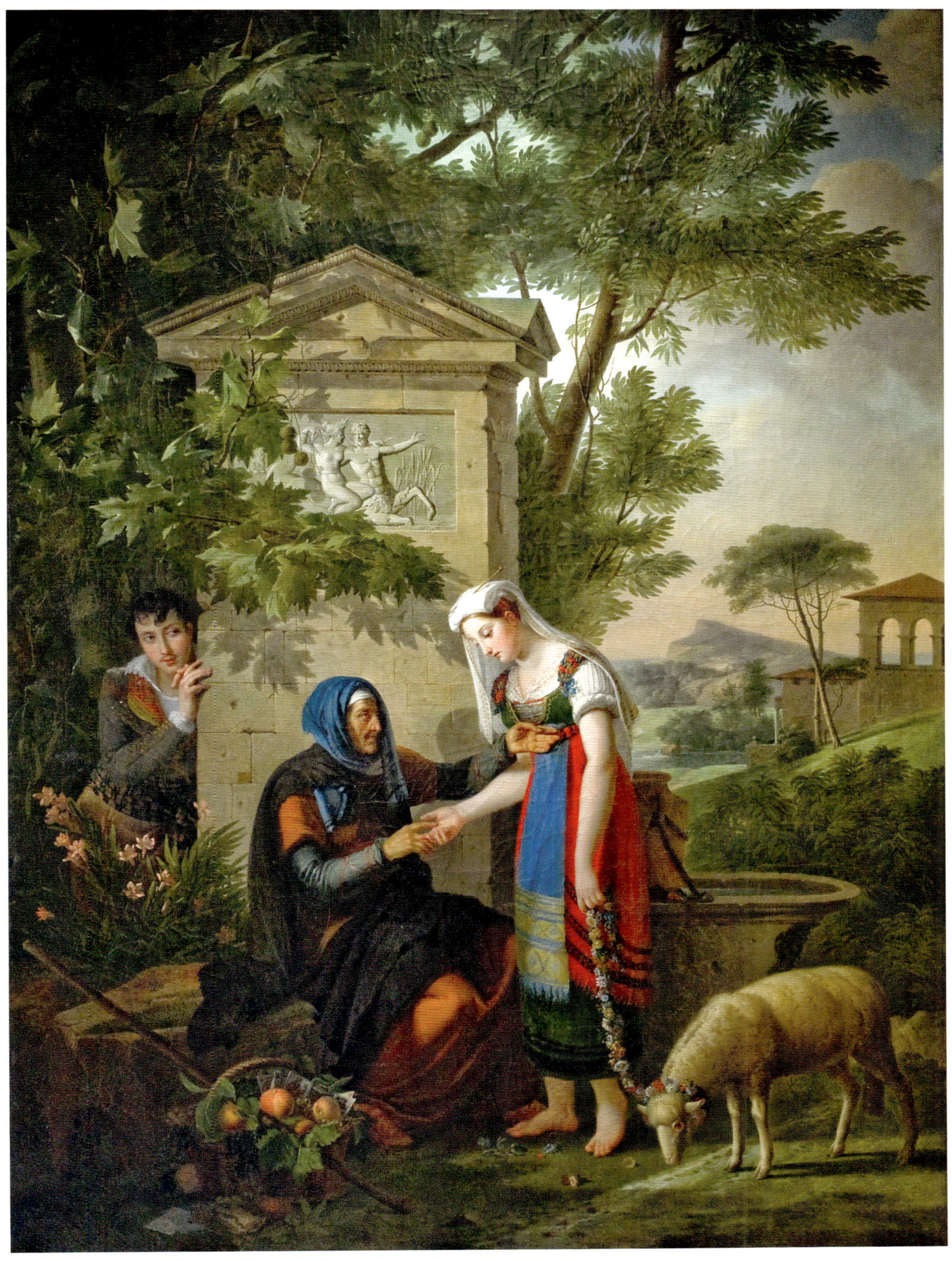

CAT. 20. MARIE GUILHELMINE BENOIST (1768–1826), *The Consultation, or The Fortune-Teller*, 1812. Oil on canvas.
Musée de la ville, Saintes

next year Vallayer-Coster and Suzanne Roslin were added to the ranks of the Académie, a development that was immediately followed by the official policy that restricted the number of female members to four. Like most professional artists of the time, Brossard de Beaulieu and Allais had to carry out their careers by making the most of the opportunities that were available to them outside the charmed circle of the royal institutions. These opportunities did not make them famous or gain them a place in traditional histories of art, but these women were nonetheless recognized by their contemporaries and able to participate as professional artists in the rich visual culture of their own time. In this broader milieu, other women — one thinks particularly of Marguerite Gérard (1761 – 1837), about the 1780s (see fig. 2.2) — even managed to establish themselves as highly successful artists, on a par with "the three Graces," entirely without the imprimatur of the Académie.

The Showing of Women Elsewhere

During the second half of the eighteenth century, there were a number of alternative venues in Paris that were open to women. These included the expositions sponsored by the Académie de Saint-Luc between 1751 and 1774; the biweekly Salon de la Correspondance, mounted by the entrepreneur Pahin de la Blancherie between 1777 and 1787; and the one-time Exposition du Colisée, in 1776. But the exhibition that was for the longest time of special importance for women artists took place in the place Dauphine. This was an open-air exhibition, held on the day of Corpus Christi, called the Exposition de la jeunesse. As early as 1760, a certain Demoiselle Allais (and another named Girouard) were mentioned among the young artists showing there. By the 1780s women's increasingly significant participation in the exhibition made it a hot topic in the press.[12]

From 1789 until the end of its existence, in 1791, the Exposition de la jeunesse was moved indoors, to the lavish new showroom of the art dealer Jean Baptiste Pierre Le Brun (1748 – 1813). Thanks to Le Brun's detailed catalogue of the 1791 show, we know that fifteen of the seventy-nine exhibitors (19 percent) were women.[13] With his connections and exhibition spaces, Le Brun would be instrumental in helping to launch the career of his wife, Élisabeth Louise Vigée-LeBrun. She displayed works in his first gallery, at the Hôtel de Lubert, in 1779 and 1785. Le Brun also handled the work of Marguerite Gérard (see cats. 7, 12, 14, 19, 21, 39 and pp. 2, 3), who had her first public showing in his gallery in the 1789 exposition. Le Brun also featured Gérard's work in at least one of his later exhibitions.[14] Brossard de Beaulieu (who also showed at the alternative venues, including Le Brun's), followed the enterprising example of her teacher Greuze, holding her own private studio exhibitions during the 1780s. These shows of her work were announced, and received positive press, in widely read newspapers and gazettes.

Along with listings in almanacs and biographical dictionaries, such notices were a precious source of publicity for artists of all kinds: in 1759, for example, the *Feuille nécessaire* announced in glowing terms the recent completion of works by François Boucher (1703 – 1770), Jean Baptiste Henri Deshays (1729 – 1765), Suzanne Roslin, and Marie Thérèse Vien.[15] In 1757 the *Mercure de France* noted that a Mademoiselle de Briancourt had presented two allegories to Queen Marie Leszczińska that celebrated the dauphin's recent recovery from illness, with which the queen and her daughters were "very pleased."[16] Such private viewings at court were relatively rare, but could certainly open doors for an aspiring artist. Mlle de Briancourt does not seem to have gained anything but publicity out of it, since we almost never hear of her again.[17] But the strategy of making a gift of one's work to potential clients (such as the queen), or to venerated institutions such as the Académie française, was one that was pursued to great effect by Vigée-LeBrun, among others. In 1775, at the beginning of her career, she attracted a good deal of attention by presenting the Académie française with portraits of former academicians, setting her firmly on the path to success.[18]

Conclusion: Looking Elsewhere

The examples I have outlined here of women's artistic engagements offer tantalizing glimpses behind the scenes of the traditional history of eighteenth-century art. They point to how much is to be gained by continuing to re-frame and fill out our picture of art history—a project that American and European scholars began in earnest in the 1970s. Continuing to recover artists who have been lost to art history, and looking beyond the usual official sources, is essential to writing the much-needed histories of the art world that have remained hidden. Looking elsewhere helps us to see that, as was undoubtedly known in the eighteenth century, *women* were never elsewhere. They were always there.

Notes

I thank the University of Florida Office of Research and Graduate Programs for providing generous funding for this essay through the Fine Arts Scholarship Enhancement Fund.

1. Madame de Coicy, *Les femmes comme il convient de les voir, ou Aperçu de ce que les femmes ont été, de ce qu'elles sont, et de ce qu'elles pourroient être* (Paris and London, 1785), vol. 2, pp. 61–71, cited in Mary D. Sheriff, *The Exceptional Woman: Elisabeth Vigée-Lebrun and the Cultural Politics of Art* (Chicago, 1996), p. 263.

2. See Eik Kahng et al., *Anne Vallayer-Coster, Painter to the Court of Marie-Antoinette*, exh. cat. (New Haven, 2002), and Joseph Baillio, *Elisabeth Louise Vigée Le Brun, 1755–1842*, exh. cat. (Fort Worth, 1982).

3. See Laura Auricchio, "Portraits of Impropriety: Adélaïde Labille-Guiard and the Careers of Professional Women Artists in Late Eighteenth-Century Paris" (PhD diss., Columbia University, 2000), p. 92. On Labille-Guiard, see also Auricchio's *Adélaïde Labille-Guiard: Artist in the Age of Revolution* (Los Angeles, 2009).

4. On the liberalization of the Salon, see Margaret A. Oppenheimer, "Women Artists in Paris, 1791–1814" (PhD diss., New York University, 1996); Vivian P. Cameron, "Woman as Image and Image-Maker in Paris during the French Revolution" (PhD diss., Yale University, 1983); and Auricchio, "Portraits of Impropriety."

5. On the Silvestres, see Roger-Armand Weigert, "Femmes peintres du XVIIIe siècle: Les deux Marie Silvestre," *Archives de l'art français*, nouv. pér., 22 (1959), pp. 129–35, and the informative Web site maintained by their descendants, http://israel .silvestre.free.fr/israel/israel.php.

6. See Melissa Lee Hyde and Jennifer Milam, eds., *Women, Art and the Politics of Identity in Eighteenth-Century Europe*, Women and Gender in the Early Modern World (Aldershot, 2003).

7. For an illustration of this work, see Auricchio, *Adélaïde Labille-Guiard*, p. 41, fig. 30.

8. Reproduced in *Importants tableaux anciens*, sale cat., Sotheby's, Monaco, June 15, 1990, lot 289.

9. Auricchio offers a different reading of the Vestier portrait in "Self-Promotion in Adélaïde Labille-Guiard's 1785 *Self-Portrait with Two Students*," *The Art Bulletin* 89, no. 1 (March 2007), p. 56.

10. For a discussion of Brossard de Beaulieu, with bibliography, see Melissa Lee Hyde, "Women and the Visual Arts in the Age of Marie-Antoinette," in Kahng, *Vallayer-Coster*, p. 80.

11. The letter is summarized in Neil Jeffares, *Dictionary of Pastellists before 1800* (London, 2006), p. 31.

12. Prosper Dorbec, "L'Exposition de la jeunesse au XVIIIe siècle," *Gazette des beaux-arts*, July 1905, p. 466. For an in-depth discussion of the Exposition de la jeunesse and the Salon de la Correspondance, see Auricchio, "Self-Promotion," pp. 55–56, and Laura Auricchio, "Pahin de la Blancherie's Commercial Cabinet of Curiosity (1779–87)," *Eighteenth-Century Studies* 36, no. 1 (Fall 2002), pp. 47–61.

13. Oppenheimer, "Women Artists," p. 9.

14. One of those exhibitions, in 1798, included paintings by Jacques-Louis David (1748–1825) and Louis Léopold Boilly (1761–1845). See Carol S. Eliel, "Genre Painting during the Revolution and the Goût Hollandais," in *1789: French Art during the Revolution*, ed. Alan Wintermute, exh. cat. (New York, 1989), p. 55. See also Sally Wells-Robertson, "Marguerite Gérard" (PhD diss., New York University, 1978), vol. 1, pp. 1, 112, and Carole Blumenfeld, "Marguerite Gérard et la peinture de genre de la fin des années 1770 aux années 1820" (PhD diss., Université de Lille 3, 2011).

15. *La feuille nécessaire*, April 2, 1759, p. 118. For more on the women artists listed in almanacs, see Sheriff, *Exceptional Woman*, p. 263, and Hyde, "Women and the Visual Arts."

16. Cited in Jean Chatelus, *Peindre à Paris au XVIIIe siècle* (Nîmes, 1991), p. 26.

17. Briancourt's (untraced) portrait of Madame Latour de Franqueville is discussed in correspondence between the sitter and Jean-Jacques Rousseau. See *Correspondance originale et inédite de Jean-Jacques Rousseau avec Mme Latour de Franqueville et M. de Peyrou* (Paris, 1803), vol. 1, p. 292.

18. For these portraits and the works she exhibited chez Le Brun, see Baillio, *Vigée Le Brun*, pp. 12–13.

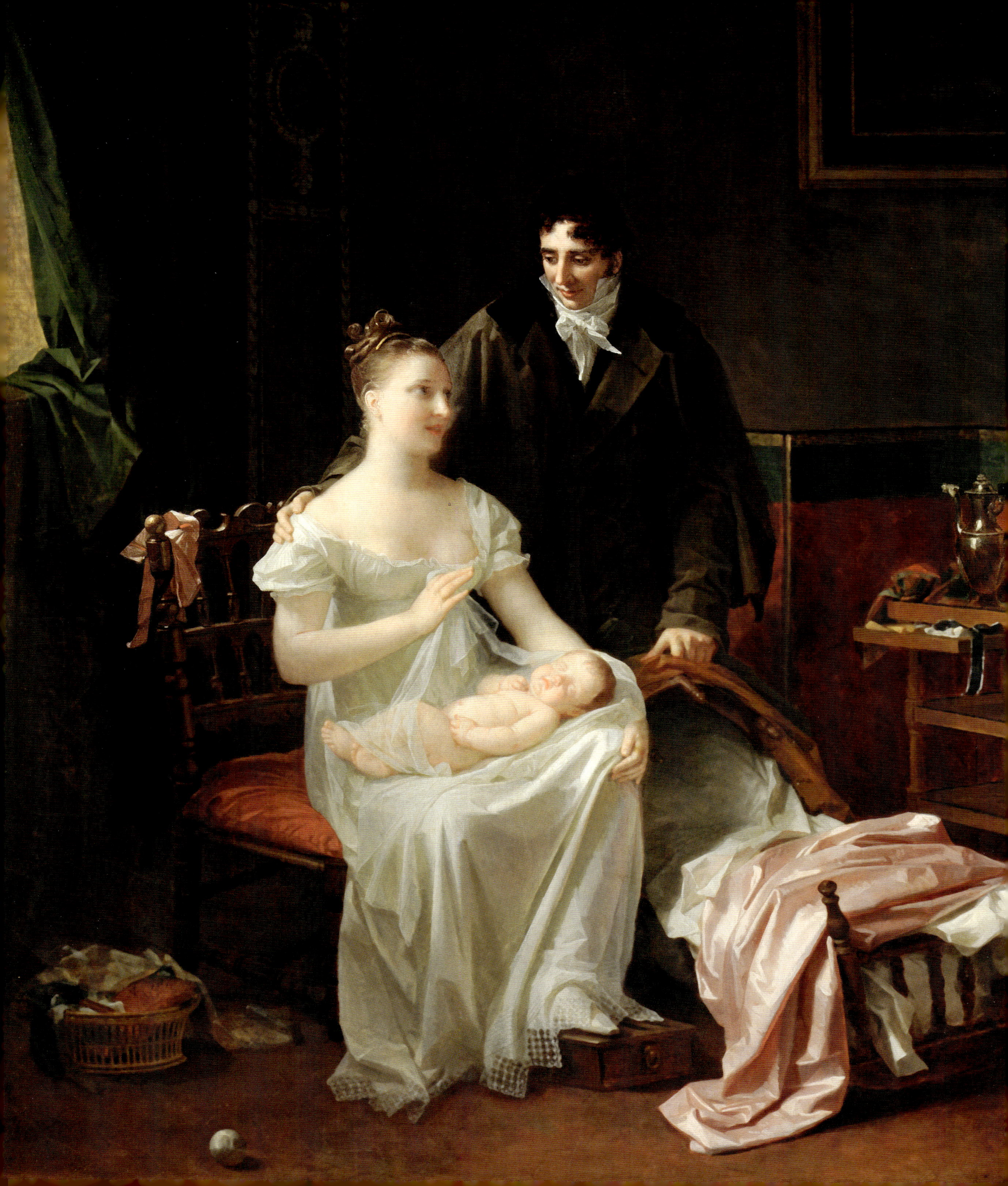

The Woman-Artist Question | *Mary D. Sheriff*

THE WOMAN-ARTIST QUESTION TOOK ON PARTICULAR urgency in the eighteenth century as scientists and philosophers proposed new theories of sexual difference that touched all Frenchwomen, royalists and revolutionaries alike. Medical men located mental development—and with it, the potential for artistic creativity—in the biological "facts" of the body, in its nerves, fibers, organs, and, above all, *sensibilité* (sensibility or sensitivity). Writers such as the surgeon Pierre Fabre (1716–?1791), in his 1785 *Essai sur les facultés de l'âme considérées dans leurs rapports avec la sensibilité et l'irritabilité de nos organes* (Essay on the faculties of the mind considered in relation to the sensibility and irritability of our organs), proposed that exquisite *sensibilité* was the key to genius; without it, a man could never become a Raphael or a Rubens.[1] But what about a woman? Was it likely that *her* exquisite *sensibilité* could lead to greatness?

Developed in the 1740s and 1750s, the concept of *sensibilité* dominated French medical literature into the nineteenth century.[2] *Sensibilité* was a property of *all* living bodies and allowed them to perceive and respond to the impressions of external objects and stimuli.[3] Although the degree of *sensibilité* could vary from individual to individual, bodies were endowed with more or less *sensibilité* depending on the softness and impressionability of their nerves and organs and on the speed with which the nerve and muscle fibers vibrated. These factors correlated with age and sex. According to the theory of *sensibilité* popularized in the *Encyclopédie* (1751–72), the great compendium of knowledge of the French Enlightenment, children were more sensitive than adults, which accounted for the frequent convulsions they experienced at the least emotional disturbance. "As to women," Henri Fouquet claimed in his *Encyclopédie* entry, "their constitution approaches, as one knows, that of children. Women's passions are much livelier, in general, than those of men."[4] The *sensibilité* that enabled women to feel emotion keenly also made them prone to mental illness. With the physician Edmé Pierre Chauvot de Beauchêne (1748–1824), doctors found that woman's equilibrium was easily upset, her functions easily deranged, because her "sensitive internal organs and more rapid movements of nerve and muscle fibers made her more susceptible to the effects of passion."[5]

Differences in *sensibilité* also ensured that men and women did not develop the same powers of reason and imagination. The physiologist Pierre Roussel (1742–1802) took on the question of woman's mental development in his influential *Système physique et moral de la femme* (Physical and moral system of the woman), first published in 1775 and reissued throughout the nineteenth century. He found woman's sense organs to be active and impressionable, and her perceptions rapid. He noted that sensations imprinted themselves on her imagination organs with

CAT. 21. MARGUERITE GÉRARD (1761–1837), *Motherhood*, 1815–20. Oil on canvas. Musée des beaux-arts, Lyon

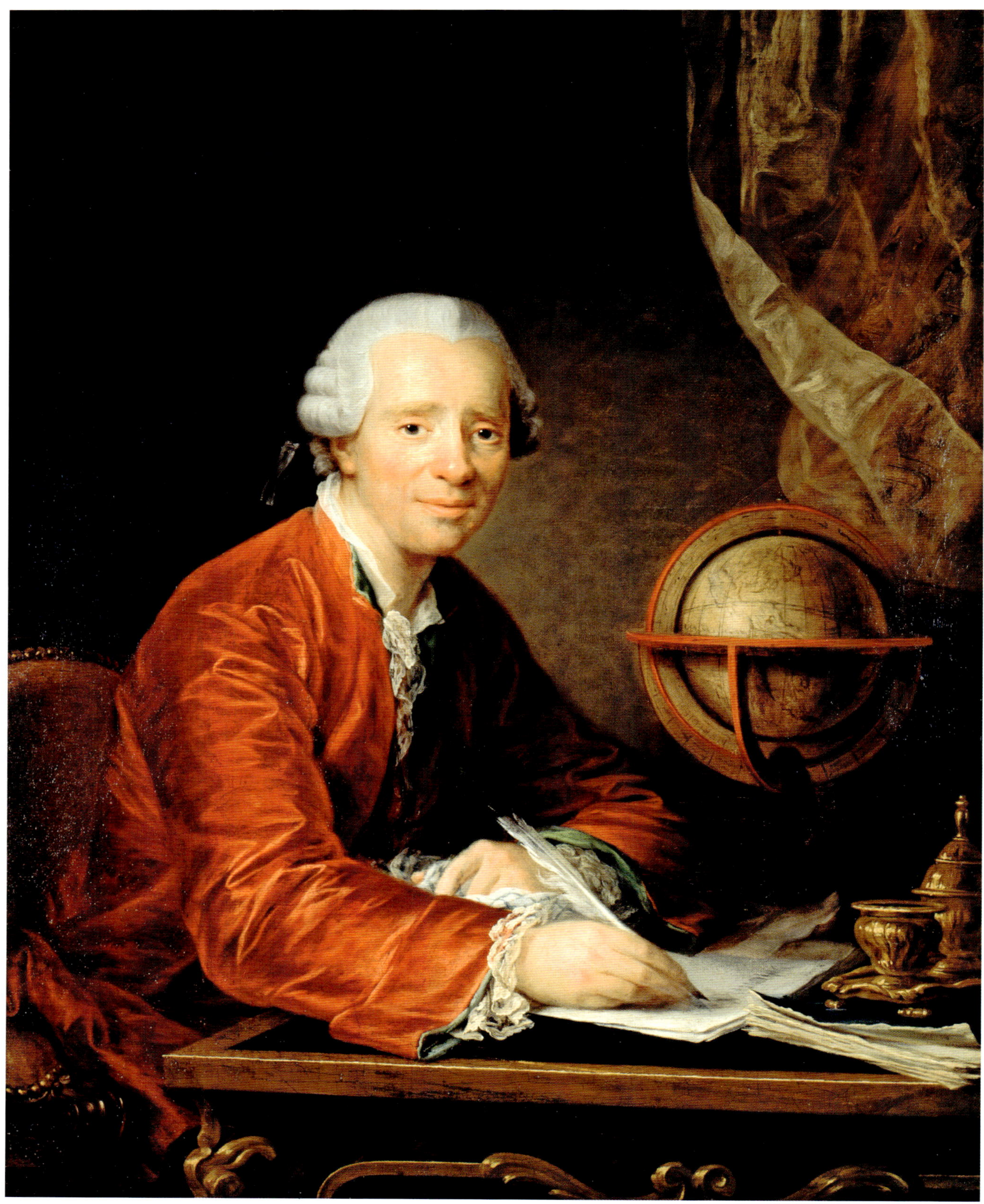

great facility. Yet because in women the variety of sensations was much greater than their duration, women were constantly distracted and never developed strong powers of reflection or reason.[6] The *Encyclopédie* article "Femme" (Woman) promoted the medicine of *sensibilité* in noting that although the "delicacy of their organs" (*la délicatesse de leur organisation*) gave women a livelier imagination, it rendered them less capable of attention. Women could perceive more quickly than men, but because they could not consider anything for any length of time, they never developed the powers of reflection necessary to good reason.[7]

In the eighteenth and nineteenth centuries, the ability to imagine vividly *and* to experience vicariously the emotions appropriate to the subject portrayed marked the artistic temperament.[8] It would seem, then, that women, whose heightened *sensibilité* endowed them with these qualities, were biologically destined to make art. Their *sensibilité*, however, was not exquisite but excessive; it was not adequately controlled by reason. Woman's *sensibilité* thus led not to creative endeavor but to the "vapors" and "hysteria," mental illnesses that presented particular dangers for the female sex. There were, of course, doctors like Julien d'Offray La Mettrie (1709–1751) who did not stress sexual difference in articulating the effects of *sensibilité*, but they were few and far between. And in this new era of *sensibilité* it was difficult to claim, as did the Cartesian François Poullain de la Barre (1647–1725), that the mind—which in his philosophy was independent of the body—had no sex.[9] The discourse of *sensibilité* was even used to limit the imaginative power of the female mind and thus to push women further from cultural production. It is here that the collusion between philosophy and medicine is most evident.

In his treatise on women, Roussel specifically distinguished the female imagination from that of the true artist: "[Woman's] imagination, more lively than stable, lends itself little to those true and picturesque expressions that are the sublime of the arts of imitation. More able to sense than to create, she receives more easily in her mind the images of objects that she cannot reproduce."[10] In finding woman more capable of "sensing than creating," Roussel differentiates between an imagination that mirrors perception and one that creates ideas; the first belonged to women, the second to men. Roussel did not, however, invent this distinction. Rather, he "verified" scientifically what philosophers had already posited, and he refers his readers to the 1772 discourse on women written by the minor philosopher Antoine Léonard Thomas (1732–1785).[11] In his *Essai sur le caractère, les mœurs et l'esprit des femmes dans les différents siècles* (Essay on the character, morals, and mind of women in different centuries), Thomas offered the conventional wisdom that imagination, not reason, dominated women: "The real world is not sufficient for them; they love to create an imaginary world; they live in it and embellish it."[12] He justifies his assessment by recourse to the science of *sensibilité:* sensations strongly affect women, whose imaginations are lively and represent sensations rapidly. Yet for Thomas, woman's imagination is not strong but lively and light; it is adapted to feminine weakness. He concludes his discussion by observing that woman's imagination resembles a "mirror that reflects everything but creates nothing."[13]

The woman-artist question is implicit in the writings of Thomas, Roussel, and others of their ilk. It was left to the physician Beauchêne, however, to state directly what was at stake. Women, he admitted, had a lively spirit that effortlessly produced the most wonderful images and animated them in the most seductive colors. Yet their bursts of imagination and their exquisite sensibility were only compensation for "that which is lacking in the profundity of their ideas, in the force of their reason, and in creative genius, which by right belong to man."[14] "By right" is a telling phrase, for this right was claimed long before the science of *sensibilité* claimed to prove it empirically.

Cat. 22. Catherine Lusurier (1752–1781), *Portrait of Jean Le Rond d'Alembert*, 1777. Oil on canvas. Musée Carnavalet–Histoire de Paris

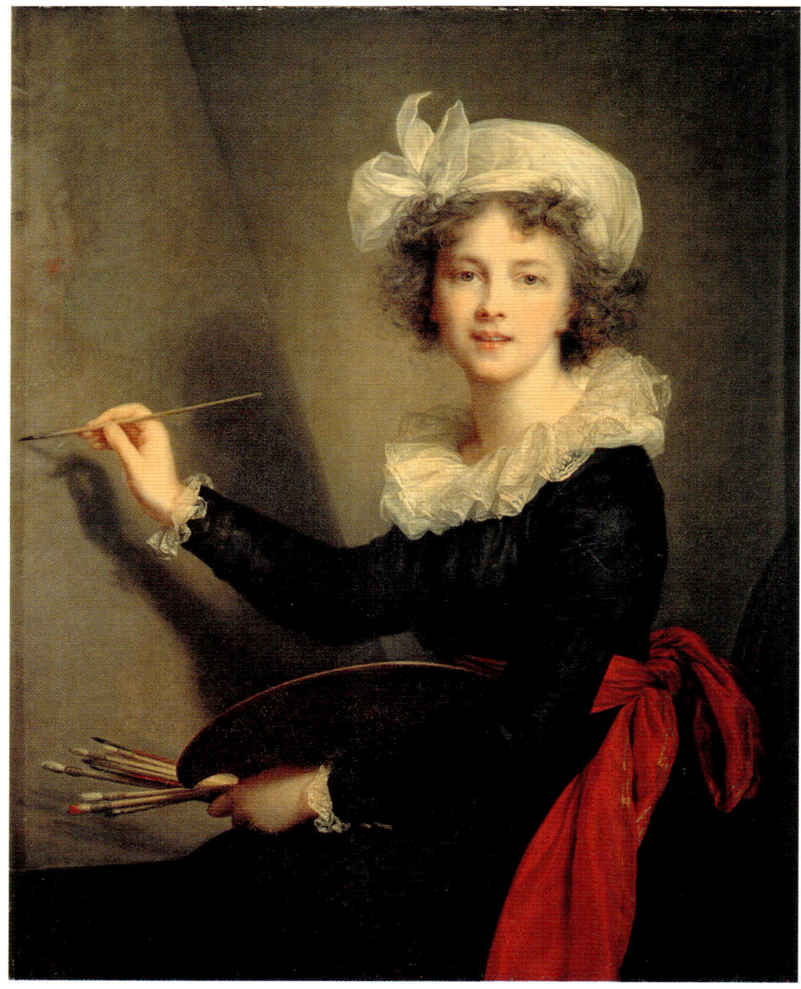

Figure 3.1. Élisabeth Louise Vigée-LeBrun (1755–1842). *Self-Portrait*, 1790. Oil on canvas, 39⅜ × 31⅞ in. (100 × 81 cm). Galleria degli Uffizi, Florence

Women who wanted to refute the claims of Roussel, Beauchêne, and Thomas were at a disadvantage. They could not offer their own scientific proof because the dictates of modesty that society imposed on women excluded them from serious study of biology and medicine. But women in the eighteenth and nineteenth centuries did talk back. They drew on logic, noting contradictions in theories of *sensibilité*. They drew on reports of travelers who observed "savages" thought to be close to the state of nature. They drew on history and experience to counter generalizations about woman's abilities, recalling many examples that did not fit the proposed models. They found allies in thinkers like Poullain de la Barre and physicians like La Mettrie whose theories of mental development did not stress sexual difference, and in writers like Ambroise Riballier (1712–1785) who attributed to educational systems the differences between men's and women's achievements.[15]

Madame d'Épinay (1726–1783), a writer and friend of the Encyclopedists, responded this way in 1772 to Thomas's discourse on women: "It is quite evident that men and women are of the same nature and the same constitution. The proof is that savage women are as robust, as agile as savage men; so the weakness of our constitution and of our organs belongs surely to our education and is a result of the condition that we have been assigned in society."[16] In her 1785 *Les femmes comme il convient de les voir* (Women as it is appropriate to see them), Madame de Coicy (d. 1841) attributed the difference between the sexes to differences in education and societal expectations. She dares to challenge science, and alluding to Poullain de la Barre, writes that "the most precise anatomy has not been able to show any difference between the head of a woman and the head of a man; their brains are entirely the same; they see, they hear by organs that are exactly the same. They receive sense impressions and conserve them in the same way.... All physical difference resides in sexual organs that have nothing to do with understanding."[17] And Madame de Genlis (Stéphanie Félicité, comtesse de Genlis, 1746–1830), in her 1826 *De l'influence des femmes sur la littérature française* (On the influence of women on French literature), noted that genius was composed of

Cat. 23. Élisabeth Louise Vigée-Lebrun (1755–1842), *Portrait of Joseph Vernet*, 1778. Oil on canvas. Musée du Louvre, Département des peintures, Paris

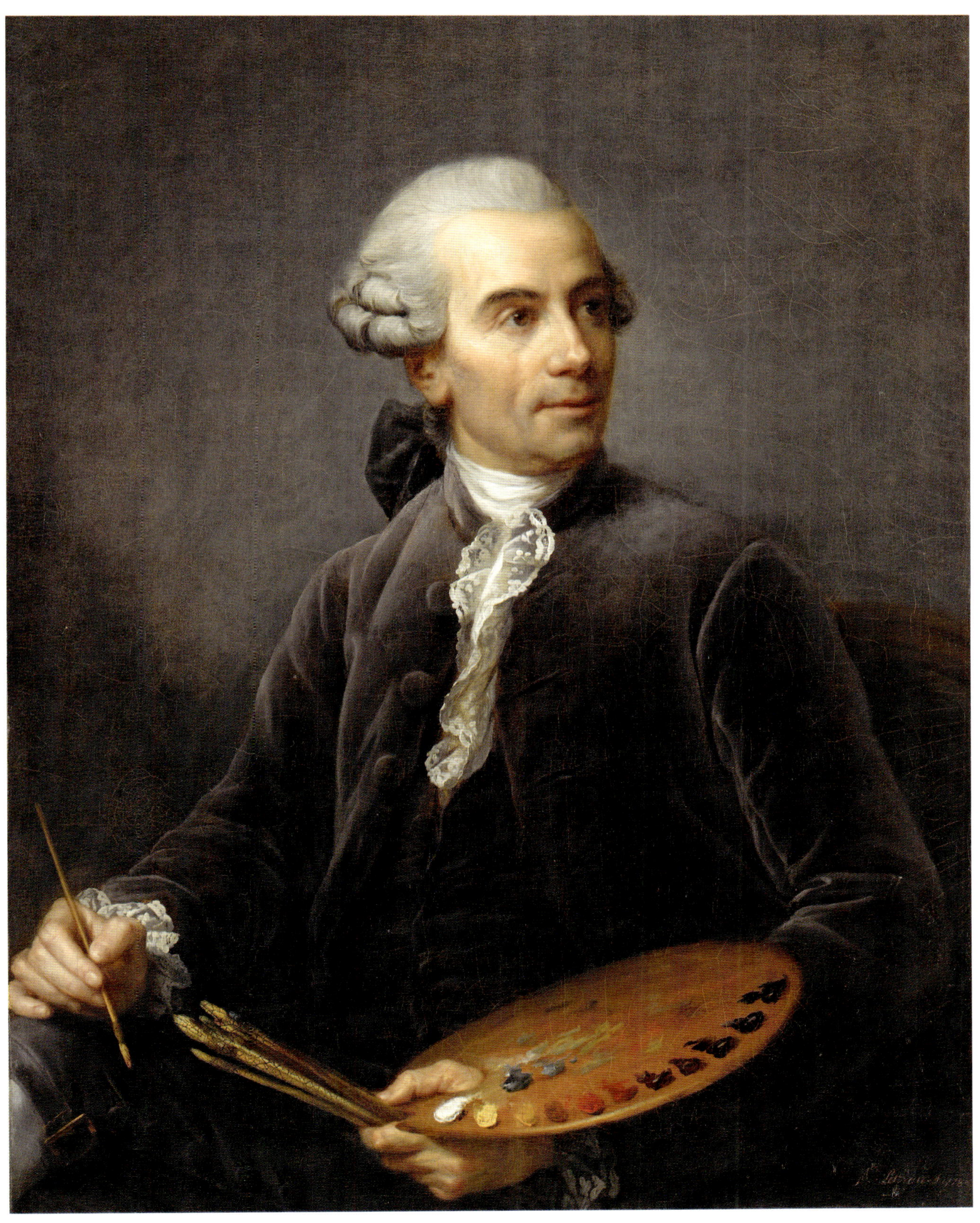

imagination, *sensibilité*, and an elevated mind and that women possessed those qualities in the highest degree. Although women writers had not achieved the same greatness as men, it did not follow, she argued, that "a woman's organs must be inferior to those of a man."[18] Genlis, like Épinay and Coicy, attributes women's plight to their lack of education and to the rules that society imposes on them.

Élisabeth Louise Vigée-LeBrun (1755–1842; see cats. 11, 23, 63) also responded to the woman-artist question, both in painted self-portraits and in her autobiographical *Souvenirs* (1835–37). Take, for example, the self-portrait of 1790 (fig. 3.1). It was made while she was living in Italy, for a gallery of self-portraits representing celebrated European artists. The image shows Vigée-LeBrun seated by an easel on which she has sketched from memory the portrait of Marie-Antoinette. The artist includes in this self-image an unusual feature—the shadow cast by her hand and arm on the canvas. The shadow alludes to painting's mythical origin as told in the ancient tale of the Corinthian maiden Dibutades, who invents painting by tracing the shadow cast on a wall by her sleeping lover. The figure of Dibutades had a special resonance for the woman-artist question. In 1783 one art critic transformed her into a character that he called on to assess the exhibition of that year, an exhibition marked by the unprecedented participation of three women, including Vigée-LeBrun. The critic makes Dibutades a woman artist, but has her refute the claim to be the inventor of painting. She associates herself, rather, with the physionotrace, a profile portrait made mechanically by tracing the sitter's shadow projected on a planar surface. In view of contemporaneous writing about woman's imagination, this Dibutades is significant. She is designed to verify the claims of those like Thomas and Roussel who argued that woman's imagination produced nothing new; it created mental images that, like shadows on a wall, re-presented an object rather than reinventing or idealizing it.

The Dibutades crafted to denigrate women painters at the Salon of 1783 was distant from the Dibutades French academicians took as an allegory of their own painting practice. Charles Nicolas Cochin (1715–1790), an officer of the Académie royale de peinture et de sculpture, created an image of Dibutades in 1769 that carried this exhortation: "Draw in your mind, that is the primary canvas" (*Dessine en ton cerveau, c'est la première toile*). The line is taken from Antoine-Marin Lemierre's 1769 poem *La peinture* (Painting), which challenges the artist not to trace the outline of objects from life but to imagine that outline, to draw it in the mind. Given these different interpretations of Dibutades, Vigée-LeBrun's self-portrait, with its clearly rendered shadow, might be understood to suggest that the artist was a mere tracer of shadows—that her imagination reflected but did not create. The artist short-circuits this interpretation, however: she shows herself not tracing a shadow but, rather, sketching the portrait of the absent Marie-Antoinette. The self-portrait suggests that Vigée-LeBrun sketches from memory the queen's image, that she draws it in her mind before tracing it on the canvas. The self-portrait thwarts any suggestion that the woman artist merely copies, for projected on the canvas pictured in Vigée-LeBrun's self-portrait is a distinct shadow, which she does not trace, and her sketch of a queen whom she cannot see.[19]

Vigée-LeBrun takes on medical science more directly in her *Souvenirs*, for there she describes a visit made in 1792 to the cabinet of Felice Fontana (1730–1805), the celebrated Florentine anatomist and maker of wax models. How much of this record is remembered and how much is invented we cannot know. But that it so neatly refutes the position of science on the woman-artist question suggests that it imagines rather than mirrors reality. As told in the *Souvenirs*, the artist notices among the wax models one of a reclining woman. "Fontana told me to approach this figure, then, raising a kind of cover, he offered to my regards all the intestines, turned as in our bodies. This sight made such an impression on me that I sensed myself near to being sick."[20] She then tells us that on later outings "it was impossible to distract myself from it, to the point that I could not see a person without mentally stripping her of her clothing and of her skin, which put me into a deplorable nervous state."[21]

To be cured of her deplorable nervous state, Vigée-LeBrun returns to Fontana's cabinet: "When I revisited M. Fontana I asked him his advice to deliver me from the troublesome susceptibility of my organs. I hear everything, I told him, I see too much, and I sense all from a mile away."[22] Here the artist appears to accept the discourse on *sensibilité* in which her "troublesome susceptibility" leads to her derangement. But the answer put into the anatomist's mouth reveals the contradictions in the discourse of sensibility: "What you consider as a weakness and as an evil is your force and talent; however, if you want to diminish the inconveniences of that susceptibility, paint no longer."[23]

The artist concludes the account with a commentary: "You will easily believe that I was not tempted to follow his advice; to paint and to live have only ever been a single and identical word for me, and I have quite often rendered thanks to Providence for having given me this excellent sight, of which I had taken it into my head to complain like a fool to the celebrated anatomist."[24] Vigée-LeBrun admits to an error, but it is not connected to the impression that deranged her imagination. Rather, she errs in doubting her gift — in making herself momentarily blind to the source of her talent, of which the obsessed imagination is a symptom. The point of the story is clear: it is an affirmation of Vigée-LeBrun's acute sensibilities and artistic talent. The story addresses the question of the woman artist, making *sensibilité* the basis of talent rather than the cause of illness.

That medical findings and philosophical theories helped to justify the exclusion of women from all realms of creative endeavor there can be no doubt. The historical record, however, shows that individual women did not passively accept the lot that medical science assigned to women as a group. Like Vigée-LeBrun, royalists and revolutionaries together contributed substantially to literature, painting, and sculpture despite the writings of those who warned against the troublesome susceptibility of their organs.

Notes

1. Pierre Fabre, *Essai sur les facultés de l'âme considérées dans leurs rapports avec la sensibilité et l'irritabilité de nos organes* (Paris and Amsterdam, 1785), p. 140.

2. For an extended discussion of these ideas, see Mary D. Sheriff, *The Exceptional Woman: Elisabeth Vigée-Lebrun and the Cultural Politics of Art* (Chicago, 1996), pp. 13–38, and Sheriff, *Moved by Love: Inspired Artists and Deviant Women in Eighteenth-Century France* (Chicago, 2004), pp. 15–50.

3. Henri Fouquet, "Sensibilité, Sentiment, (Médecine)," in *Encyclopédie, ou Dictionnaire raisonné des sciences, des arts et des métiers*, ed. Denis Diderot and Jean Le Rond d'Alembert, microfiche facsimile of the 1751–72 edition (Zug, Switzerland, 1967), vol. 15, p. 38.

4. Ibid., p. 47: "Quant aux femmes, leur constitution approche beaucoup, comme on sait, de celle des enfans; les passions sont chez elles extrêmement plus vives en général que chez les hommes."

5. Edmé Pierre Chauvot de Beauchêne, *De l'influence des affections de l'âme dans les maladies nerveuses des femmes, avec le traitement qui convient à ces maladies* (Montpellier and Paris, 1781), pp. 19–20.

6. Pierre Roussel, *Système physique et moral de la femme* (Paris, 1775), pp. 30–31.

7. Louis de Jaucourt, "Femme," in *Encyclopédie*, vol. 6, p. 472.

8. Sheriff, *Moved by Love*, pp. 15–40.

9. Poullain de la Barre put forward these ideas in *De l'égalité des deux sexes: Discours physique et moral, où l'on voit l'importance de se défaire des préjugez* (On the equality of the two sexes: A physical and moral discourse showing the importance of relinquishing one's prejudices), first published in Paris in 1673.

10. Roussel, *Système*, p. 31: "[S]on imagination, plus vive que soutenue, se prête peu à ces expressions vraies et pittoresques qui sont le sublime des arts d'imitation, et que, plus capable de sentir que de créer, elle reçoit plus facilement dans son âme les images des objets, qu'elle ne peut les reproduire."

11. Antoine Léonard Thomas, *Essai sur le caractère, les mœurs et l'esprit des femmes dans les différents siècles*, in *Qu'est-ce qu'une femme? Un débat*, introduction by Elisabeth Badinter (Paris, 1989), pp. 108–9.

12. Ibid., p. 109: "Le monde réel ne leur suffit pas; elles aiment à se créer un monde imaginaire; elles l'habitent et l'embellissent."

13. Ibid., p. 110: "[un] miroir qui réfléchit tout, mais ne crée rien."

14. Beauchêne, *De l'influence*, p. 17: "ce qui leur manque du côté de la profondeur des idées, de la force de la raison, du génie créateur, qui sont l'apanage de l'homme."

15. See, for example, La Mettrie's *L'homme machine* (Machine man), of 1748, and Riballier's *De l'éducation physique et morale des femmes* (On the physical and moral education of women), of 1779.

16. Louise-Florence-Pétronille de la Live d'Épinay, letter to the abbé Galiani, March 14, 1772, in *Qu'est-ce qu'une femme?*, p. 193: "Il est bien constant que les hommes et les femmes sont de même nature et de même constitution. La preuve en est que les femmes sauvages sont aussi robustes, aussi agiles que les hommes sauvages: ainsi la faiblesse de notre constitution et de nos organes appartient certainement à notre éducation, et est une suite de la condition qu'on nous a assignée dans la société."

17. Madame de Coicy, *Les femmes comme il convient de les voir, ou Apperçu de ce que les femmes ont été, de ce quelles sont, et de ce qu'elles pourroient être* (Paris and London, 1785), vol. 1, pp. 7–8: "L'anatomie la plus exacte n'a pu encore remarquer aucune différence entre la tête de la femme et la tête de l'homme. Leur cerveau est enti[è]rement semblable; ils voyent, ils entendent par des organes qui sont exactement les mêmes; les impressions des sens se reçoivent, se rassemblent, se conservent de la même mani[è]re. …[T]oute la différence qui est entre'eux, se trouve dans les organes qui sont nécessaires à la production de l'espèce, ce qui n'a rien de commun avec l'entendement."

18. Stéphanie Félicité, comtesse de Genlis, *De l'influence des femmes sur la littérature française comme protectrices des lettres et comme auteurs, ou Précis de l'histoire des femmes françaises les plus célèbres* (Paris, 1826), vol. 1, pp. ix–x: "il [ne] faut pas conclure que l'organisation des femmes soit inférieure à celle des hommes."

19. This analysis is condensed from Sheriff, *Exceptional Woman*, pp. 227–39.

20. A longer discussion of this visit can be found in Sheriff, *Exceptional Woman*, pp. 13–30. Élisabeth Louise Vigée-LeBrun, *Souvenirs*, ed. Claudine Herrmann (Paris, 1986) vol. 1, p. 238: "Fontana me dit de m'approcher de cette figure, puis, levant une espèce de couvercle, il offrit à mes regards, tous les intestins, tournés comme sont les nôtres. Cette vue me fit une telle impression, que je me sentis près de me trouver mal."

21. Ibid.: "Pendant plusieurs séjours, il me fut impossible de m'en distraire, au point que je ne pouvais voir une personne sans la dépouiller mentalement de ses habits et de sa peau, ce qui me mettait dans un état nerveux déplorable." On my reading of *personne*, in this context, as specifically feminine, see Sheriff, *Exceptional Woman*, p. 271, n. 19.

22. Ibid.: "Quand je revis M. Fontana, je lui demandais ses conseils pour me délivrer de l'importune susceptibilité de mes organes. — J'entends trop, lui dis-je, je vois trop et je sens tout d'une lieue."

23. Ibid.: "— Ce que vous regardez comme une faiblesse et comme un malheur, me répondit-il, c'est votre force et c'est votre talent; d'ailleurs, si vous voulez diminuer les inconvénients de cette susceptibilité, ne peignez plus."

24. Ibid.: "On croira sans peine que je ne fus pas tentée de suivre son conseil; peindre et vivre n'a jamais été qu'un seul et même mot pour moi, et j'ai bien souvent rendu grâces à la Providence de m'avoir donné cette vue excellente, dont je m'avisais de me plaindre comme une sotte au célèbre anatomiste."

ARTIST BIOGRAPHIES

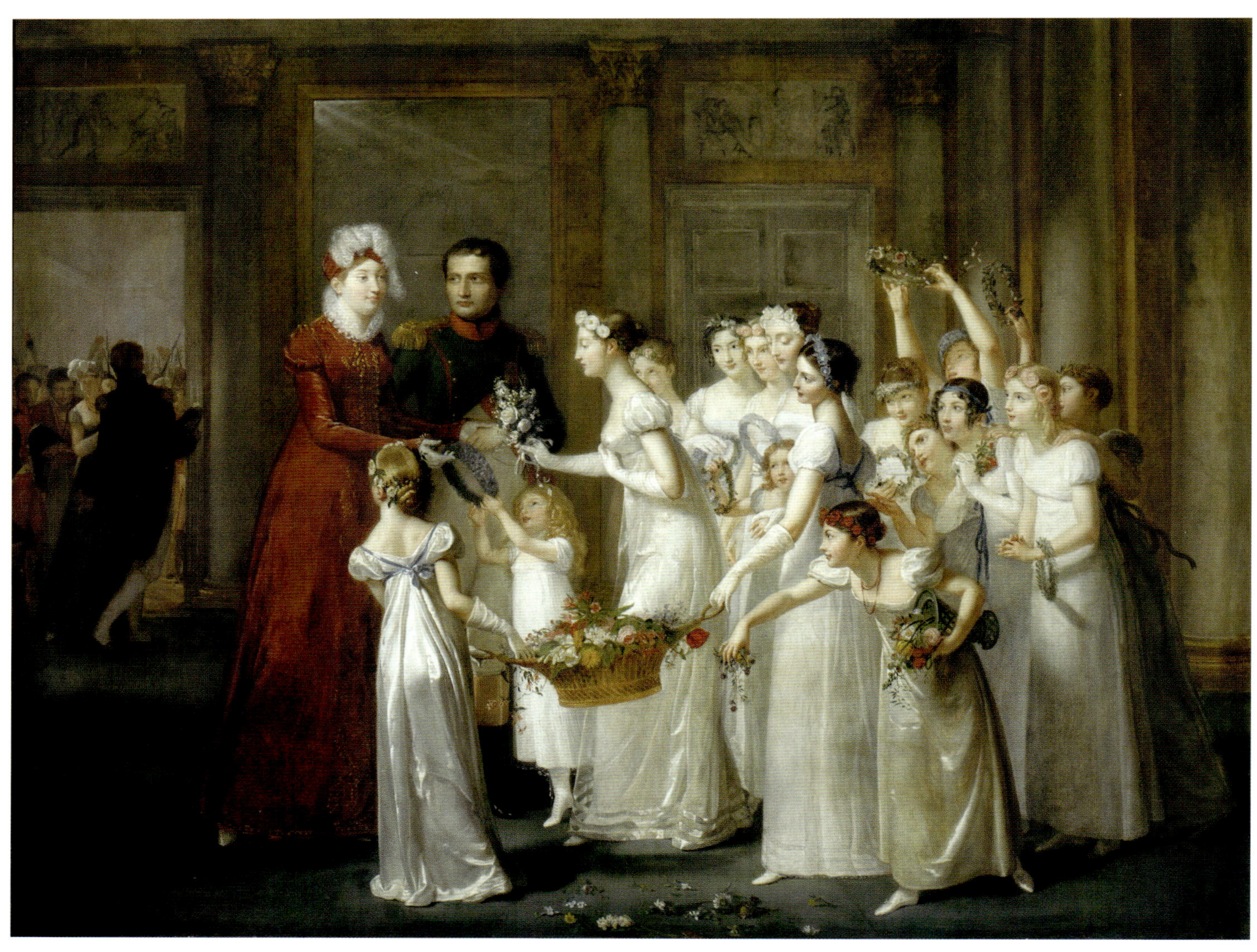

CAT. 24. PAULINE AUZOU (1775–1835), *The Arrival at Compiègne of Empress Marie-Louise*, 1810. Oil on canvas. Musée national des châteaux de Versailles et de Trianon

Pauline Auzou, née Jeanne-Marie-Catherine Desmarquest

(Paris, 1775 – Paris, 1835)

PAULINE AUZOU ESTABLISHED a reputation as a painter of portraits, scenes from everyday life, and history paintings — large-scale, narrative canvases that ranked at the top of the "hierarchy of genres" codified by the Académie royale de peinture et de sculpture. In the 1780s she trained with Jean-Baptiste Regnault (1754 – 1829), a history painter and member of the Académie.[1] Although women were not permitted to study in the prestigious schools run by the Académie, Regnault and several other academicians welcomed female students to their private studios. Under Regnault's tutelage, Auzou appears to have participated in modified life-drawing classes where women studied nude male and female models who posed with their genitals covered.[2]

Auzou was among the hundreds of artists of both sexes who began exhibiting at the Louvre Salons after 1791, when the National Assembly passed legislation requiring the exhibition, previously limited to Académie members, to open its doors to all artists. She first exhibited in 1793.[3] That year Auzou was also admitted to the Commune générale des arts, which briefly replaced the Académie, but she was excluded a few months later when the organization banned women. In December 1793 Auzou married a paper merchant, Charles-Marie Auzou, with whom she raised four children. She exhibited in all but one of the Salons held between 1793 and 1817.

Auzou's greatest successes came during the Napoleonic era (1799 – 1815). She received a first-class medal at the 1806 Salon, apparently for her painting *Departure for the Duel* (untraced).[4] In 1810 she exhibited a scene from the life of Empress Marie-Louise, Archduchess of Austria, who in that year became Napoléon's second wife. This work, *The Arrival at Compiègne of Empress Marie-Louise* — on view in the exhibition (cat. 24) — was followed in 1812 by *The Farewell of Marie-Louise to Her Family*. Both were purchased for the Musée Napoléon, and entered the collection of Versailles during the reign of Louis-Philippe.[5] Auzou fared less well during the restoration of the Bourbon monarchy (1815 – 30), when she repeatedly tried and failed to win government commissions. She did, however, continue to run a successful studio where she taught female students for some twenty years, publishing a book of head studies to aid in their education.

Notes

1. Biographical information on Auzou has been gleaned from Vivian P. Cameron, "Auzou, Pauline," in *Dictionary of Women Artists*, ed. Delia Gaze (London, 1997), vol. 1, pp. 199 – 201; Vivian P. Cameron, "Jeanne Marie Catherine Desmarquest," 2004 entry in *Dictionary of Women in Pre-Revolutionary France*, http://www.siefar.org/dictionnaire/en/Jeanne_Marie _Catherine_Desmarquest; *La femme artiste: D'Élisabeth Vigée-Lebrun à Rosa Bonheur*, exh. cat. (Mont-de-Marsan, 1981), pp. 35 – 39; Ann Sutherland Harris and Linda Nochlin, *Women Artists, 1550 – 1950*, exh. cat. (New York, 1976), pp. 211 – 12; and Margaret A. Oppenheimer, "Women Artists in Paris, 1791 – 1814" (PhD diss., New York University, 1996), pp. 104 – 6.

2. On female students in the studios of male academicians, see Vivian P. Cameron, "Woman as Image and Image-Maker in Paris during the French Revolution" (PhD diss., Yale University, 1983); Margaret A. Oppenheimer, "'The Charming Spectacle of a Cadaver': Anatomical and Life Study by Women Artists in Paris, 1775 – 1815," *Nineteenth-Century Art Worldwide* (Spring 2007), http://19thc-artworldwide.org/spring_07/articles/oppe .shtml; and Mary Vidal, "The 'Other Atelier': Jacques-Louis David's Female Students," in *Women, Art and the Politics of Identity in Eighteenth-Century Europe*, ed. Melissa Lee Hyde and Jennifer Milam (Aldershot, 2003), pp. 237 – 52.

3. For a complete list of Auzou's exhibitions and known works, see Cameron, "Desmarquest."

4. The untraced status of this work is reported by Cameron (ibid.).

5. Claire Constans, *Musée national du château de Versailles: Les peintures*, introduction by Jean-Pierre Babelon (Paris, 1995), vol. 1, p. 55. The *Farewell of Marie-Louise* is illustrated in Germaine Greer, *The Obstacle Race: The Fortunes of Women Painters and Their Work* (New York, 2001), p. 302.

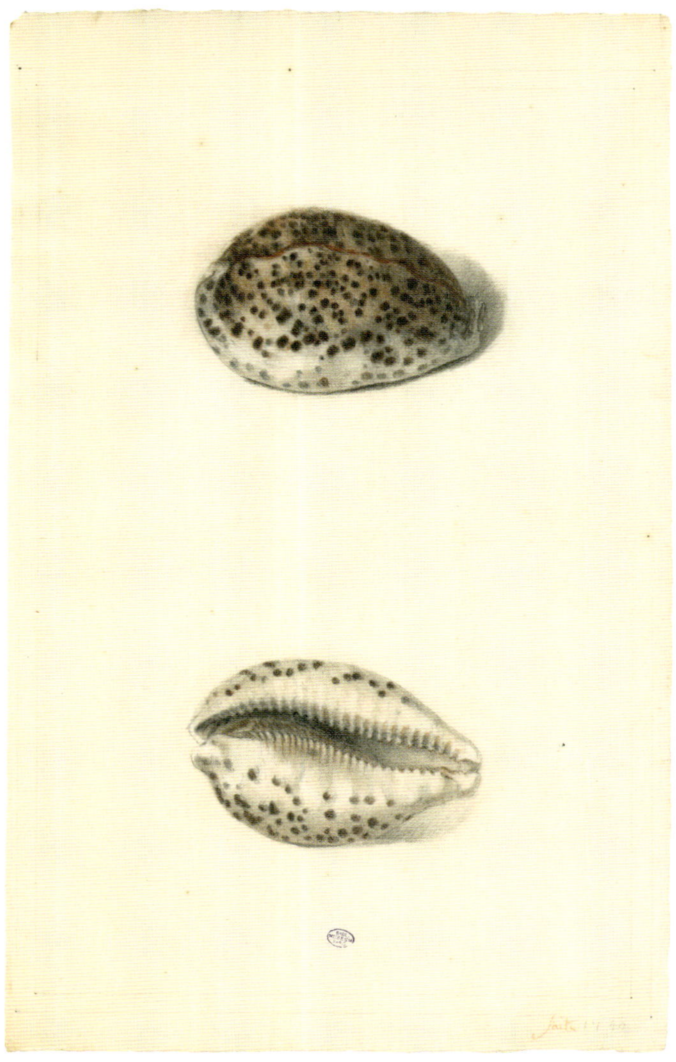

CAT. 25. MADELEINE FRANÇOISE BASSEPORTE (1701–1780), *Patella*, 1747. Red chalk on paper. Bibliothèque centrale du Muséum national d'histoire naturelle, Paris

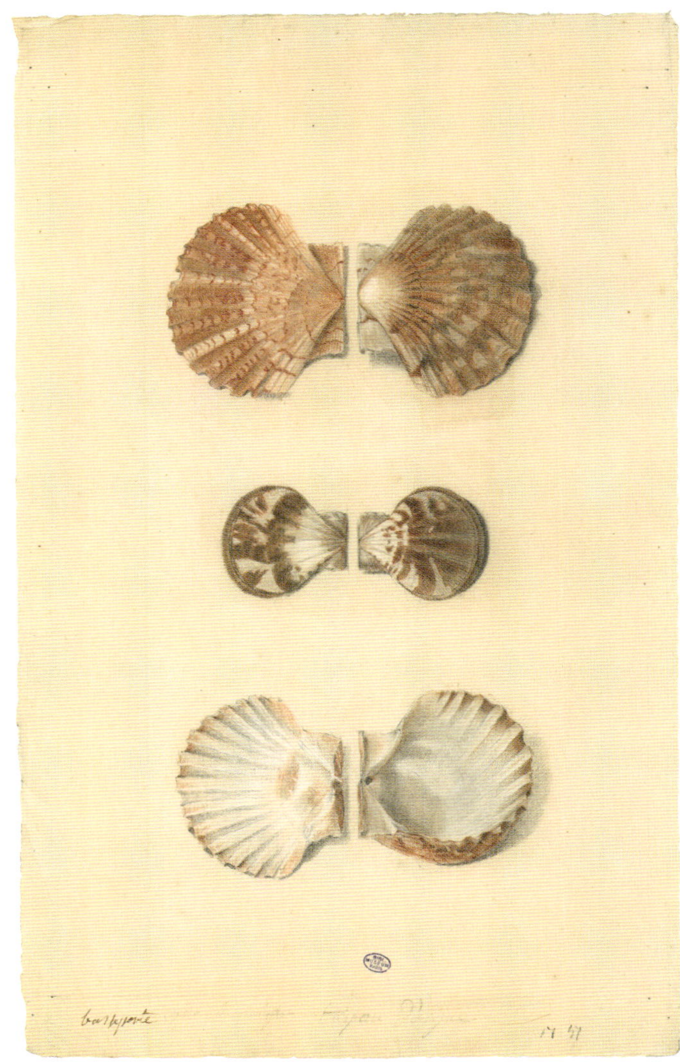

CAT. 26. MADELEINE FRANÇOISE BASSEPORTE (1701–1780), *Pectinidae*, 1747. Red chalk on paper. Bibliothèque centrale du Muséum national d'histoire naturelle, Paris

Madeleine Françoise Basseporte

(Paris, 1701 – Paris, 1780)

ALTHOUGH MADELEINE BASSEPORTE initially studied with a history painter, she became a botanical illustrator whose work stands at the intersection of art and science.[1] Her first teacher was the painter and engraver Paul-Ponce-Antoine Robert, known as Robert de Séry (1686–1733), who enjoyed the patronage of Cardinal de Rohan, the scion of an influential noble family of Breton origin. Through Robert, Basseporte was able to study the collections of old master paintings housed at Rohan's *hôtel* in the Marais district of Paris.[2] Robert had close relationships with Basseporte and her widowed mother: he placed Basseporte at the head of a drawing school for female students, asked her to produce prints after many of his works, and entrusted both women to assist with the inventory and distribution of his possessions upon his death.

Tradition has it that Basseporte, who grew adept at the art of pastel portraiture, chose to pursue flower painting because it promised a steady income that would enable her to support her aging mother. After Robert's death, Basseporte apprenticed herself to Claude Aubriet (1665–1742), whom she succeeded in 1741 as official painter to the Jardin du roi (the king's botanical gardens in Paris). This post, which Basseporte held until 1780, obliged her to provide the crown with twelve paintings per year. Most of these are still held at the gardens, renamed the Jardin des plantes during the Revolution and today part of the Muséum national d'histoire naturelle. Several of Basseporte's drawings from the collection of the Jardin des plantes are on view in this exhibition (cats. 25, 26). Basseporte was also called upon to travel to the royal châteaus at Versailles, Compiègne, Fontainebleau, and Bellevue to record the collections of animals and plants that Louis XV and Madame de Pompadour assembled at these properties. In addition, she taught flower painting to the daughters of Louis XV,

who maintained life-long interests in both art and botany. She may also have given lessons to other women, including the future *académiciennes* Marie Thérèse Vien and Anne Vallayer-Coster, both included in the current exhibition (see cats. 16, 61, 62).

During her tenure at the Jardin du roi, Basseporte interacted with many scientific and intellectual luminaries of the era. The influential Swedish botanist Carolus Linnaeus met Basseporte in the 1730s when she was still studying with Aubriet. The French naturalist Georges-Louis Leclerc, comte de Buffon, kept up a decades-long correspondence with the artist. And the *philosophe* Jean-Jacques Rousseau reportedly exclaimed that "nature gave plants their existence" but "Mademoiselle Basseporte preserved it for them."[3]

Notes

1. The most thorough biography of Basseporte remains "Nécrologe," *Revue universelle des arts* 13 (1861), pp. 139–47. The present text also draws upon Émile Bellier de la Chavignerie, *Dictionnaire général des artistes de l'école française depuis l'origine des arts du dessin jusqu'à nos jours: Architectes, peintres, sculpteurs, graveurs et lithographes* (1882–85; rpr., Paris, 1997), vol. 1, p. 50, and Augustin Jal, *Dictionnaire critique de biographie et d'histoire: Errata et supplément pour tous les dictionnaires historiques d'après des documents authentiques inédits* (Paris, 1867), p. 124.

2. All information concerning Basseporte's work with Robert de Séry is based on Henri Bourin, *Paul-Ponce-Antoine Robert (de Séry) peintre du Cardinal de Rohan (1686–1733)* (Paris, 1907).

3. "Nécrologe," p. 142. According to the author, Rousseau famously said "la nature donnait l'existence aux plantes, mais… mademoiselle [*sic*] Basseporte la leur conservait."

Marie Guilhelmine Benoist, née Leroulx de la Ville

(Paris, 1768 – Paris, 1826)

THE CAREER OF Marie Guilhelmine Benoist was profoundly entwined with the politics of the Revolutionary era. In the 1780s Benoist and her sister, Marie-Élisabeth Leroulx de la Ville (1770–1842), studied with Jacques-Louis David (1748–1825) and Élisabeth Louise Vigée-LeBrun (see cats. 11, 23, 63).[1] A controversy arose in July 1787, when the young women's presence in David's Louvre studio troubled the comte d'Angiviller, the director of the Batîments du roi (the royal arts administration), who objected to the mingling of the sexes in a royal palace.[2] Benoist's romantic attachment to the poet Charles-Albert Demoustier (1760–1801) also attracted attention in these years; Demoustier's 1786 *Lettres à Émilie sur la mythologie* (Letters to Émilie on [Greek] mythology) were reportedly inspired by her.

Barred from the Académie royale de peinture et de sculpture, which reached its quota of four female members in 1783, Benoist exhibited at the annual outdoor exhibitions held at the place Dauphine, on the Île de la Cité, from 1784 to 1789. There she displayed pastel studies as well as self-portraits, portraits, and sentimental genre scenes painted in oil. In 1791 she took advantage of the Salon's open exhibition policy, exhibiting three narrative paintings in the Louvre that year.

Royalist allegiances generated problems, however. Benoist's father, René Leroulx-Delaville, served in Louis XVI's administration, and in 1793 the artist married Pierre-Vincent Benoist, who fled France later that year to avoid arrest; he was accused, in a warrant signed by Jacques-Louis David, of plotting to rescue Marie-Antoinette from prison. In 1795, with hostilities ended, Madame Benoist was reunited with her husband, exhibited at the Salon (after a hiatus), received a financial award from the government, and was granted coveted lodgings in the Louvre.

The nineteenth century brought still greater successes. Benoist's best-known work, the *Portrait of a Negress* (Musée du Louvre, Paris),[3] caused a stir at the 1800 Salon. Following Napoléon's coup d'état of 18 Brumaire (November 9, 1799), Monsieur Benoist was appointed to the Ministry of the Interior, and Madame joined the cadre of artists disseminating images of Napoléon and the imperial family throughout the First Empire. Several of these state portraits appeared at Salons, where they attracted additional commissions. Benoist earned a second-class medal at the 1804 Salon and opened a school for girls in the same year. She turned increasingly to genre painting at this time, creating works like *Reading from the Bible* (1810) and *The Consultation, or The Fortune-Teller* (1812), both seen in this exhibition (cats. 20, 28).

In 1815 the restored Bourbon monarchy appointed Monsieur Benoist to the Council of State. In the interest of decorum, Marie Guilhelmine Benoist abruptly ended her career. She never exhibited again.

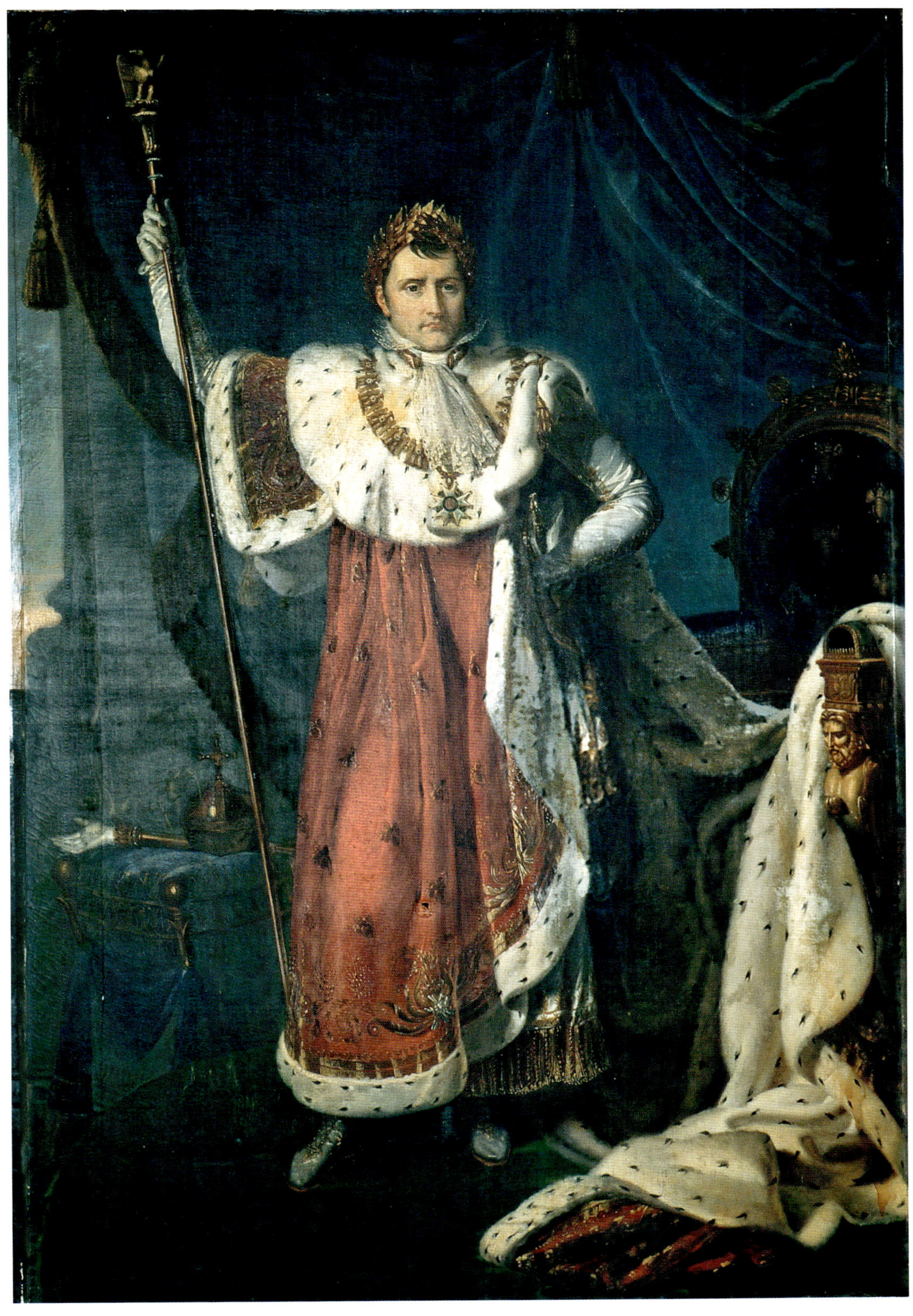

CAT. 27. MARIE GUILHELMINE BENOIST (1768–1826), *Portrait of Napoléon*, 1809. Oil on canvas. Musées d'Angers

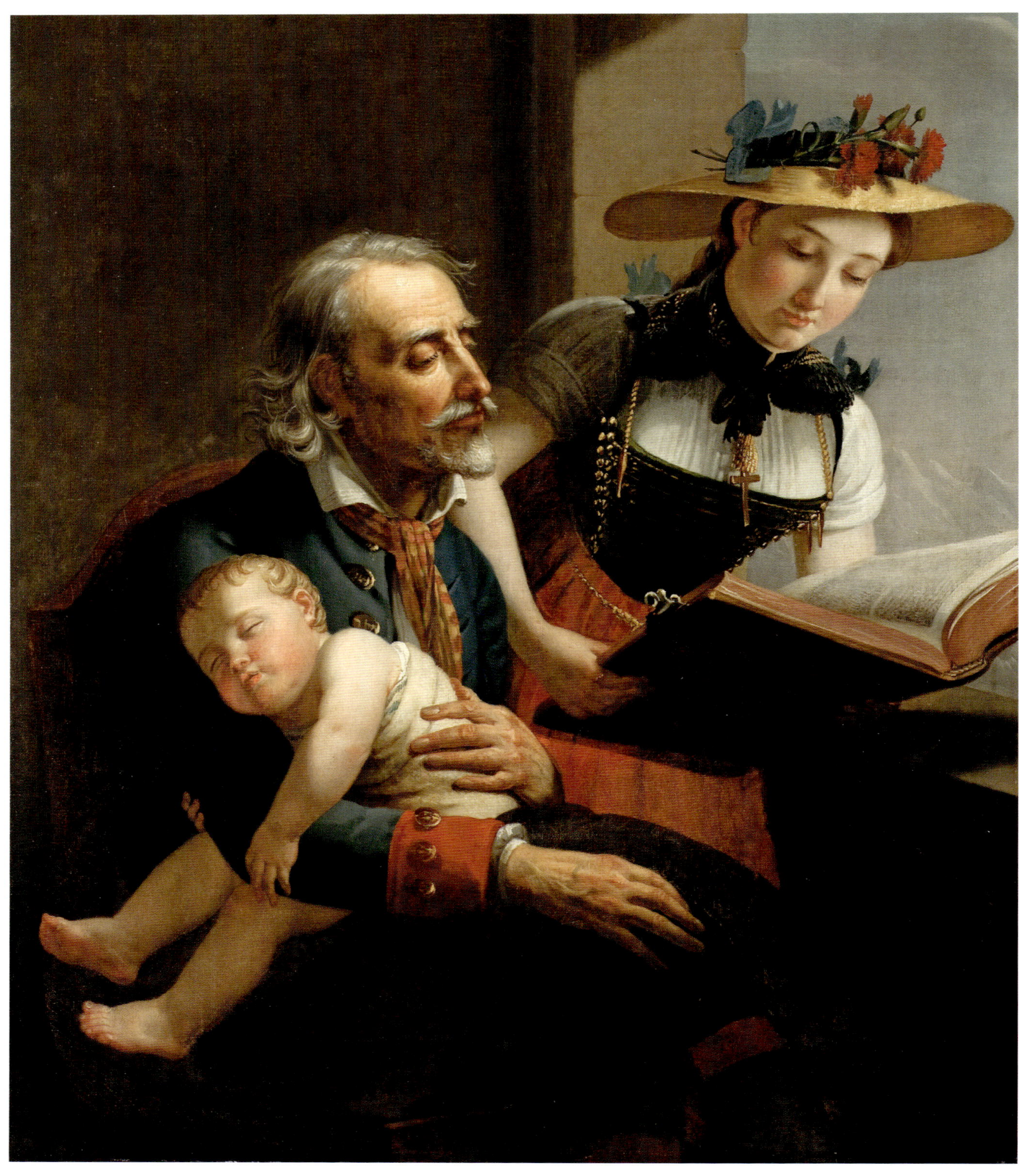

CAT. 28. MARIE GUILHELMINE BENOIST (1768–1826), *Reading from the Bible*, 1810. Oil on canvas. Musée de Louviers

Notes

1. The seminal source on Benoist is Marie-Juliette Ballot, *Une élève de David, la comtesse Benoist, l'Émilie de Demoustier, 1768–1826* (Paris, 1914). The present account is also indebted to Vivian P. Cameron, "Benoist, Mme," in *Dictionary of Women Artists*, ed. Delia Gaze (London, 1997), vol. 1, pp. 244–47; Gen Doy, *Women and Visual Culture in Nineteenth-Century France, 1800–1852* (London and New York, 1998), pp. 34–36; Ann Sutherland Harris and Linda Nochlin, *Women Artists, 1550–1950*, exh. cat. (New York, 1976), pp. 209–10; Margaret A. Oppenheimer, "Three Newly Identified Paintings by Marie-Guillemine Benoist," *Metropolitan Museum Journal* 31 (1996), pp. 143–50; and Margaret A. Oppenheimer, "Women Artists in Paris, 1791–1814" (PhD diss., New York University, 1996), pp. 110–14.

2. See Mary Vidal, "The 'Other Atelier': Jacques-Louis David's Female Students," in *Women, Art and the Politics of Identity*, ed. Melissa Lee Hyde and Jennifer Milam (Aldershot, 2003), pp. 237–52. Portions of the relevant correspondence are published in J. J. Guiffrey, "Écoles de demoiselles dans les ateliers de David et de Suvée au Louvre," in *Nouvelles archives de l'art français* (Paris, 1874–75), pp. 394–401.

3. Benoist's *Portrait of a Negress* is reproduced in Germaine Greer, *The Obstacle Race: The Fortunes of Women Painters and Their Work* (New York, 2001), p. 299.

Marie Geneviève Bouliar

(Paris, 1763 – château d'Arcy, Saône-et-Loire, 1825)

DURING HER LIFETIME Marie Geneviève Bouliar,[1] a talented painter of portraits, history paintings, and head studies, was an active participant in the lively artistic milieus of Revolutionary and Directory Paris.[2] She regularly showed her work in the government-sponsored Salons at the Louvre (1791–1817), as well as in the privately run Expositions des amis des arts (1791–93), and garnered accolades in the burgeoning French press. Bouliar's talent also received official recognition. In 1792 her *Head of a Young Woman Crowned with Roses* was selected by a jury of artists over entries by, among others, Adélaïde Labille-Guiard (see cats. 8, 13, 17, 45) for a third-class prize in the category of genre painting. This state-sponsored award carried a stipend of 1,000 livres and funded the production of Bouliar's *Aspasia*, a depiction of the Athenian courtesan reputed to have advised Pericles and tutored Sophocles that entered the Republican government's growing art collection and is included in the present exhibition (cat. 29).[3] The state also accorded her a coveted, rent-free apartment in the Louvre from early 1797; in 1801, when the palace was vacated by Napoleonic decree, the Ministry of the Interior granted her a life-long annual indemnity of 300 francs to offset housing costs.[4]

From 1793 Bouliar was described in the Salon *livrets*, or brochurelike printed catalogues, as the student of Joseph-Siffrède Duplessis (1725–1802); although later art historians have suggested that she also studied with other leading artists, including Jean-Baptiste Greuze (1725–1805), no documentary evidence exists to support these claims. Given Duplessis's status as an acclaimed portraitist, it is likely that Bouliar's affiliation with him conferred legitimacy in the eyes of clients such as those depicted in the imposing group painting known as the *Portrait of Monsieur Olive, Treasurer of the Legislative Assembly of Brittany, with His Family* (cat. 5). In any case,

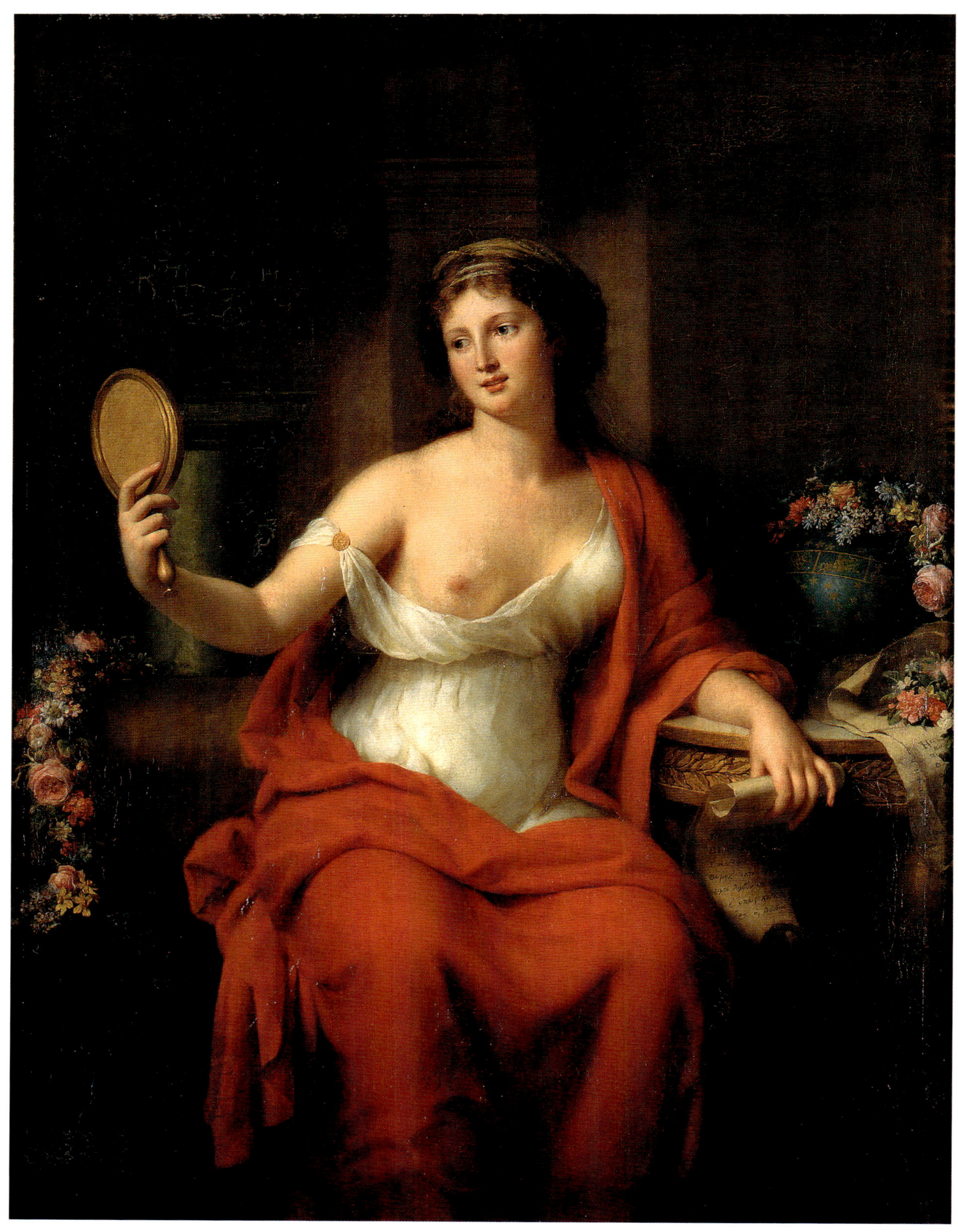

CAT. 29. MARIE GENEVIÈVE BOULIAR (1763–1825), *Aspasia*, 1794. Oil on canvas. Musée des beaux-arts, Arras

Duplessis doubtless had a hand in Bouliar's acquisition of a 1796 commission for double portraits representing Alexandre Lenoir (1762–1839), son of the Madame Lenoir whose portrait Duplessis himself had produced in 1764, and his wife, Adélaïde Binard (1771–1832).[5] The latter, an affectionate depiction of another practicing artist (Binard studied with Jean-Baptiste Regnault and exhibited regularly in the Salons from 1795 to 1817), appears in the current exhibition (cat. 18).

Confusion over the spelling of Bouliar's surname, both in contemporary literature and in subsequent art-historical accounts, has led scholars to suggest familial relationships with the engraver Jacques Bouliard or the wood sculptor Joseph Bouliart.[6] Nonetheless, unlike many of her female counterparts, Bouliar did not originate from an artistic milieu. Her father, Antoine Bouliar, was a tailor, and occupations mentioned in notarized documents for her maternal relatives include those of farmer, hired soldier, and master cutler. However, Bouliar, an only child who never married, seems to have consciously asserted her ties to the art world in, for instance, her double portrait of the children of the painter Carle Vernet (1758–1835), the youngest child of the famous painter of landscapes and seascapes Claude-Joseph Vernet (1714–1789), now in a private collection in France.[7] Bouliar also appears to have cultivated this milieu on a personal level. She died during a stay at the château d'Arcy, in the Saône-et-Loire department, where her hostess, Marie-Anne Jacqueline de Saint-Cyr, herself an amateur sculptor, habitually entertained a diverse mix of artists and intellectuals.

Notes

1. The spelling of the artist's surname has long been an object of scholarly debate, and she continues to be referenced as both Bouliar and Bouliard in art-historical literature, with predictably confusing results. The present catalogue prefers the spelling Bouliar (without the final *d*) on the basis of the archival documentation and arguments advanced most recently in Yuriko Jackall, "Recovering the Work of Marie-Geneviève Bouliar (1763–1825): The Invention of Self in Revolutionary France," *Cahiers de l'histoire de l'art* 7 (2009), pp. 48–60.

2. Biographical information is compiled from Louis Govier, "Bouliar, Marie-Geneviève," in *Dictionary of Women Artists*, ed. Delia Gaze (London, 1997), vol. 1, pp. 295–97; Ann Sutherland Harris and Linda Nochlin, *Women Artists, 1550–1950*, exh. cat. (New York, 1976), pp. 202–4; Jackall, "Recovering the Work of Bouliar"; Henry Jouin, *Mademoiselle Marie-Geneviève Bouliard* (Paris, 1891); and Françoise Maison, "Marie-Geneviève Bouliar," in *Peinture française, 1770–1830*, Trésors des musées du nord de la France 2, exh. cat. (Paris, 1975), p. 46.

3. This painting is sometimes described as a self-portrait of the artist but the *livrets* of the Salons of 1795 and 1796 — the exhibitions at which the painting was shown — indicate that the work was never identified as such during the eighteenth century. Rather, the painting must be understood as Bouliar's ambitious attempt to assert herself in the intellectual genre of history painting. For an analysis of the critical reception accorded *Aspasia* in this regard, see Louis Govier, "Contemplating Contradictions: Re-Viewing Marie-Geneviève Bouliar's *Aspasie*," *Object* 1 (1998–99), pp. 23–44. On the *prix d'encouragement*, see Marc Furcy-Raynaud, *Procès-verbaux des assemblées du jury élu par les artistes exposants au salon de 1791 pour la distribution des prix d'encouragement* (Paris, 1906), p. 69.

4. *Jacques-Louis David, 1748–1825*, exh. cat. (Paris, 1989), p. 593. On the lodging indemnity, see Archives Nationales, Paris, Series F/21, dossiers 1, 4, 5, and 6.

5. On Duplessis, see Jules Belleudy, *J.-S. Duplessis, peintre du roi (1725–1802)* (Chartres, 1913). Bouliar's portrait of Alexandre Lenoir, the founder of the Parisian Musée des monuments français, is now in the Musée Carnavalet, Paris; it is illustrated, and discussed together with the portrait of Binard, in Angela Rosenthal, *Angelica Kauffman: Art and Sensibility* (New Haven, 2006), p. 100, fig. 40. For a comparison of Bouliar's portraits of Lenoir and Binard with portraits of the couple by David, see Philippe Bordes, *Jacques-Louis David: Empire to Exile*, ext. cat. (New Haven, 2005), pp. 158–60.

6. See, for instance, Harris and Nochlin, *Women Artists*, p. 202, n. 1.

7. For a reproduction of this work, see Jackall, "Recovering the Work of Bouliar," p. 55, fig. 11.

Henriette Jacotte Cappelaere

(act. 1846–59)

WE KNOW ONLY A FEW rudimentary facts about Henriette Jacotte Cappelaere. Born in Paris, she studied with the Romantic painter Léon Cogniet (1794–1880) and exhibited portraits, genre scenes, and dog paintings at the Salons of 1846, 1848, 1849, and 1859.[1] At the time of the 1850 Salon, Cappelaere was living at 22, rue Godot-de-Mauroy, today part of the ninth arrondissement—an area of Paris that was being rapidly transformed under the auspices of Baron Haussmann, Louis-Napoléon's prefect of the Seine.

This exhibition includes Cappelaere's best-known paintings: *Ham, the Dog of Louis-Napoléon* (p. 136) and *Portrait of Elisabeth-Ann Haryett, Called Miss Harriet Howard, Wife of Trelawny, comtesse de Beauregard* (cat. 30). Exhibited at the 1850 Salon, both works depict companions of Louis-Napoléon (Napoléon III) who were instrumental in his rise to the imperial throne. Ham, a black-and-white dog sometimes described as a beagle but bearing a close resemblance to a spaniel, was named for the fort in the Picardy region of northern France where Louis-Napoléon was imprisoned for six years following his unsuccessful coup d'état in 1840.

According to legend, the lovable Ham shared his master's confinement and aided in his escape by distracting the porter long enough for Louis-Napoléon to slip out undetected in the guise of a workman. Louis-Napoléon fled to London, where he met, and set up house with, the wealthy Miss Harriet Howard. Howard, a former actress whose money was inherited from a deceased lover, bankrolled his successful bid for the presidency of France. Elected in 1848, Louis-Napoléon followed in the footsteps of his late uncle when, in 1852, he declared himself Emperor of the French.

Notes

1. This biography has been compiled from the following sources: Émile Bellier de la Chavignerie, *Dictionnaire général des artistes de l'école française depuis l'origine des arts du dessin jusqu'à nos jours: Architectes, peintres, sculpteurs, graveurs et lithographes* (Paris, 1882), vol. 1, p. 197; *Explication des ouvrages de peinture, sculpture, architecture, gravure et lithographie des artistes vivants, exposés au Palais national le 26 décembre 1850* (Paris, 1850), p. 58; Jean-Marie Moulin, "Musée national du château de Compiègne: Acquisitions récentes (1978–1986) pour le Musée du second empire," *La revue du Louvre et des musées de France* 1 (1988), pp. 43–52; and Ulrich Thieme and Felix Becker, eds., *Allgemeines Lexikon der bildenden Künstler von der Antike bis zur Gegenwart* (Leipzig, 1911), vol. 5, p. 547.

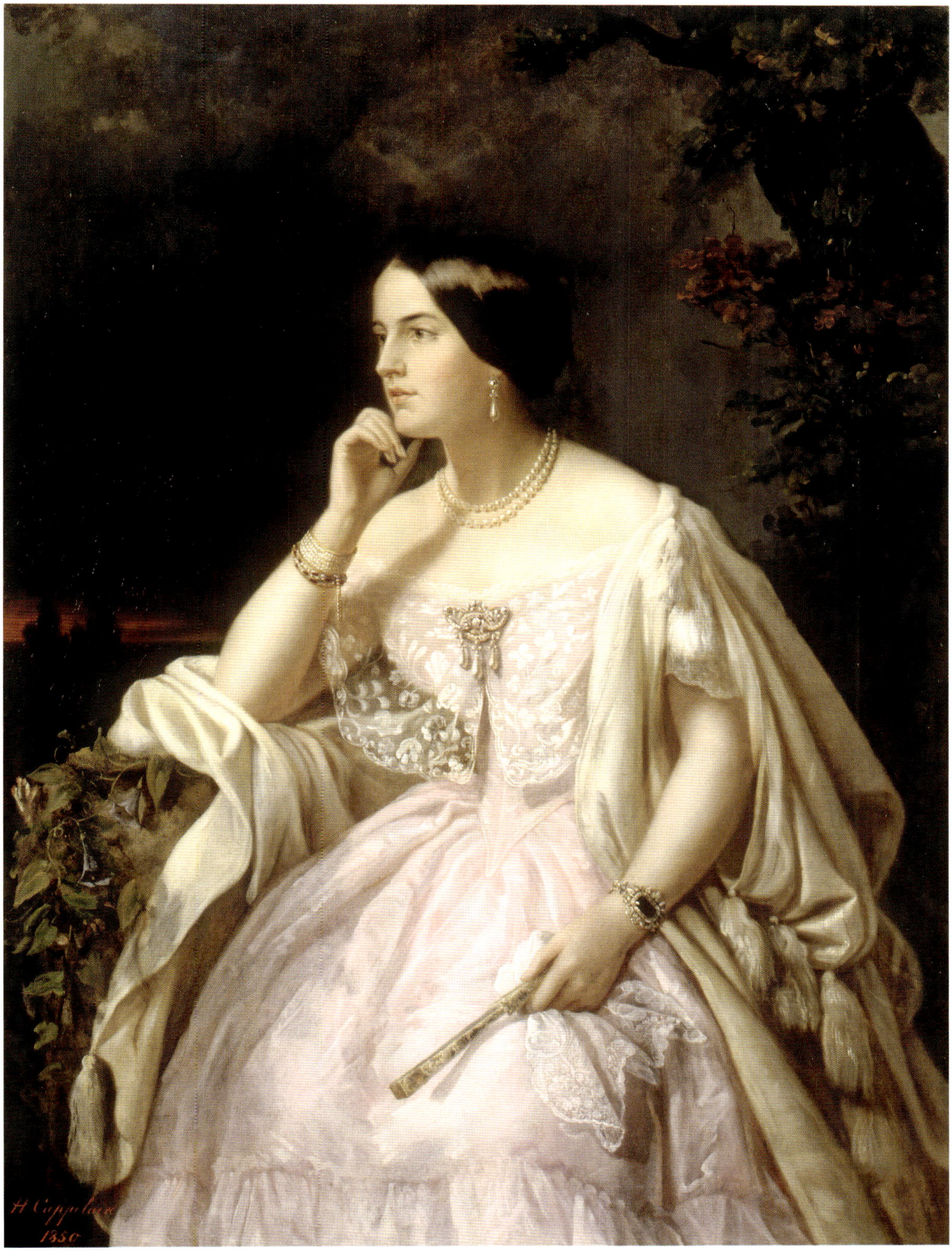

Cat. 30. Henriette Jacotte Cappelaere (act. 1846–59), *Portrait of Elisabeth-Ann Haryett, Called Miss Harriet Howard, Wife of Trelawny, comtesse de Beauregard*, 1850. Oil on canvas. Musée national du château de Compiègne

Constance Marie Charpentier, née Blondelu

(Paris, 1767–Paris, 1849)

CONSTANCE MARIE CHARPENTIER exhibited at least thirty works at the Paris Salons from 1795 to 1819, yet she is remembered almost exclusively as the painter of *Melancholy* (1801), included in the present exhibition (cat. 31).[1] Sound information about her training is scant; lists of her teachers traditionally include the history painters Jacques-Louis David (1748–1825) and François Gérard (1770–1837), as well as Louis Lafitte (1770–1828), who is best known for his decorative work, and the painter and engraver Pierre Bouillon (1776–1831).[2] A final name is variously given as that of the printmaker Johan-Georg Wille (1715–1808) or his son, the painter and sculptor Pierre-Alexandre Wille (1748–1821), or an artist identified only as Wilk.

Charpentier's family history is better documented. In the year of her birth, her father, a Parisian merchant named Pierre-Alexandre-Hyacinthe Blondelu, was taken to court by the apothecaries' guild for abrogating its privilege to formulate and sell medication.[3] In 1793 the artist married Victor-François Charpentier, a government employee who worked for the prefecture of Paris and department of the Seine. Her husband's brother-in-law, the Revolution's fiery orator Georges Danton (1759–1794), sat for a portrait by Charpentier.

Charpentier met with considerable success at the Salons, where she exhibited primarily portraits and domestic genre scenes. In 1798 her pendant paintings *Widow of a Day* and *Widow of a Year* earned a *prix d'encouragement*, a commission for a painting to be purchased by the state for 1,500 francs. *Melancholy*, Charpentier's only known history painting, fulfilled this commission, and its appearance at the 1801 Salon prompted an admiring poet to declare: "this painting lets us discover / Charm in melancholy."[4] Charpentier went on to win a gold medal at the Paris Salon of 1814, and a silver medal at the 1821 Salon exhibition at Douai, in

northern France. Although she ceased exhibiting after 1821, she was still teaching ten years later when a dictionary of artists announced that she "receives, three times a week, young women who wish to follow her advice on drawing and painting" at her residence on the rue du Pot de fer Saint-Sulpice (part of the modern-day rue Bonaparte, in the sixth arrondissement of Paris).[5]

Notes

1. Thirty is the number given by Valerie Mainz, "Charpentier, Constance," in *Dictionary of Women Artists*, ed. Delia Gaze (London, 1997), vol. 1, pp. 381–82.

2. See, for instance, E. Bénézit, *Dictionary of Artists* (Paris, 2006), vol. 3, p. 807; *French Painting, 1774–1830: The Age of Revolution*, exh. cat. (Detroit, 1975), pp. 345–47; Charles Gabet, *Dictionnaire des artistes de l'école française, au XIXᵉ siècle* (Paris, 1831), pp. 132–33; Ann Sutherland Harris and Linda Nochlin, *Women Artists, 1550–1950*, exh. cat. (New York, 1976), p. 207; Jean-François Heim, Claire Béraud, and Philippe Heim, *Les salons de peinture de la Révolution française, 1789–1799* (Paris, 1989), p. 163; and Margaret A. Oppenheimer, "Women Artists in Paris, 1791–1814" (PhD diss., New York University, 1996), pp. 136–37. Except where noted, this biography is based on Oppenheimer's work.

3. Oppenheimer ("Women Artists," p. 136) gives her parents' names. The lawsuit is documented in "Procès des maîtres et gardes apothicaires contre Pierre Alexandre Hyacinthe Blondelu, pour préparation et vente de drogues," 1767–68, Archives et manuscrits de la Bibliothèque interuniversitaire de pharmacie, Paris, AE/12.

4. *Arlequin chasse du muséum par un artiste: Critique en prose et en vaudeville* (Paris, [1801]), as translated and quoted in Matthieu Pinette, *From the Sun King to the Royal Twilight: Painting in Eighteenth-Century France from the Musée de Picardie, Amiens*, exh. cat. (New York, 2000), p. 177. Quoted in the original French, with citation, in Matthieu Pinette, *Peintures françaises des XVIIᵉ et XVIIIᵉ siècles des musées d'Amiens* (Paris, 2006), pp. 252–53: "Et ce tableau nous fait trouver / Du charme à la mélancolie."

5. Gabet, *Dictionnaire*, pp. 132–33. Quotation from p. 133: "Mme Charpentier reçoit, trois fois par semaines [*sic*], les jeunes personnes qui désirent suivre ses conseils pour le dessin et la peinture."

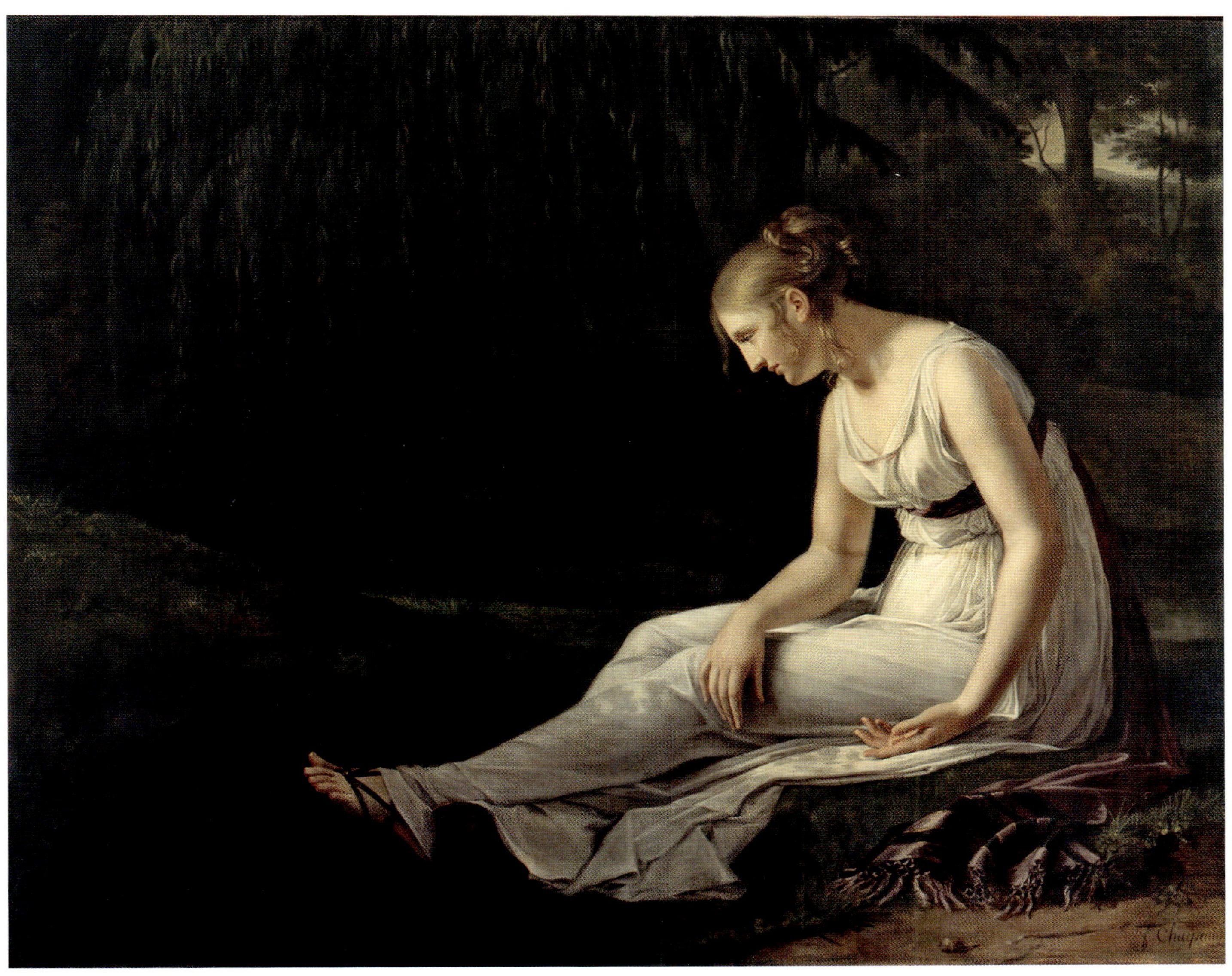

CAT. 31. CONSTANCE MARIE CHARPENTIER (1767–1849), *Melancholy*, 1801. Oil on canvas. Musée de Picardie, Amiens

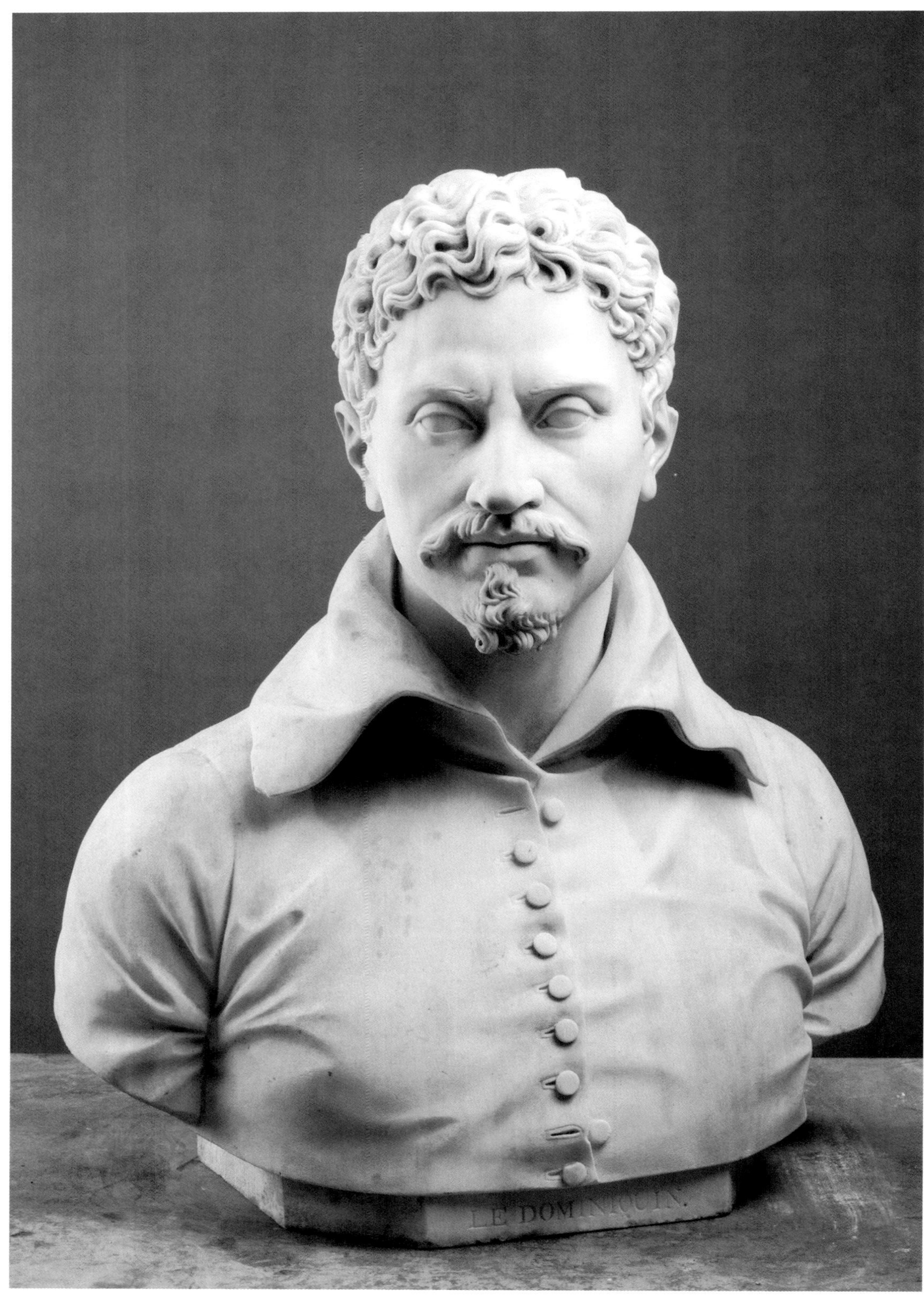

CAT. 32. JULIE CHARPENTIER (1770–1843), *Bust of Domenico Zampieri (1581–1641)*, 1818. Marble. Musée du Louvre, Département des sculptures, Paris

Julie Charpentier

(Paris, 1770 – Paris, 1843)

THE SCULPTOR JULIE CHARPENTIER grew up amid artists and artisans in the Palais du Louvre, where her father, François-Philippe Charpentier (1734 – 1817), enjoyed government-sponsored lodgings.[1] An inventor of a new engraving technique that earned him the title of *mécanicien du roi*, Charpentier, *père*, also developed machines for fabricating lace, laminating veneers, and facilitating other production processes. Julie Charpentier, whose sister Adélaïde also pursued the arts, learned to draw from her father and received lessons from the sculptor and Académie royale member Augustin Pajou (1730 – 1809).

Charpentier began exhibiting in 1787, when the entrepreneur known as Pahin de la Blancherie included her bust of Adélaïde in the guise of a vestal virgin and her bas-relief of the duc d'Orléans (both untraced) at his Salon de la Correspondance.[2] As announced by Pahin, whose newsletter had previously discussed the inventions of François-Philippe, the relief was in the collection of Mademoiselle, daughter of the duc d'Orléans, who supported Charpentier with a pension.[3] Charpentier debuted at the Louvre Salon in 1793, showing busts, medallions, and statuettes in terra-cotta and stone. She went on to send works in these media and in plaster to every Salon from 1798 to 1824.

Many of Charpentier's sculptures were commissioned by government agencies. For instance, her marble bust of the Bolognese painter Domenico Zampieri (Domenichino) (1581 – 1641), included in the current exhibition (cat. 32), was created for the Grand Gallery of the Louvre in 1818. Other state commissions were intended for public sculptures in Paris: two bas-reliefs (untraced) for a never-completed fountain in the shape of an elephant planned for the place de la Bastille, and four of the 425 bronze bas-reliefs that decorate the Austerlitz column in the center of the place Vendôme.[4]

Although Charpentier and her family worked diligently and remained in government-owned housing, they struggled financially. Her father ultimately returned to his native Blois, where he died in 1817. In 1801 the artist offered her services to the Parisian Muséum d'histoire naturelle, explaining that her skills at drawing and sculpting could be applied to taxidermy. For the next twenty-five years she completed piecework assignments for the museum, mounting a range of birds and quadrupeds. At last, in 1826, she received a salaried post at the museum, but her earnings remained insufficient. She died in poverty in the Salpêtrière, a public hospital in Paris.

Notes

1. This biography is based primarily on Anastasia Easterday, "'Labeur, Honneur, Douleur': Sculptors Julie Charpentier, Félicie de Fauveau, and Marie d'Orléans," *Women's Art Journal* 18, no. 2 (Fall 1997-Winter 1998), pp. 11 – 12; Charles Gabet, *Dictionnaire des artistes de l'école française, au XIXe siècle* (Paris, 1831), pp. 133 – 34; Ernest Théodore Hamy, "Julie Charpentier, sculpteur et préparateur de zoologie (1770 – 1845)," *Bulletin du Muséum d'histoire naturelle* 5, no. 7 (November 28, 1899), pp. 329 – 34; and Margaret A. Oppenheimer, "Women Artists in Paris, 1791 – 1814" (PhD diss., New York University, 1996), pp. 139 – 41.
2. Margaret A. Oppenheimer, "Julie Charpentier," 2007 entry in *Dictionnaire des femmes de l'ancienne France*, http://www.siefar.org/dictionnaire/fr/Julie_Charpentier, indicates in her complete list of Charpentier's work that these sculptures are untraced.
3. Claude-Mammès Pahin de la Blancherie, "Salon de la correspondance pour les sciences et les arts," *Nouvelles de la république des lettres et des arts* 8, suite du no. 3 (January 11, 1787), p. 36, and Pahin de la Blancherie, "Salon de la correspondance pour les sciences et les arts," *Nouvelles de la république des lettres et des arts* 8, suite du no. 11 (March 8, 1787), p. 132.
4. Oppenheimer, "Julie Charpentier," indicates that the reliefs intended for the place de la Bastille are untraced.

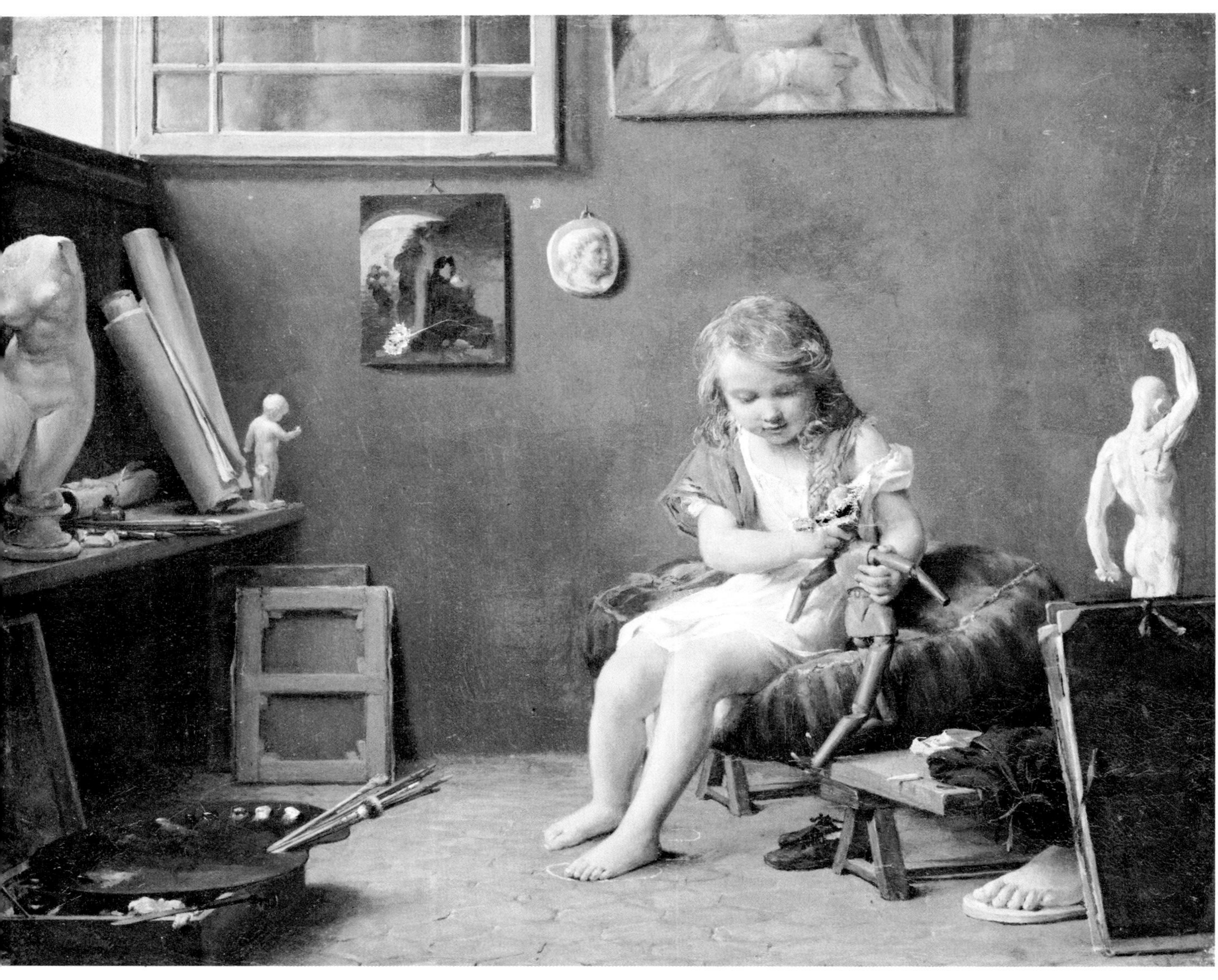

CAT. 33. MARIE-AMÉLIE COGNIET (1798–1869), *Studio Interior*, 2nd quarter of 19th century. Oil on canvas. Palais des beaux-arts, Lille

Marie-Amélie Cogniet

(Paris, 1798 – Paris, 1869)

MARIE-AMÉLIE COGNIET studied and worked with her brother, Léon (1794 – 1880), a Rome Prize – winner who produced portraits, genre scenes, and history paintings.[1] Like his contemporary Eugène Delacroix (1798 – 1863), a leading figure in the French Romantic movement, Léon developed an affinity for exotic narratives of the Middle East, often taken from English literature or the reports of Napoleonic expeditions, rendered on canvas in a brushy, coloristic style.

Amélie Cogniet made her Salon debut in 1831 with five paintings that revealed the breadth of her abilities. In addition to a portrait and a kitchen scene, she displayed two works on military themes: a bivouac and an image of Ali-Hamet, described in the *livret* as an "Egyptian, former Mameluk of the Imperial Guard, wounded twice on July 28 while fighting with the Parisians."[2] Cogniet's *Studio Interior*, included in this exhibition (cat. 33), was also on view in the 1831 Salon. Léon, an active teacher, maintained two studios in Paris throughout his career. In 1831 his atelier for male students, which he oversaw, was located at 9, rue Grange-aux-Belles, near the canal Saint-Martin, and his studio for women, supervised by Amélie, was situated at 50, rue des Marais-Saint-Martin.[3] This painting appears to depict Léon's atelier; the only woman present is believed to be a self-portrait of Amélie.[4]

Amélie Cogniet went on to participate in six additional Salon exhibitions between 1833 and 1843, with portraiture constituting the bulk of her work on view. She won a second-class medal in 1833. In 1838 she received commissions from the Maison du roi to copy two royal portraits; in one case, the portrait of Eugénie-Adélaïde-Louise d'Orléans (1777 – 1848), the original had been painted by her brother. Both of these paintings remain in the collection of the Musée national des châteaux de Versailles et de Trianon.[5]

Notes

1. Émile Bellier de la Chavignerie, *Dictionnaire général des artistes de l'école française depuis l'origine des arts du dessin jusqu'à nos jours: Architectes, peintres, sculpteurs, graveurs et lithographes* (Paris, 1882), vol. 1, p. 272.

2. *Explication des ouvrages de peinture, sculpture, gravure, lithographie et architecture exposés au Musée royal le 1ᵉʳ mai 1831* (Paris, 1831), p. 28: "égyptien, ancien mameluck de la garde impériale, blessé deux fois le 28 juillet en combattant avec les Parisiens."

3. The addresses are given in ibid. and in Charles Gabet, *Dictionnaire des artistes de l'école française, au XIXᵉ siècle* (Paris, 1831), p. 154. In *The Obstacle Race: The Fortunes of Women Painters and Their Work* (New York, 2001), p. 321, Germaine Greer lists several of the women who studied with the Cogniets. Among their students was Léon's future wife, Catherine-Caroline Thévenin (1813 – 1892).

4. See Alexandra K. Wettlaufer, *Portraits of the Artist as a Young Woman: Painting and the Novel in France and Britain, 1800 – 1860* (Columbus, OH, 2011), p. 276, n. 34. Wettlaufer observes a striking similarity between the woman depicted here and the woman in a drawing by Léon Cogniet, *Portrait of the Artist's Sister*, auctioned at Sotheby's, New York, January 27, 2005, sale No8062, "Art of the Enlightenment," lot 10A.

5. Claire Constans, *Musée national du château de Versailles: Les peintures*, introduction by Jean-Pierre Babelon (Paris, 1995), vol. 1, pp. 170 – 71.

Césarine Henriette Flore Davin, née Mirvault

(Paris, 1773 – Paris, 1844)

CÉSARINE DAVIN enjoyed modest success as a painter of portraits and narrative paintings in both oils and miniatures. Having studied miniature painting with Jean-Baptiste-Jacques Augustin (1759 – 1832) and oil painting with two rival history painters, Joseph-Benoît Suvée (1743 – 1807) and Jacques-Louis David (1748 – 1825), she regularly exhibited in both media at the Louvre Salons from 1798 to 1822.[1] Her work garnered two awards: a second-class medal at the 1804 Salon and a gold medal at the 1814 Salon. The 1814 prize acknowledged her painting of the *Death of Malek-Adhel* (untraced), which must have been an exotic scene based on the popular 1805 novel *Mathilde, ou Mémoires tirés de l'histoire des croisades* (Mathilde, or Memoirs from the history of the Crusades) by Sophie Cottin.[2]

Davin, whose brother held a position in the Finance Ministry under Napoléon, also received some recognition from government authorities. In 1807 she delivered a portrait (Musée national des châteaux de Versailles et de Trianon) of François-Joseph Lefebvre, Marshal of the Empire, which had been commissioned for the Gallery of Marshals at the Palais des Tuileries. In 1825 she was asked to copy a portrait of Louis XVIII. The painting included in the current exhibition, the *Portrait of Askar Khan, Ambassador from Persia, in 1808* (cat. 34), exhibited at the Salon of 1810, was purchased for the museum at Versailles in 1836.[3]

Davin seems to have been married for several years by the time of her first exhibition, as her 1798 Salon offerings included *Maternal Tenderness*, a family portrait depicting the artist with her husband and their children.[4] She is known to have been a regular guest at weekly soirées held by Adélaïde-Marie-Castellas Moitte (1747 – 1807), wife of the sculptor and object designer Jean-Guillaume Moitte (1746 – 1810), and to have joined in social events at the home of her teacher David.

Musicians, too, figured among Davin's acquaintances. Madame Moitte reports seeing the violinist Antonio Bartolomeo Bruni (1751 – 1821) perform at a soirée chez Davin. Several portraits of musicians testify to such connections, including a portrait of Bruni in the Frick Collection, New York. Formerly attributed to David, this work was firmly identified by Georges Wildenstein as one of Davin's 1804 Salon offerings.[5]

Like many female artists of the time, Davin supplemented her income by teaching young women. Her school, which opened in 1805, was reportedly still operating in the year of her death some four decades later.

Notes

1. Davin's biography is based on Nathalie Lemoine Bouchard, *Les peintres en miniature actifs en France, 1650 – 1850* (Paris, 2008), p. 181; Amy M. Fine, "Césarine Davin-Mirvault: 'Portrait of Bruni' and Other Works by a Student of David," *Women's Art Journal* 4, no. 1 (Spring-Summer 1983), p. 16; Margaret A. Oppenheimer, "Women Artists in Paris, 1791 – 1814" (PhD diss., New York University, 1996), pp. 155 – 57; Mary Vidal, "The 'Other Atelier': Jacques-Louis David's Female Students," in *Women, Art and the Politics of Identity in Eighteenth-Century Europe*, ed. Melissa Lee Hyde and Jennifer Milam (Aldershot, 2003), p. 257; and Georges Wildenstein, "Un tableau attribué à David rendu à Mme Davin-Mirvault: 'Le portrait du violoniste Bruni' (Frick Collection)," *Gazette des beaux-arts*, 6th ser., 59 (February 1962), pp. 93 – 98.

2. Émile Bellier de la Chavignerie, *Dictionnaire général des artistes de l'école française depuis l'origine des arts du dessin jusqu'à nos jours* (1882 – 85; rpr., Paris, 1997), vol. 1, p. 362, reports that the painting is untraced.

3. Claire Constans, *Musée national du château de Versailles: Les peintures*, introduction by Jean-Pierre Babelon (Paris, 1995), vol. 1, p. 225.

4. Jean-François Heim, Claire Béraud, and Philippe Heim, *Les salons de peinture de la Révolution française, 1789 – 1799* (Paris, 1989), p. 177.

5. Wildenstein, "Tableau attribué à David." The painting is illustrated in Fine, "Césarine Davin-Mirvault," p. 16, fig. 1.

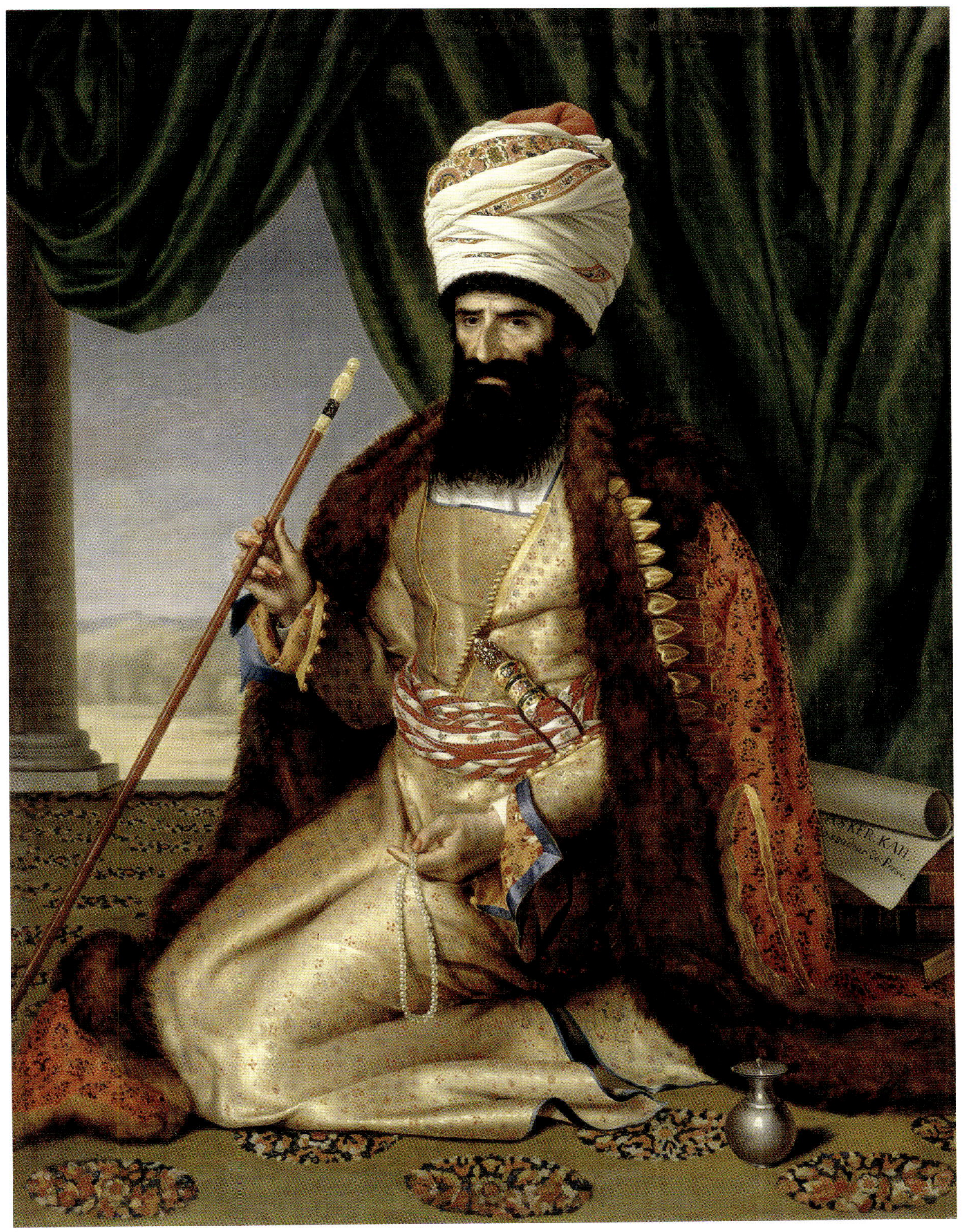

CAT. 34. CÉSARINE HENRIETTE FLORE DAVIN (1773–1844), *Portrait of Askar-Khan, Ambassador from Persia, in 1808*, 1808. Oil on canvas. Musée national des châteaux de Versailles et de Trianon

Herminie Dehérain, née Lerminier
(Abbeville, 1798 – Paris, 1839)

HERMINIE DEHÉRAIN was a painter of portraits, historical narratives, and religious paintings who studied with Antoine Cécile Hortense Haudebourt-Lescot, also included in the present exhibition (see cats. 1, 3, 9, 42, 43).[1] Her husband, Alexandre Dehérain, was a magistrate who presided over the Paris court of appeals before his death in 1837. Their son, Pierre Paul Dehérain, became a noted botanist specializing in plant physiology, and their daughter became a professional portraitist.

Dehérain exhibited regularly at the Paris Salons between 1827 and 1839, winning a second-class medal in 1831. The current exhibition includes one of the four works that she displayed in 1833 — a portrait of the painter and sculptor Antonin Moine (1796–1849) (cat. 35). Writing of the works by female artists in that year's Salon, the critic Augustin Jal concluded that "women do not lack strength."[2] One of the paintings that Jal singled out for praise was Dehérain's *Louis XIV and Mademoiselle Mancini*; he declared that Dehérain "is no longer an amateur who tries her hand with spirit, but an artist who produces with talent."[3] In 1834 the author Hilaire Léon Sazerac fondly remembered the previous year's *Portrait of Antonin Moine*, which, he recalled, possessed so much "intelligence and truth" that "art proved itself to be the happy rival of nature."[4]

Dehérain was especially appreciated in her own time for her many religious paintings, which included *Christ in the Garden of Olives* (1834 Salon; installed in the Abbeville cathedral), *Martha and Mary* (1838 Salon; untraced), and *The Education of the Virgin* (1839 Salon; untraced).[5] Shortly before her death, she published a volume of *Pious Images* featuring lithographs after her drawings by Pierre Joseph Challamel. As an obituary observed, it was "almost unprecedented in the arts to see a woman take on religious painting, and succeed in every one of her works."[6]

The same obituary contains a tantalizing reference to a collection of unpublished writings found among her effects. These included fragmentary manuscripts dealing with subjects such as the influence of women in the arts and letters, observations on Spain's Royal Museum of Painting and Sculpture, and the beginnings of a novel. The whereabouts of these items is unknown.

Notes

1. Biographical information has been compiled from the *Allgemeines Künstlerlexikon: Die bildenden Künstler aller Zeiten und Völker* (Munich, 2000), vol. 25, p. 253; Émile Bellier de la Chavignerie, *Dictionnaire général des artistes de l'école française depuis l'origine des arts du dessin jusqu'à nos jours: Architectes, peintres, sculpteurs, graveurs et lithographes* (Paris, 1882), vol. 1, p. 377; E. Bénézit, *Dictionnaire critique et documentaire des peintres, sculpteurs, dessinateurs, et graveurs de tous les temps et de tous les pays par un groupe d'écrivains spécialistes français et étrangers*, new ed. (Paris, 1999), vol. 4, p. 589; and M. L. Maquenne, "P.-P. Dehérain — Notice nécrologique," *Nouvelles archives du Muséum d'histoire naturelle*, ser. 4, 5 (1903), p. iii.

2. Augustin Jal, *Salon de 1833: Les causeries du Louvre* (Paris, 1833), pp. 233–34. The quotation is on p. 233: "La force ne manque pas aux femmes."

3. Ibid., p. 341: "ce n'est plus un amateur qui s'essaie avec esprit, c'est une artiste qui produit avec talent."

4. Hilaire Léon Sazerac, *Lettres sur le salon de 1834* (Paris, 1834), p. 178: "tant il y avait d'intelligence et de vérité dans cette figure d'homme, tant l'art s'y montrait le rival heureux de la nature."

5. This paragraph and the next are based on Louis Batissier, "Mme Dehérain," *L'artiste*, ser. 2, 3, no. 1 (1839), pp. 72–73. Both paintings are listed as untraced in Bellier de la Chavignerie, *Dictionnaire général*, vol. 1, p. 377.

6. Batissier, "Mme Dehérain," p. 72: "C'était presque une chose nouvelle dans les arts que de voir une femme s'attaquer à la peinture religieuse, et réussir dans chacune de ses oeuvres."

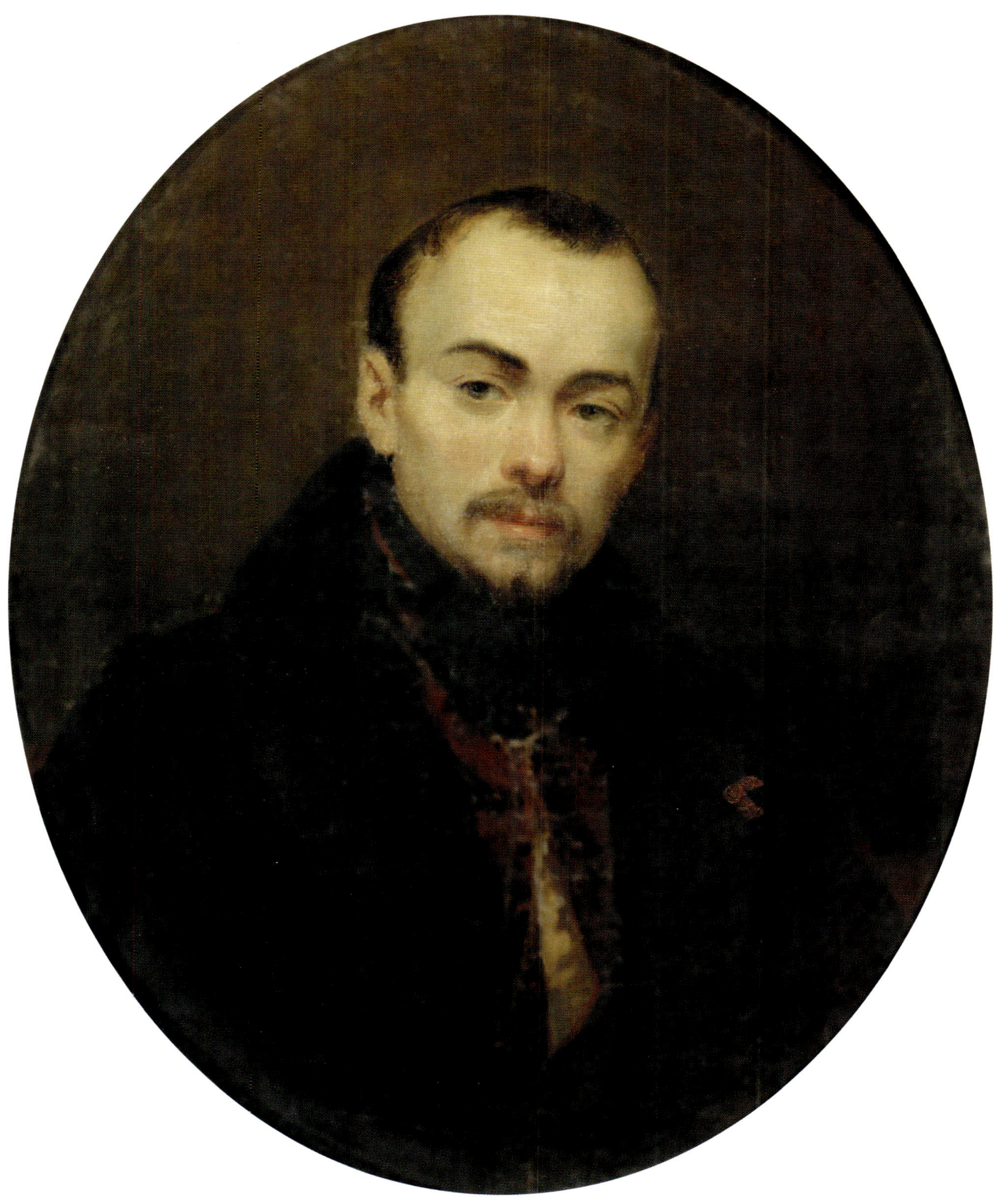

CAT. 35. HERMINIE DEHÉRAIN (1798–1839), *Portrait of Antonin Moine*, 1833. Oil on canvas.
Musée national des châteaux de Versailles et de Trianon

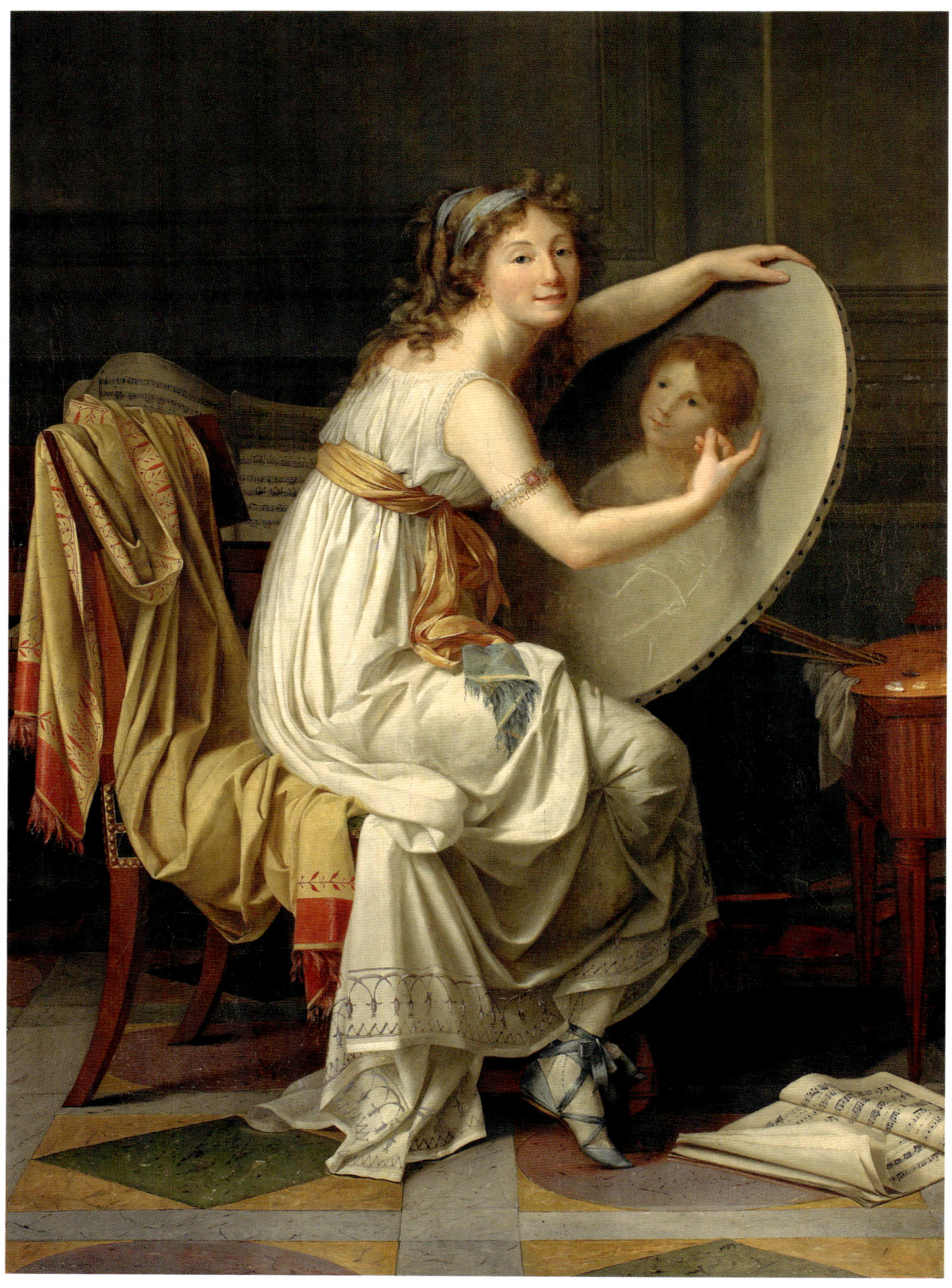

CAT. 36. ROSE ADÉLAÏDE DUCREUX (1761–1802), *Portrait of the Artist*, ca. 1799. Oil on canvas.
Musée des beaux-arts, Rouen

Rose Adélaïde Ducreux

(Paris, 1761 – Saint-Domingue, 1802)

ROSE ADÉLAÏDE DUCREUX was the eldest of six children in the Parisian household of portraitist Joseph Ducreux (1735 – 1802) and his wife, Philippine Rose Cosse.[1] Having learned to paint in her father's studio, Ducreux participated in her first exhibition in 1786. That January she sent a self-portrait to one of the biweekly exhibitions organized by the entrepreneur known as Pahin de la Blancherie in his commercial venue, the Salon de la Correspondance. Her father, whose difficult personality had evidently prevented him from winning admission to the Académie royale de peinture et de sculpture, also exhibited occasionally at this alternative space.

Father and daughter made their joint debut at the Louvre Salon in 1791, when Académie membership ceased being a prerequisite for participation. Rose Ducreux displayed two paintings: a portrait of a young woman and a life-size, standing self-portrait, painted in a Neoclassical style, depicting the artist playing a harp, now in the collection of the Metropolitan Museum of Art (fig. 1.1).[2] She went on to exhibit at the Louvre in 1793, 1795, 1798, and 1799, showing at least a half dozen paintings and studies, most of which remain untraced. The self-portrait in the current exhibition (cat. 36) is dated to around 1799 based on its furnishings and fashions: the white, unstructured, *néo-grec* dress, the mustard-colored cashmere shawl, and the saber-shaped chair legs all point to this period.

In 1801 Ducreux became engaged to François-Jacques Lequoy de Montgiraud (1748 – 1804), a colonial prefect sent by Napoléon to Saint-Domingue (modern-day Haiti) to help restore order on the island, which was in the throes of revolution.[3] After crossing the Atlantic, she contracted typhoid fever and died in 1802.

Notes

1. This biography is based on Joseph Baillio, "Une artiste méconnue, Rose Adélaïde Ducreux," *L'œil* 399 (October 1988), pp. 20 – 27; Neil Jeffares, *Dictionary of Pastellists before 1800*, online edition, updated May 18, 2010, http://www.pastellists.com/Articles/DucreuxR.pdf; and Margaret A. Oppenheimer, "Women Artists in Paris, 1791 – 1814" (PhD diss., New York University, 1996), pp. 171 – 72. On Joseph Ducreux, see Neil Jeffares, "Ducreux, Joseph," *Dictionary of Pastellists before 1800*, online edition, updated March 23, 2011, http://www.pastellists.com/Articles/Ducreux.pdf; and Georgette Lyon, *Joseph Ducreux, premier peintre de Marie-Antoinette (1735 – 1802): Sa vie, son œuvre* (Paris, 1958).

2. Jean-François Heim, Claire Béraud, and Philippe Heim, *Les salons de peinture de la Révolution française, 1789 – 1799* (Paris, 1989), p. 194.

3. On Lequoy de Montgiraud in Saint-Domingue, see Jean-Marcel Champion, "30 Floréal Year X: The Restoration of Slavery by Bonaparte," in *The Abolitions of Slavery: From L.L.F. Sonthonax to Victor Schoelcher, 1793, 1794, 1848*, ed. Marcel Dorigny (Paris and Oxford, 2003), p. 231.

Félicie de Fauveau

(Florence, 1801 – Florence, 1886)

THE SCULPTOR Félicie de Fauveau was an ardent royalist whose renegade spirit garnered her as much renown as did her art.[1] Born in Florence to French émigré parents, she moved with her family to the French town of Besançon, near the Swiss border, near the end of Napoléon's reign.[2] In the 1820s, following the death of her father, Fauveau relocated to Paris with her mother, brother, and two sisters.[3]

There she befriended some of the most prominent artists and writers of the Restoration. She studied with the portraitist and history painter Louis Hersent (1777–1860) and socialized with the staunch Neoclassicist Jean-Auguste Dominique Ingres (1780–1867) and the Romantics Paul Delaroche (1797–1856) and Ary Scheffer (1795–1858); Scheffer painted a striking 1829 portrait of Fauveau with short-cropped hair (Musée du Louvre, Paris). Authors including Stendhal (1783–1843), Honoré de Balzac (1799–1850), and Alexandre Dumas (1802–1870) knew and praised her work.

Royalist to the core, Fauveau explained in unpublished memoirs that she was moved to trade painting for carving by the sight of sculptures defaced by Revolutionary iconoclasts. She shared the fascination with the medieval and Renaissance past that suffuses the so-called Troubadour paintings of Scheffer and Delaroche, filling sketchbooks with historical costumes and ornaments that she adapted to her new medium.[4] Her 1827 Salon debut included a plaster relief depicting the seventeenth-century subject *Queen Christina of Sweden Refusing to Spare the Life of Her Equerry Monaldeschi* (Musée municipal, Louviers), which won a second-class medal.

When the revolution of July 1830 placed Louis-Philippe d'Orléans on the throne abandoned by his Bourbon cousin Charles X, Fauveau became active in legitimist conspiracies. Accompanied by her dear friend Félicie de Duras, comtesse de la Rochejaquelein, she joined in counterrevolutionary activities in the Vendée region of western France. The women were arrested, and Fauveau was imprisoned for seven months. In 1832 they returned on horseback to the Vendée and took up arms on behalf of the duchesse de Berry, daughter-in-law of Charles X, whose son claimed the throne. Their forces routed, they fled the country. Fauveau, tried in absentia, faced life in prison if she returned to France.

Fauveau went to Florence, setting up a home and studio in a former convent. There she welcomed streams of visitors and produced stone sculptures and decorative arts for European nobility. The present exhibition features a stellar example of her metalwork: a letter opener in the shape of a dagger, with scenes from *Romeo and Juliet*, made for the daughter of Czar Nicholas I (cat. 37).[5]

Notes

1. Fauveau has recently received renewed attention with the publication of her first book-length biography: Emmanuel de Waresquiel, *Une femme en exil: Félicie de Fauveau, artiste, amoureuse et rebelle* (Paris, 2010). According to Waresquiel (ibid., p. 215, n. 2), an exhibition and catalogue organized by Sylvain Bellenger, Jacques de Caso, and Christophe Vital are forthcoming.

2. Biographical information has been assembled from E. Bénézit, *Dictionary of Artists* (Paris, 2006), vol. 5, pp. 513–14; Anastasia Easterday, "'Labeur, Honneur, Douleur': Sculptors Julie Charpentier, Félicie de Fauveau, and Marie d'Orléans," *Women's Art Journal* 18, no. 2 (Autumn 1997-Winter 1998), pp. 11–16; Erika Naginski, "Fauveau's Dame Clémence, or Personifying Romanticism," in *Early Modern Visual Allegory: Embodying Meaning*, ed. Cristelle Baskins and Lisa Rosenthal (Aldershot, 2007), pp. 197–216; Nancy Proctor, "Fauveau, Félicie de," in *Dictionary of Women Artists*, ed. Delia Gaze (London, 1997), vol. 1, pp. 511–13; Waresquiel, *Femme en exil*; and Charlotte Yeldham, *Women Artists in Nineteenth-Century France and England* (New York, 1984), vol. 1, pp. 329–65.

3. Various dates have been given for her father's death and her family's move to Paris. Bénézit (*Dictionary*, p. 513) indicates that Monsieur de Fauveau died in 1822; Proctor ("Fauveau," p. 511)

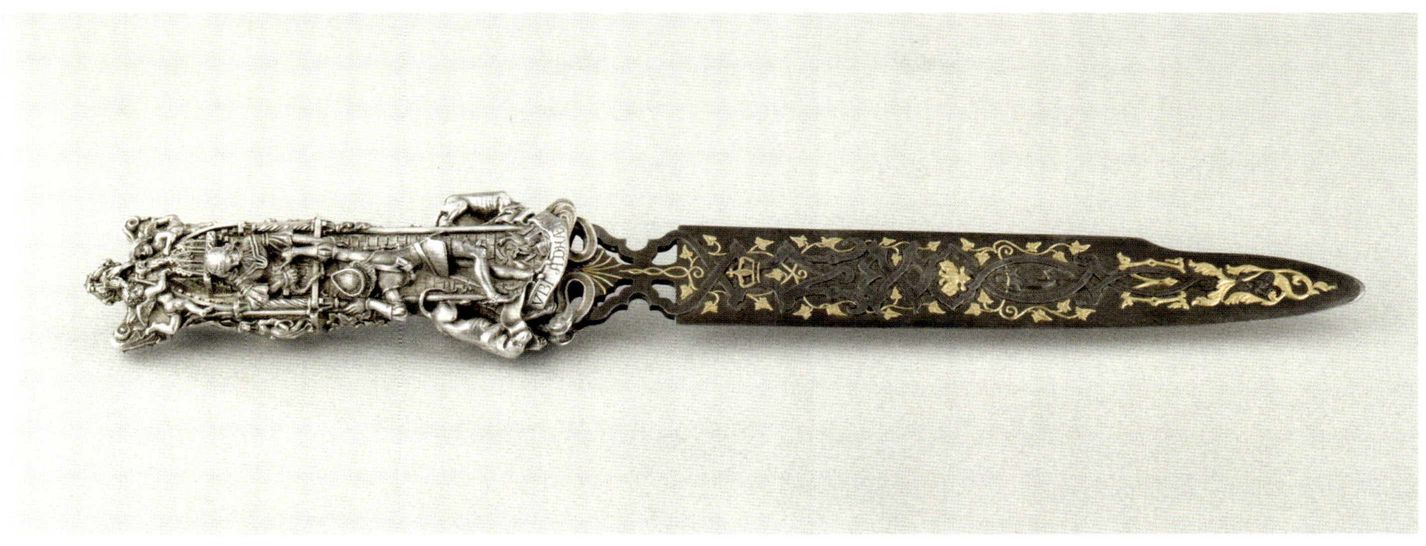

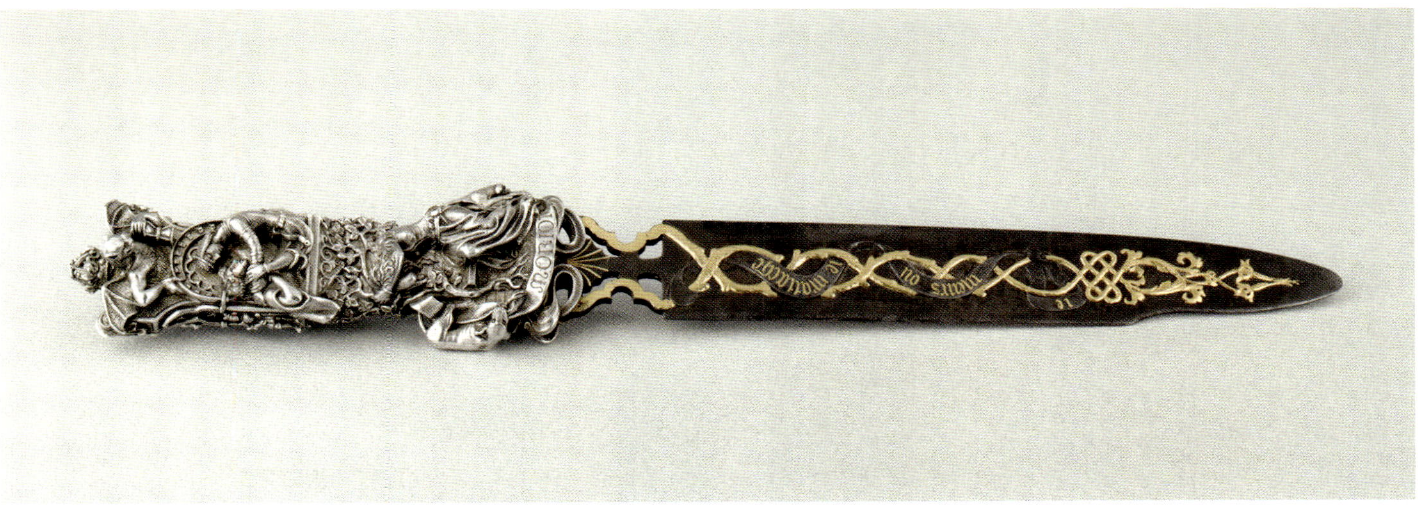

CAT. 37. FÉLICIE DE FAUVEAU (1801–1386), *Letter Opener in the Shape of a Dagger (of the Grand Duchess Maria Nikolaevna?)*, ca. 1850 (two views). Steel, gold, oxidized silver. Musée du Louvre, Département des objets d'art, Paris

and Yeldham (*Women Artists*, p. 329) place the death in 1824; and Waresquiel (*Femme en exil*) states that he died in October 1826.

4. See Gert Schiff, "The Sculpture of the 'Style Troubadour,'" *Arts Magazine* 58, no. 10 (June 1984), pp. 102–10.

5. See Juliette Barbotte, "La dague de Félicie de Fauveau," *La revue du Louvre et des musées de France* 33, no. 2 (1983), pp. 122–25.

Anne Rosalie Filleul, née Bocquet

(Paris, 1752 – Paris, 1794)

BORN IN PARIS to the family of a merchant, Anne Rosalie Filleul was a frequent companion of Élisabeth Louise Vigée-LeBrun (see cats. 11, 23, 63).[1] Vigée-LeBrun's memoirs describe the two attractive adolescents garnering admiring looks as they traversed the gardens of the Palais-Royal en route to the studio of their teacher Gabriel Briard (1725 – 1777).[2] Filleul, who painted in both oils and pastels, received a warm reception when she sent a still life and several portraits to the 1774 exhibition sponsored by the Académie de Saint-Luc. The following year she was admitted to that institution.

After marrying Louis Filleul de Besne, concierge of the royal château de la Muette, in 1777, she ceased exhibiting but continued to paint. One of the many women befriended by Benjamin Franklin during his time in Paris, Filleul painted Franklin's portrait in oil. The original (Philadelphia Museum of Art) was recorded in her lodgings upon her death, but prints after the work, engraved in 1779 by Louis Jacques Catehlin (1738 – 1804), circulated widely.[3] From 1781 to 1783 Filleul produced numerous pastels and oils of the children of the comte d'Artois, the king's youngest brother who reigned as Charles X in the nineteenth century. The portrait of Louis-Antoine d'Artois, duc d'Angoulême (1775 – 1844), in the current exhibition depicts the eldest of Artois's children (cat. 38).

When Louis Filleul died in 1788, Madame Filleul took over as keeper of the château and continued to live in an *hôtel* given to the couple by the king. In 1794 she was arrested, tried, and executed as a leading player in the Affaire de la Muette.[4] The charge was theft: evidently, she had been selling items from the *hôtel*, which now belonged to the nation. But the judgment against her also excoriated her character, declaring it "natural" that a woman who was "a servant of the court, a friend of [Marie-]Antoinette," and an ally of Artois would be a "counter-Revolutionary." Her mother, too, was condemned to death in the *affaire*, as was Émilie Félicité Chalgrin, daughter of the landscape painter Joseph Vernet. As Vigée-LeBrun remembered it, Chalgrin had celebrated her daughter's wedding at La Muette in June 1794, and "the very next day, the Revolutionaries didn't hesitate to arrest both Mme Filleul and Mme Chalgrin on the charge of 'burning the nation's candles.'"[5] They perished on the guillotine the following month.

Notes

1. This biography is based on Neil Jeffares, "Filleul, Mme, née Anne-Rosalie Bocquet," in *Dictionary of Pastellists before 1800*, online edition, updated March 23, 2011, http://www.pastellists .com/Articles/Filleul.pdf; and Xavier Salmon, *Les pastels* (Paris, 1997), pp. 76 – 78. Salmon directed me to the archival sources listed below, which I subsequently consulted.

2. *The Memoirs of Elisabeth Vigée-Le Brun*, trans. Siân Evans (London, 1989), p. 19. Vigée-LeBrun's *Souvenirs* were first published between 1835 and 1837. I refer throughout to the first unabridged English translation.

3. Advertisements for the print appeared in the *Journal de Paris*, July 3, 1779, and the *Gazette de France*, July 6, 1779. The inventory of Madame Filleul's home, including her portrait of Franklin, valued at 120 livres, is housed in the Archives Nationales, Paris, F 17/1267, no. 139.

4. The trial records are housed in the Archives Nationales, Paris, W431/148, no. 96.

5. *Memoirs of Vigée-Le Brun*, p. 19. For the original text, see Élisabeth Louise Vigée-LeBrun, *Souvenirs*, ed. Claudine Hermann (Paris, 1986), vol. 1, pp. 41 – 42: "le lendemain, les révolutionnaires n'en vinrent pas moins arrêter madame Filleul et madame Chalgrin, qui, disait-on, avaient *brûlé les bougies de la nation*."

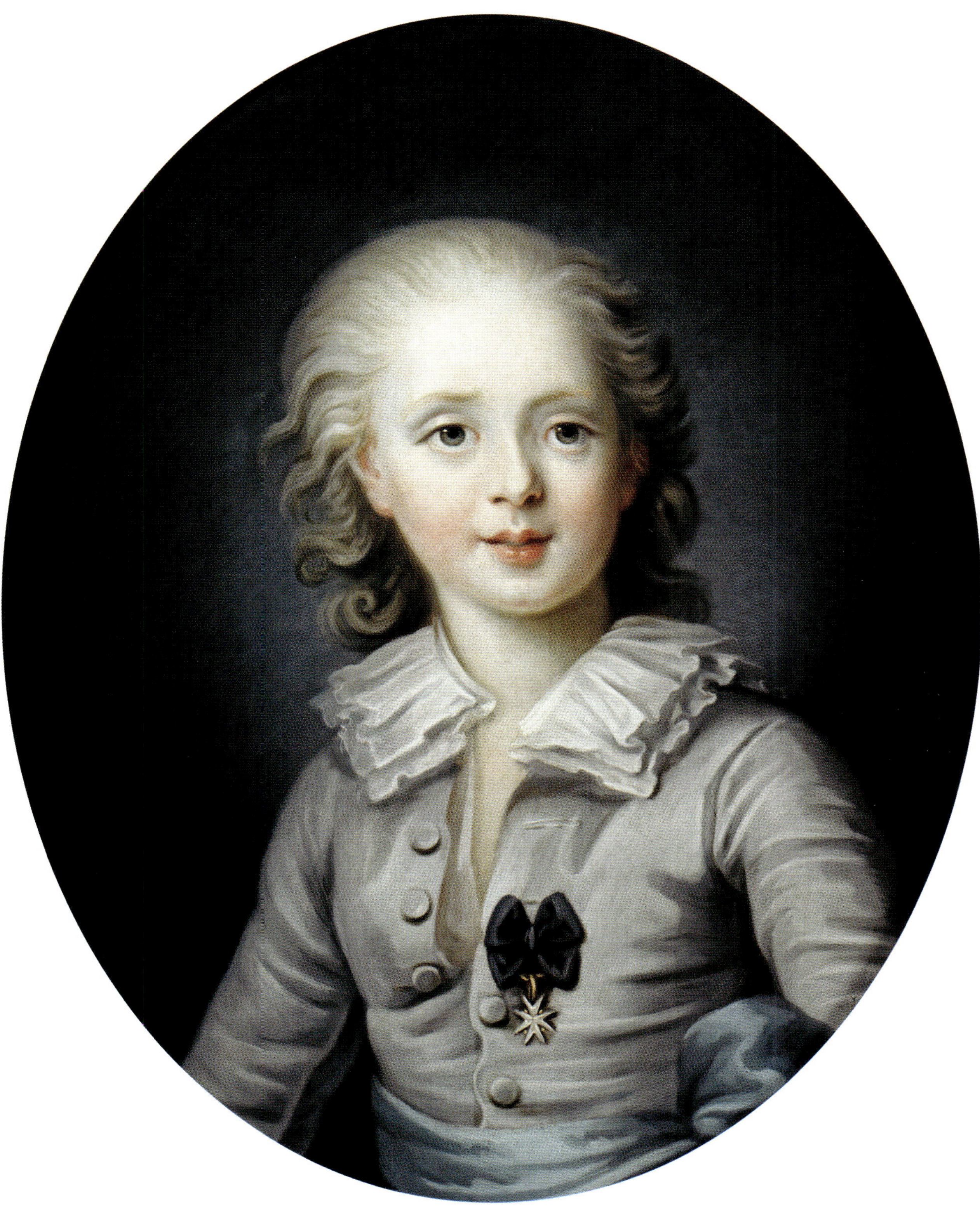

CAT. 38. ANNE ROSALIE FILLEUL (1752–1794), *Louis-Antoine d'Artois, duc d'Angoulême (1775–1844)*, ca. 1785.
Oil on canvas. Musée national des châteaux de Versailles et de Trianon

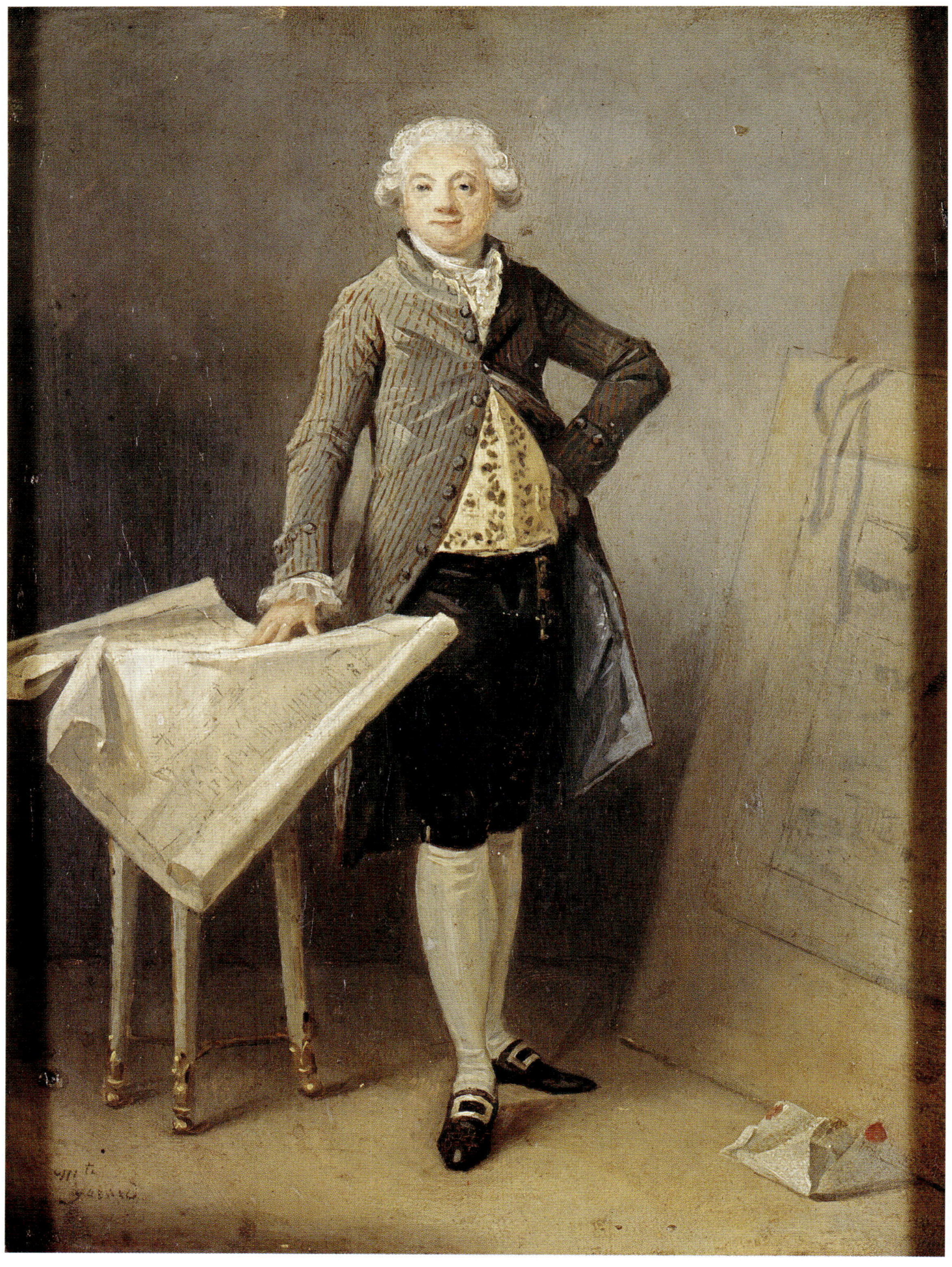

CAT. 39. MARGUERITE GÉRARD (1761–1837), *Portrait of Claude-Nicolas Ledoux*, 1787–90. Oil on wood.
Musée Cognacq-Jay, Paris

Marguerite Gérard

(Grasse, 1761–Paris, 1837)

MARGUERITE GÉRARD has always been closely associated with the renowned Rococo painter Jean-Honoré Fragonard (1732–1806). Gérard, the youngest of seven children, was living in Paris when her mother died, in 1775.[1] Rather than join her father, a perfume maker, in her native Grasse, Gérard entered the household of her sister Marie-Anne, a painter of miniatures who was married to Fragonard.

Gérard quickly became a full-fledged member of Fragonard's studio. Her earliest signed works are engravings after paintings by Fragonard; the 1778 *Honoring the Genius of Franklin*, included in the current exhibition (cat. 19), ranks among them. Her brother Henri also joined the workshop as an engraver, but Marguerite alone pursued oil painting. Following a traditional studio model, she made her first forays into the medium as small contributions to her teacher's canvases. In the 1780s, however, she and Fragonard developed a more unusual collaborative process. Together they produced midsize genre scenes painted in a style reminiscent of that of the seventeenth-century Dutch masters, such as Gerard Ter Borch (1617–1681) and Gabriel Metsu (1629–1667), who were enjoying a surge in popularity in late-eighteenth-century Paris.

By the eve of the French Revolution, Gérard was widely admired, but she did not participate in the open Salons until 1799. She would send some forty-two paintings to eleven Salon exhibitions between 1799 and 1824.[2] Three received awards, and one — *The Clemency of Napoléon* (1808 Salon) — was purchased by the emperor. She also pursued book illustration, providing six images for a 1796 edition of Choderlos de Laclos's libertine novel, *Les liaisons dangereuses*.

The paintings by Gérard on view in the present exhibition exemplify her oeuvre. The portrait of the architect Claude-Nicolas Ledoux (cat. 39) and the presumed portrait of the painter Jean-Jacques Lagrenée (cat. 7) belong to a series of at least thirty-five portraits of painters, actors, and patrons that Gérard produced between 1787 and 1791.[3] Intimate portraits intended to be viewed by friends and family, these works offer full-length views of casually posed subjects presented with attributes of their occupation: an architectural plan in the portrait of Ledoux and a canvas in the portrait of Lagrenée. The genre paintings included here are also typical, with three depicting the scenes of maternal domesticity for which Gérard is best remembered (cats. 14, 21 and p. 2).[4] The *Presumed Portrait of Mesdames Tallien and Récamier* (p. 3) hovers between portraiture and genre painting, featuring a touching scene of female companionship — another important theme in Gérard's work.[5]

Notes

1. Although traditional accounts assert that Gérard traveled to Paris after the death of her mother, Carole Blumenfeld has unearthed unpublished documents that place the family in Paris upon the mother's death. Carole Blumenfeld, "Marguerite Gérard et ses portraits de société," in *Marguerite Gérard: Artiste en 1789, dans l'atelier de Fragonard*, exh. cat. (Paris, 2009), p. 8. Except where noted, all information herein is drawn from this catalogue.

2. *French Painting, 1774–1830: The Age of Revolution*, exh. cat. (Detroit, 1975), p. 440.

3. This series forms the focus of Blumenfeld, "Marguerite Gérard," pp. 17–40. The Ledoux and Lagrenée portraits are discussed in *Marguerite Gérard*, pp. 78, cat. no. 8, 105, cat. no. 21, respectively.

4. On the popularity of this theme, see Carol Duncan, "Happy Mothers and Other New Ideas in French Art," *The Art Bulletin* 55, no. 4 (December 1973), pp. 570–83.

5. The role of female intimacy in Gérard's oeuvre is discussed in Mary D. Sheriff, "Gérard, Marguerite," in *Dictionary of Women Artists*, ed. Delia Gaze (London, 1997), vol. 1, pp. 580–82.

Marie Éléonore Godefroid

(Paris, 1778 – Paris, 1849)

THE PORTRAITIST AND copyist Marie Éléonore Godefroid lived at the center of the Parisian art world for much of the late-eighteenth and early-nineteenth centuries.[1] She spent her first decade in the Louvre, where her paternal grandmother, Marie-Jacobe van Merle, *veuve* (widow) Godefroid, had been granted lodgings and studio space in recognition of her work as restorer to the royal painting collection. Marie Éléonore's father, Joseph-Ferdinand-François Godefroid, carried on the restoration business after his mother's death, and his family enjoyed the Louvre rooms until he died, in 1788. Marie Éléonore received training from artists who worked and socialized at the Louvre, notably François Gérard (1770–1837) and Jean-Baptiste Isabey (1767–1855), and studied music with the composer Étienne-Nicolas Méhul (1763–1817). Her brother Ferdinand-Nicolas became a student of Jacques-Louis David (1748–1825).

In 1795 Godefroid was hired to teach drawing and piano at the school for girls operated by Madame Campan (1752–1822), former lady-in-waiting to Marie-Antoinette, west of Paris at Saint-Germain-en-Laye. She was still residing at the school when she debuted at the Paris Salon in 1800 with a drawing entitled *Portrait of a Young Girl at the Piano* (untraced).[2] Her next exhibition came in 1806, one year after she had returned to Paris and taken up a position as studio assistant to Gérard, who was by then an accomplished history painter and a sought-after portraitist. Godefroid lived with Gérard and his wife, helping to host their fashionable assemblies of artists, politicians, and other celebrated figures.

Godefroid was a regular fixture at the Paris Salons between 1806 and 1847, with portraits constituting the bulk of her exhibited work. She won two medals: one in 1812, for portraits including that of Hortense, Queen Consort of Holland (Napoléon's step-daughter and sister-in-law),[3] and one in 1824. Godefroid was frequently called upon to produce copies after works by Gérard and others, with some of these paintings serving as cartoons for tapestries produced at the Gobelins manufactory. The present exhibition includes Godefroid's portrait of Jacques-Louis David (cat. 40). The painting is said to have been copied after an 1817 portrait by François-Joseph Navez (1787–1869), but Clotilde Schwab-Pourbaix recently suggested that it may have been inspired by one or more of the many prints after the Navez original.

After Gérard died, Godefroid continued to live with his family. Along with his nephew Henri Gérard, she compiled a complete catalogue of his work. She died of cholera in 1849 in Henri's Auteuil home.

Notes

1. This biography is based primarily on the most recent publication on Godefroid, which corrects errors found in previous texts: Clotilde Schwab-Pourbaix, "Marie-Éléonore Godefroid et ses portraits conservés au Musée national des châteaux de Versailles et de Trianon," *La revue des musées de France* 58, no. 5 (December 2008), pp. 63–71. Older sources consulted include Léon Arbaud, "Mademoiselle Godefroid," *Gazette des beaux-arts*, 2nd ser., 1 (1869), pp. 38–52, 512–22; E. Bénézit, *Dictionnaire critique et documentaire des peintres, sculpteurs, dessinateurs, et graveurs de tous les temps et de tous les pays par un groupe d'écrivains spécialistes français et étrangers*, new ed. (Paris, 1999), vol. 6, p. 358; *La femme artiste: D'Élisabeth Vigée-Lebrun à Rosa Bonheur*, exh. cat. (Mont-de-Marsan, 1981), p. 45; and Margaret A. Oppenheimer, "Women Artists in Paris, 1791–1814" (PhD diss., New York University, 1996), pp. 96, 187–89.

2. The work is listed as untraced in Émile Bellier de la Chavignerie, *Dictionnaire général des artistes de l'école française depuis l'origine des arts du dessin jusqu'à nos jours* (1882–85; rpr., Paris, 1997), vol. 1, p. 670.

3. At auction, Drouot Richelieu, salles 5 and 6, Paris, Wednesday, December 12, 2001.

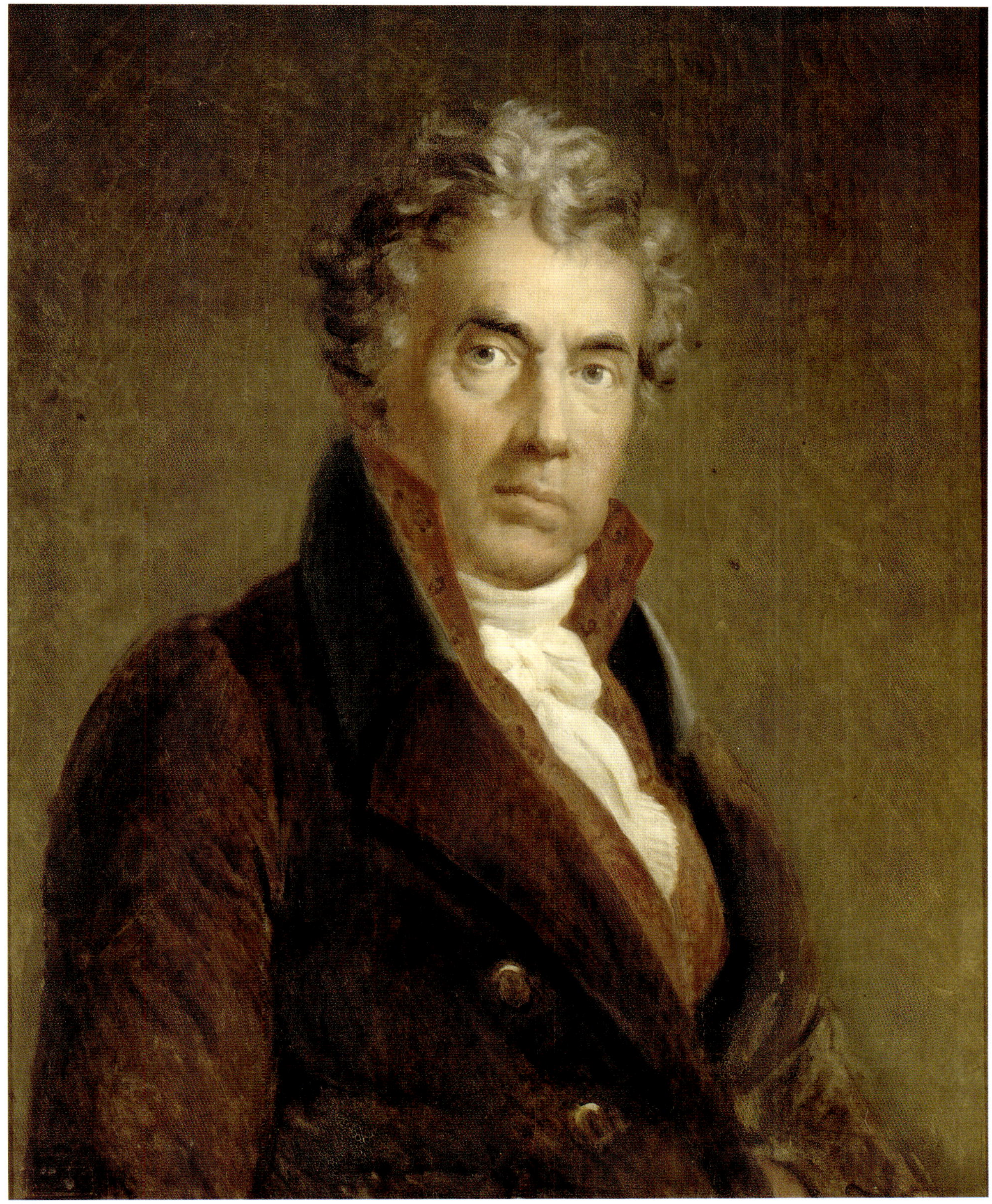

CAT. 40. MARIE ÉLÉONORE GODEFROID (1778–1849), *Portrait of Jacques-Louis David (1748–1825)*, 1843/1848. Oil on canvas. Musée national des châteaux de Versailles et de Trianon

Adrienne Marie Louise Grandpierre-Deverzy

(Tonnere, 1798 – Paris, 1869)

A PROLIFIC AND recognized artist, Grandpierre-Deverzy was a student, a colleague, and, from 1856 until her death, the second wife of the history painter Abel de Pujol (1787 – 1861).[1] From 1822 to 1855 she exhibited regularly at the Paris Salons, sending portraits, genre scenes, and history paintings. Her narrative paintings generally feature subjects selected from modern European history and literature, and associated with the Troubadour style. Her 1824 Salon offerings included the deceptively titled *View of a Portion of the Château of Fontainebleau* (untraced), which depicts the seventeenth-century queen Christina of Sweden having Monaldeschi, her equerry, murdered (a subject treated by Félicie de Fauveau, among others), and a scene (untraced) from the picaresque eighteenth-century novel *The Adventures of Gil Blas of Santillane*.[2] In 1828 she received a silver medal from the Société des amis des arts of Cambrai.

Grandpierre-Deverzy was also a committed teacher who gave lessons and assisted Pujol during the separate studio hours that he maintained for female pupils. Her 1822 *Studio of Abel de Pujol*, displayed at her Salon debut and included in the exhibition (cat. 41), depicts the seated Pujol critiquing a drawing held on his lap while more than a dozen young women, scattered about the space, paint, chat, select pigments, or, at the right, simply gaze out the window.[3] Gender-appropriate instructional aids abound, including the clothed female model seated in the left rear corner, copies after three identifiable religious paintings by Pujol, who specialized in that genre, and a shelf of plaster casts with a male nude torso turned decorously, if playfully, toward the wall. Grandpierre-Deverzy reprised the theme of the atelier twice: once at the 1836 Salon, which included the scene of Pujol's male studio also in the exhibition (cat. 15), and once in 1855. The 1836 painting includes a nude female model who, posing for the male artist at the left, maintains decorum by turning her back to the viewer.[4]

These studio scenes are Grandpierre-Deverzy's best-known paintings. The 1822 painting became emblematic of the very idea of women's artistic practice when it served as the cover image for the catalogue of the groundbreaking 1976 exhibition *Women Artists, 1550 – 1950*, curated by Ann Sutherland Harris and Linda Nochlin.

Notes

1. All sources consulted for this biography concur that Grandpierre-Deverzy studied with Pujol. These include E. Bénézit, *Dictionnaire critique et documentaire des peintres, sculpteurs, dessinateurs, et graveurs de tous les temps et de tous les pays par un groupe d'écrivains spécialistes français et étrangers*, new ed. (Paris, 1999), vol. 6, p. 569; Gen Doy, *Women and Visual Culture in Nineteenth-Century France, 1800 – 1852* (London and New York, 1998), pp. 38 – 39; *La femme artiste: D'Élisabeth Vigée-Lebrun à Rosa Bonheur*, exh. cat. (Mont-de-Marsan, 1981), pp. 57 – 59; Charles Gabet, *Dictionnaire des artistes de l'école française, au XIXᵉ siècle* (Paris, 1831), p. 325; and Ann Sutherland Harris and Linda Nochlin, *Women Artists, 1550 – 1950*, exh. cat. (New York, 1976), pp. 219 – 21. However, Elizabeth E. Guffey, *Drawing an Elusive Line: The Art of Pierre-Paul Prud'hon* (Newark, DE, 2001), p. 169, additionally refers to Grandpierre-Deverzy as a "former student of David," though her name does not appear in the list of David's female students published in Mary Vidal, "The 'Other Atelier': Jacques-Louis David's Female Students," in *Women, Art and the Politics of Identity*, ed. Melissa Lee Hyde and Jennifer Milam (Aldershot, 2003), pp. 257 – 58.

2. Both of these works are listed as untraced in Émile Bellier de la Chavignerie, *Dictionnaire général des artistes de l'école française depuis l'origine des arts du dessin jusqu'à nos jours* (1882 – 85; rpr., Paris, 1997), vol. 1, p. 687.

3. This painting is discussed by the scholars cited above and by Christine Havice, "In a Class by Herself: 19th Century Images of the Woman Artist as Student," *Woman's Art Journal* 2, no. 1 (Spring-Summer 1981), p. 37, and Alexandra K. Wettlaufer, "Dibutades and Her Daughters: The Female Artist in Postrevolutionary France," *Nineteenth-Century Studies* 18 (2004), pp. 22 – 23.

4. See Susan Waller, *The Invention of the Model: Artists and Models in Paris, 1830 – 1870* (Aldershot, 2006), pp. 47 – 48.

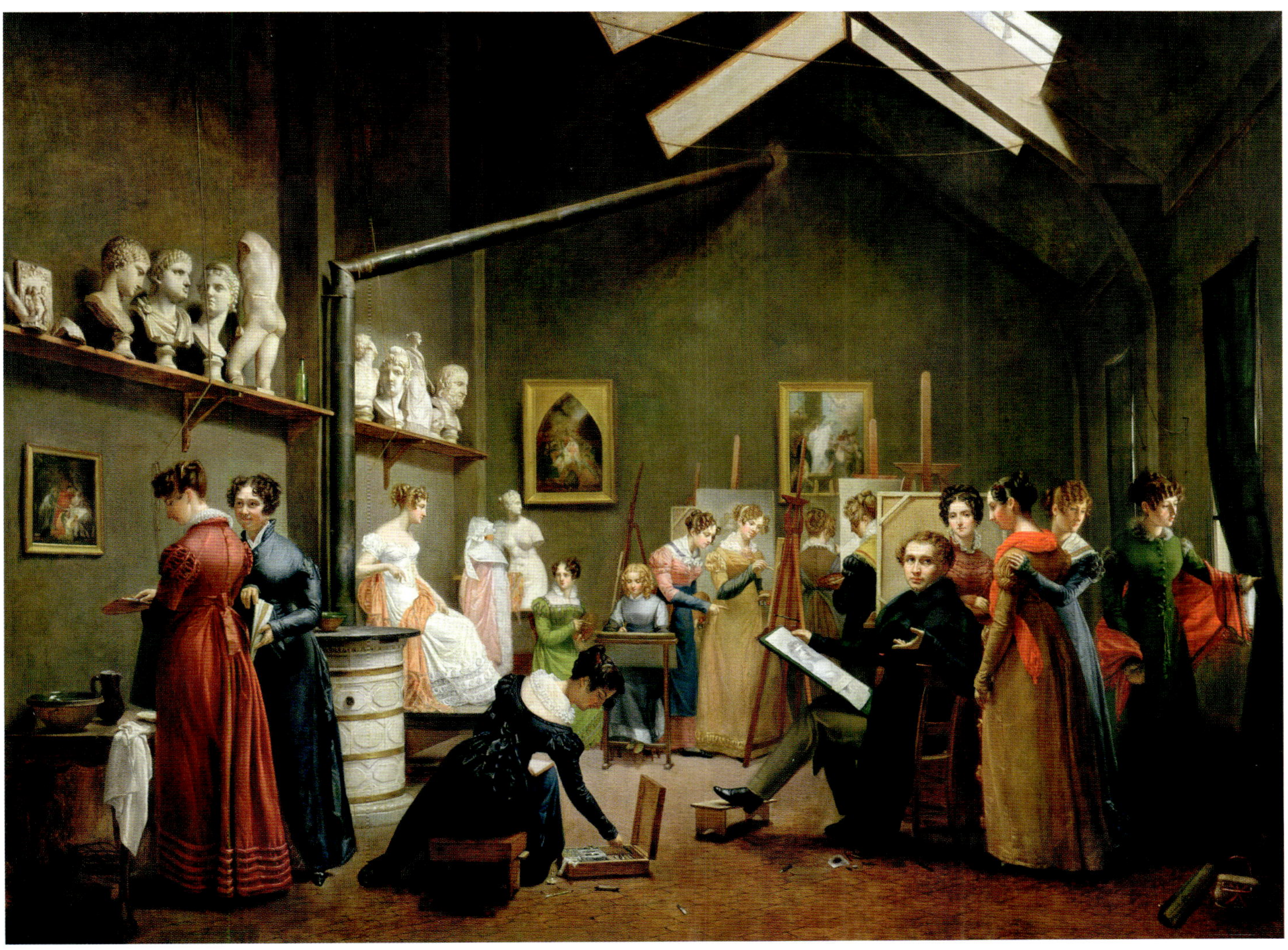

CAT. 41. ADRIENNE MARIE LOUISE GRANDPIERRE-DEVERZY (1798–1869), *The Studio of Abel de Pujol*, 1822.
Oil on canvas. Musée Marmottan Monet, Paris

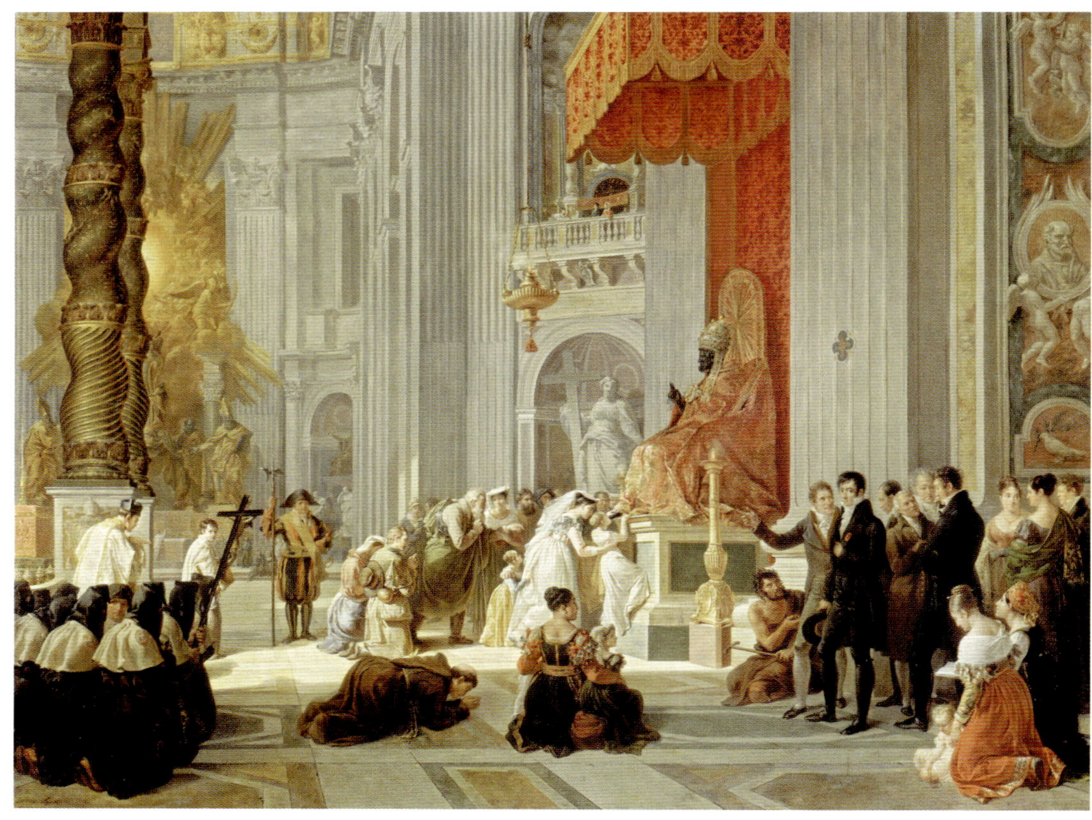

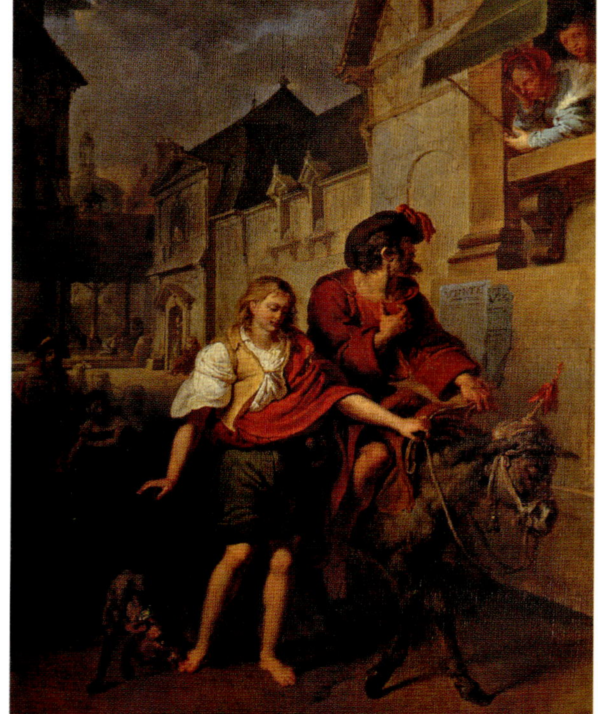

CAT. 42. ANTOINE CÉCILE HORTENSE HAUDEBOURT-
LESCOT (1784–1845), *The Kissing of the Feet in St. Peter's, Rome*,
1812. Oil on canvas. Château de Fontainebleau

CAT. 43. ANTOINE CÉCILE HORTENSE HAUDEBOURT-
LESCOT (1784–1845), *The Miller, His Son, and the Ass*, ca. 1820.
Oil on canvas. Musée Jean de La Fontaine, Château-Thierry

Antoine Cécile Hortense Haudebourt-Lescot

(Paris, 1784–Paris, 1845)

HORTENSE HAUDEBOURT-LESCOT ranks among the most versatile and prolific female artists of the early nineteenth century. She is said to have become a pupil of the Guadeloupe-born history painter Guillaume Lethière (1760–1832) at the age of ten, and to have grown into a fashionable society figure renowned for her superior dancing skills.[1] In an unprecedented move for a French woman artist, she followed Lethière to Italy after he was named director of the Académie de France in Rome in 1807.

Living in Rome until 1816, Lescot thrived within the city's vibrant community of international artists. She joined the Accademia di San Luca and befriended colleagues including the engraver Bartolomeo Pinelli (1781–1835), the sculptor Antonic Canova (1757–1822)—he is one of the artists pictured at the right foreground of Lescot's 1812 *Kissing of the Feet in St. Peter's, Rome*, seen in this exhibition (cat. 42)—and the French painter Jean-Auguste-Dominique Ingres (1780–1867). An 1814 portrait of Lescot dressed as an Italian peasant ranks among Ingres's informal drawings of fellow artists. The architect Louis-Pierre Haudebourt (1788–1849) was also studying in Rome at this time; he and Lescot married in Paris in 1820.

In 1810, while still in Rome, Lescot made her Paris Salon debut with 8 picturesque scenes of Italian life that earned a second-class medal.[2] Over the next thirty years, she went on to exhibit more than 110 portraits, genre scenes, and history paintings at the Salons, winning first-class medals in 1819 and 1827.[3] The works featured in the current exhibition exemplify her tremendous range: these include her Rembrandtesque *Self-Portrait* (cat. 1), a history painting depicting the 1558 *Capture of Thionville* (cat. 9), and a rendering of the fable *The Miller, His Son, and the Ass* (cat. 43)—a moral tale that warns against trying to please everyone.[4] Her

paintings were widely distributed in the form of prints, and collected by such eminent figures as the duc de Berry, whose wife she instructed in the art of painting, and the duc d'Orléans.[5] After Orléans ascended to the throne as King Louis-Philippe in 1830, Haudebourt-Lescot received numerous royal commissions to commemorate great moments and people in French history for the museum at Versailles (see cat. 3).

Notes

1. *Maestà di Roma: D'Ingres à Degas; Les artistes français à Rome* (Milan, 2003), p. 477, and Margaret A. Oppenheimer, "Women Artists in Paris, 1791–1841" (PhD diss., New York University, 1996), p. 194. *French Painting, 1774–1830: The Age of Revolution*, exh. cat. (Detroit, 1975), p. 486, gives her age at the time as seven. Her dancing is mentioned by Augustin Jal, *Esquisses, croquis, pochades, ou, Tout ce qu'on voudra, sur le salon de 1827* (Paris, 1828), p. 290, and by later biographers including Ann Sutherland Harris and Linda Nochlin, *Women Artists, 1550–1950*, exh. cat. (New York, 1976), p. 218. This account is indebted to the above, to the sources cited below, and to Charles Gabet, *Dictionnaire des artistes de l'école française, au XIX*e* siècle* (Paris, 1831), pp. 448–50, and Danièle Véron-Denise and Vincent Droguet, *Peintures pour un château: Cinquante tableaux (XVI*e*–XIX*e* siècle) des collections du château de Fontainebleau*, exh. cat. (Paris, 1998), pp. 110–11.

2. Nancy Heller, *Women Artists: Works from the National Museum of Women in the Arts* (Washington, D.C., 2000), p. 73.

3. Oppenheimer, "Women Artists," p. 195.

4. The 1825 *Self-Portrait*, her best-known painting, has appeared in shows ranging from Harris and Nochlin, *Women Artists*, pp. 218–19, cat. no. 75, to *Citizens and Kings: Portraits in the Age of Revolution, 1760–1830*, exh. cat. (London, 2007), pp. 337–38, cat. no. 84.

5. E. Bénézit, *Dictionnaire critique et documentaire des peintres, sculpteurs, dessinateurs, et graveurs de tous les temps et de tous les pays par un groupe d'écrivains spécialistes français et étrangers*, new ed. (Paris, 1999), vol. 6, p. 1232, states that Haudebourt-Lescot taught "noblewomen," including the duchesse de Berry.

Louise Marie Jeanne Hersent, née Mauduit

(Paris, 1784–Paris, 1862)

LOUISE MAUDUIT, as she was known for most of her exhibiting career, painted portraits, genre scenes, and history paintings that were highly prized during the Bourbon Restoration and the July Monarchy.[1] She was raised in the learned milieus of the Louvre and the Sorbonne: her father, Antoine René Mauduit, was a professor of mathematics at the Collège de France and a prolific author of books on geometry and trigonometry. Antoine René died in 1815, but Louise was still living at the Sorbonne when the next Salon opened, on April 24, 1817.[2]

Mauduit's first teacher seems to have been Guillaume Lethière (1760–1832), but the *livret* of her debut Salon, in 1810, lists her only as a student of the history painter Charles Meynier (1763–1832).[3] Mauduit went on to study with Louis Hersent (1777–1860), a history painter, portraitist, and lithographer whom she married in 1821.[4] By the time of her wedding, Madame Hersent had already enjoyed considerable success, winning medals at the Salons of 1817 and 1819.

In keeping with the period's interest in scenes from national history, many of her best-known works were inspired by episodes from the sixteenth through the eighteenth century. These include *The Dying Louis XIV Blessing His Great-Grandson* (Musée des beaux-arts, Rennes), commissioned by Louis XVIII in 1822, and *Louis XV as a Child Visiting Czar Peter I at the Hôtel de Lesdiguières, May 10, 1717* (Musée national des châteaux de Versailles et de Trianon), commissioned by Louis-Philippe in 1838. Hersent is represented in the current exhibition by *The Good Mother* (cat. 44), a genre scene that evokes the French past through such details as the young mother's spiky collar (a style popular in the seventeenth century) and the lyre (an ancient instrument) seen resting against a taboret at the right.

The 1824 Salon marked the final Paris exhibition for Louise Hersent. She participated in only one more show, winning a silver medal at the Douai Salon of 1825, before ceasing to exhibit entirely. However, she maintained a studio for female artists, and by the middle of the nineteenth century her works could be found in prominent collections including those at the châteaus of Fontainebleau and Luxembourg. Unlike many artists featured in the present exhibition, Hersent never vanished from the historical record. Nonetheless, she has not received the scholarly attention that she deserves.

Notes

1. This summary is based primarily on E. Bénézit, *Dictionnaire critique et documentaire des peintres, sculpteurs, dessinateurs, et graveurs de tous les temps et de tous les pays par un groupe d'écrivains spécialistes français et étrangers*, new ed. (Paris, 1999), vol. 7, pp. 12–13; *Encyclopédie des gens du monde: Répertoire universel des sciences, des lettres et des arts; Avec des notices sur les principales familles historiques et sur les personnages célèbres, morts et vivans* (Paris, 1840), vol. 13, p. 776; Charles Gabet, *Dictionnaire des artistes de l'école française, au XIXe siècle* (Paris, 1831), p. 350; and Margaret A. Oppenheimer, "Women Artists in Paris, 1791–1814" (PhD diss., New York University, 1996), pp. 197–99.

2. Oppenheimer ("Women Artists") lists Lethière among Hersent's teachers, and suggests that Constance Charpentier may have taught her as well. Only Meynier is named in *Explication des ouvrages de peinture, sculpture, architecture et gravure, des artistes vivans, exposés au Musée royal des arts, le 24 avril 1817* (Paris, 1817), p. 61.

3. *Explication des ouvrages de peinture, sculpture, architecture et gravure, des artistes vivans, exposés au Musée Napoléon, le 5 novembre 1810* (Paris, 1810), p. 69.

4. The year of the wedding is given in Anne-Marie de Brem, *Louis Hersent, 1777–1860: Peintre d'histoire et portraitiste*, exh. cat. (Paris, 1993), p. 161.

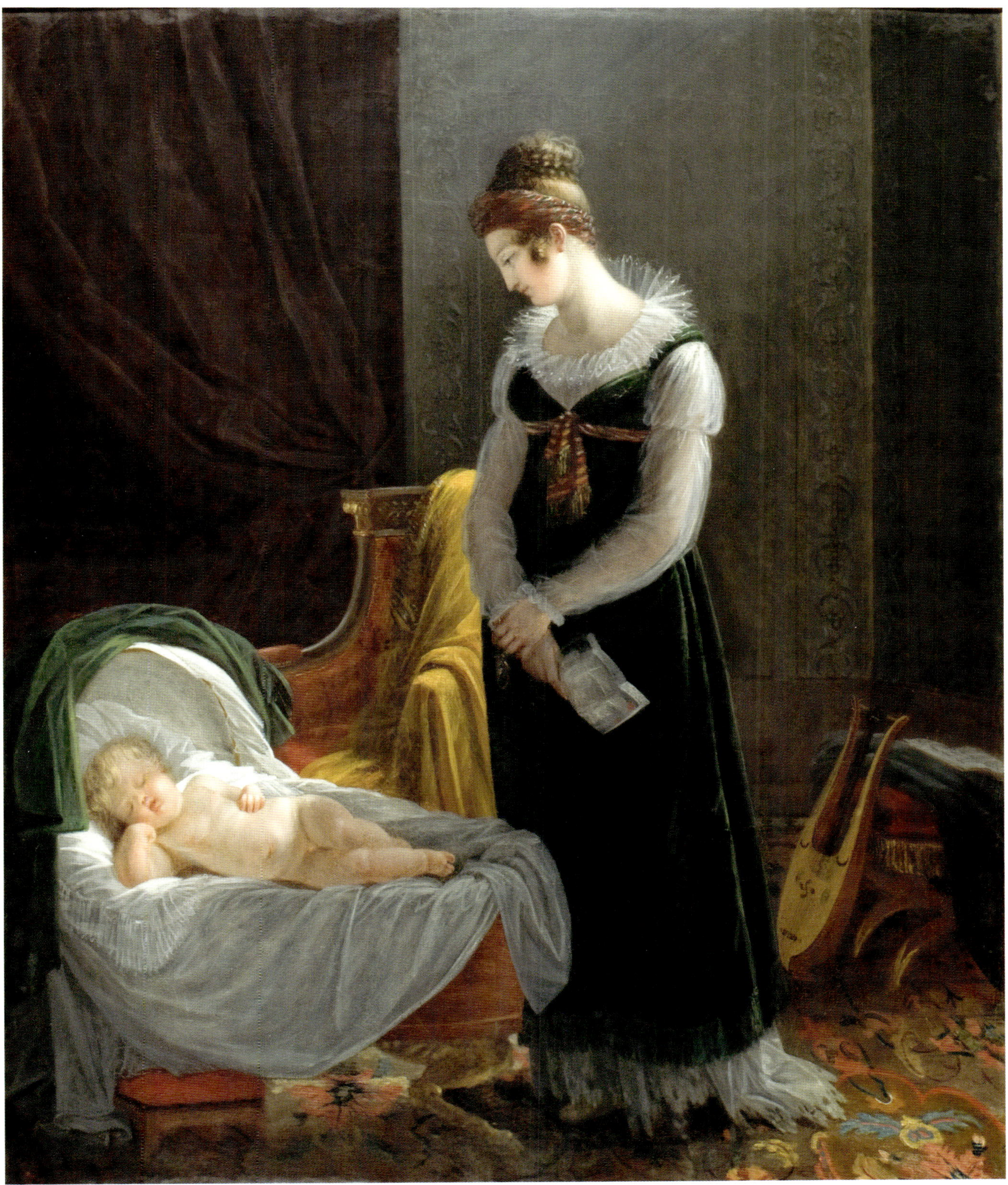

CAT. 44. LOUISE MARIE JEANNE HERSENT (1784–1862), *The Good Mother*, ca. 1815. Oil on canvas. Château-Musée de Dieppe

Adélaïde Labille-Guiard

(Paris, 1749 – Paris, 1803)

PORTRAITIST ADÉLAÏDE Labille-Guiard was the daughter of a shopkeeper whose boutique, near the Palais-Royal, stocked fashionable fabrics and trimmings.[1] She learned her considerable skills from artists in the neighborhood: she studied miniature painting with François-Élie Vincent (1708 – 1790), who taught in the Académie de Saint-Luc; she consulted academician Maurice Quentin de La Tour (1704 – 1788) for advice on pastels; and she learned oils from François-André Vincent, an academician and son of François-Élie. François-André became her second husband in 1800, seven years after she divorced Nicolas Guiard, an administrator in the treasury of the clergy.

Labille-Guiard joined the Académie de Saint-Luc in 1774, and later that year sent a pastel and a miniature to its final show. In 1782 she began exhibiting in Pahin de la Blancherie's commercial venue, the Salon de la Correspondance. Two pastels in the present exhibition — the portraits of the playwright Jean-François Ducis and the actor known as Brizard (cats. 8, 17) — first appeared in Pahin's rooms. Both were commissioned by the comtesse d'Angiviller, wife of the director of the Batîments du roi, who later helped Labille-Guiard to fend off sexually charged criticism. Six members of the Académie royale also sat for portraits by Labille-Guiard in this period; all six voted for her admission.

On May 31, 1783, Labille-Guiard and Élisabeth Louise Vigée-LeBrun (see cats. 11, 23, 63) became the twelfth and thirteenth women ever granted full membership in the Académie royale, bringing the number of female members to its limit of four. Their joint Salon debut attracted considerable attention from critics, who found the women's charms nearly as appealing as their paintings. As Labille-Guiard honed her ability to capture the look and feel of assorted materials and fashions — for instance, in her *Portrait of a Woman* (cat. 45) — she attracted the attention of Mesdames Adélaïde and Victoire, the powerful aunts of Louis XVI, who commissioned several large-scale portraits.

The outbreak of the Revolution in 1789, and Mesdames' subsequent emigration, left Labille-Guiard in a difficult position. Remaining in France, she joined the faction of academicians seeking to reform, not abolish, the institution, and affiliated with the moderate politicians known as the Feuillants. However, as radical forces gained control, she was required to submit her largest painting — a group portrait featuring the comte de Provence (the king's brother who became Louis XVIII) — to be burned. She retired to the countryside with Vincent and two students during the Reign of Terror. In 1795 Labille-Guiard returned to Paris and to the Salons, but neither her spirits nor her career ever recovered fully.

Note

1. Labille-Guiard has been the subject of three books: Laura Auricchio, *Adélaïde Labille-Guiard: Artist in the Age of Revolution* (Los Angeles, 2009); Anne-Marie Passez, *Adélaïde Labille-Guiard: Biographie et catalogue raisonné* (Paris, 1973); and Roger Portalis, *Adélaïde Labille-Guiard, 1749 – 1803* (Paris, 1902).

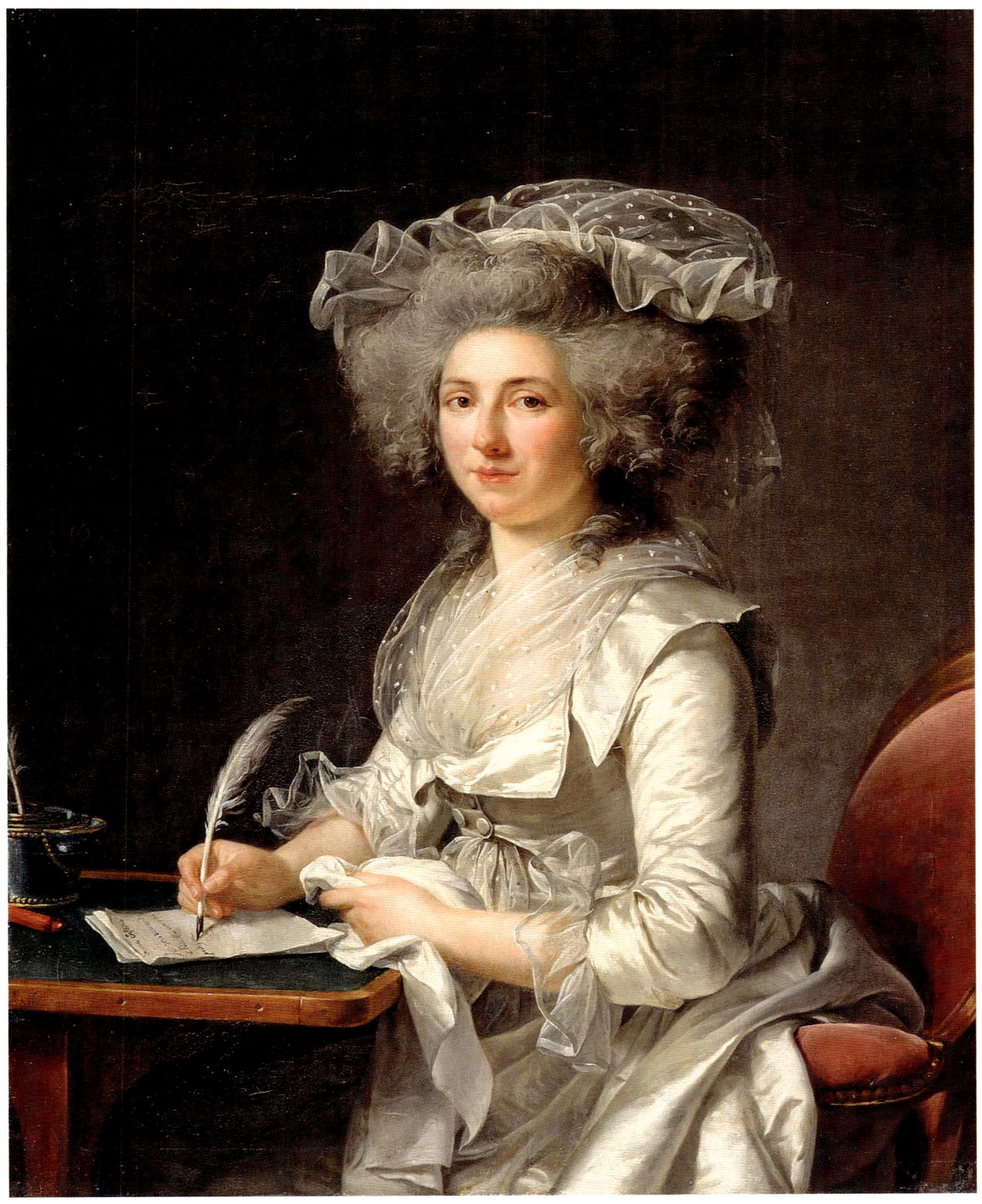

CAT. 45. ADÉLAÏDE LABILLE-GUIARD (1749–1803), *Portrait of a Woman*, 1787. Oil on canvas.
Musée des beaux-arts, Quimper

Jeanne Philiberte Ledoux

(Paris, 1767 – Belleville, 1840)

JEANNE PHILIBERTE LEDOUX enjoyed a long and largely successful career as a painter of portraits, genre scenes, and head studies.[1] Between 1793 and 1819 she exhibited regularly and prolifically in these genres at the Louvre Salons, though the broad and occasionally repetitive titles ascribed to her productions at the time of their presentation now render it difficult to determine their current locations or to ascertain whether certain of them might have been displayed twice. Moreover, as a student of Jean-Baptiste Greuze (1725 – 1805), Ledoux was stylistically linked with her teacher and produced extensively in the genre that he had popularized of single figures and heads of women and children (see cat. 46).[2] The aesthetic frontiers between Greuze and Ledoux thus have yet to be satisfactorily resolved and, notwithstanding Linda Nochlin's assertion that Ledoux's work possesses a straightforward simplicity not found in the production of the older artist, their respective oeuvres and artistic practices remain closely associated. A copy by Ledoux, subsequently retouched by Greuze, after the latter's *The Father's Curse: The Ungrateful Son* (1777), appeared on the art market in the early nineteenth century, and Ledoux also realized signed copies after, or variants of, iconic works by Greuze.[3] To a certain extent, it seems that Ledoux deliberately fostered this proximity, probably for commercial reasons, given the overwhelming popularity of Greuze's small-scale, highly sentimental art among a bourgeois clientele ill able to afford imposing history scenes. That Ledoux benefited from her affiliation with Greuze is also suggested by the fact that she certified works by him after his death, identifying herself in one instance as "his only student."[4] However, tastes had changed by the end of her career: when Ledoux, who never married, died at the age of seventy-three at the home of her brother Alcide, a retired artillery officer, the total value of her possessions was assessed at a mere eighty-one francs.

Despite the strategic assertion of a close relationship to her teacher, Ledoux appears to have been well versed in diverse styles, as indicated in the copies by her after works by Pierre Mignard (1612 – 1695) and Anne-Louis Girodet de Roussy-Trioson (1767 – 1824) listed in a catalogue of stock published in 1827 by the Maison Giroux, in the rue du Coq-Saint-Honoré.[5] It is tempting to imagine that a certain breadth of interest had been fostered by her upbringing. Her birth certificate confirms that her father was not, as is sometimes thought, the architect Claude-Nicolas Ledoux but a certain Pierre Ledoux. Margaret A. Oppenheimer proposes that the latter can be identified as Jean-Pierre Ledoux, a painter and member of the Académie de Saint-Luc in 1763.

Notes

1. Ledoux's biography is based on E. Bénézit, *Dictionnaire critique et documentaire des peintres, sculpteurs, dessinateurs et graveurs de tous les temps et de tous les pays par un groupe d'écrivains spécialistes français et étrangers,* new ed. (Paris, 1999), vol. 8, p. 414; Ann Sutherland Harris and Linda Nochlin, *Women Artists, 1550 – 1950,* exh. cat. (New York, 1976), pp. 205 – 6; and Margaret A. Oppenheimer, "Women Artists in Paris, 1791 – 1814" (PhD diss., New York University, 1996), pp. 217 – 19.

2. For a partial listing of Ledoux's exhibition activity, see Pierre Sanchez, *Dictionnaire des artistes exposant dans les salons des XVII et XVIIIème siècles à Paris et en province, 1673 – 1800* (Dijon, 2004), vol. 2, p. 1014.

3. See the image files on Ledoux conserved in the Frick Art Reference Library, the Frick Collection, New York; the Centre d'étude et de documentation du Département des peintures, Musée du Louvre, Paris; and the Documentation Marianne Roland Michel, Neuilly.

4. Jeanne Philiberte Ledoux to M. Muller, January 9, 1820. Custodia Foundation, Paris, inv.v. J. 8054c. See also the "Déclaration par Mlle Ledoux concernant un tableau de Greuze. 15 février 1835," published in *Tableau de Greuze à vendre à l'amiable* (Paris, 1863), a pamphlet advertising the sale of Greuze's *The Charitable Lady* (ca. 1772 – 75).

5. Oppenheimer, "Women Artists," p. 218.

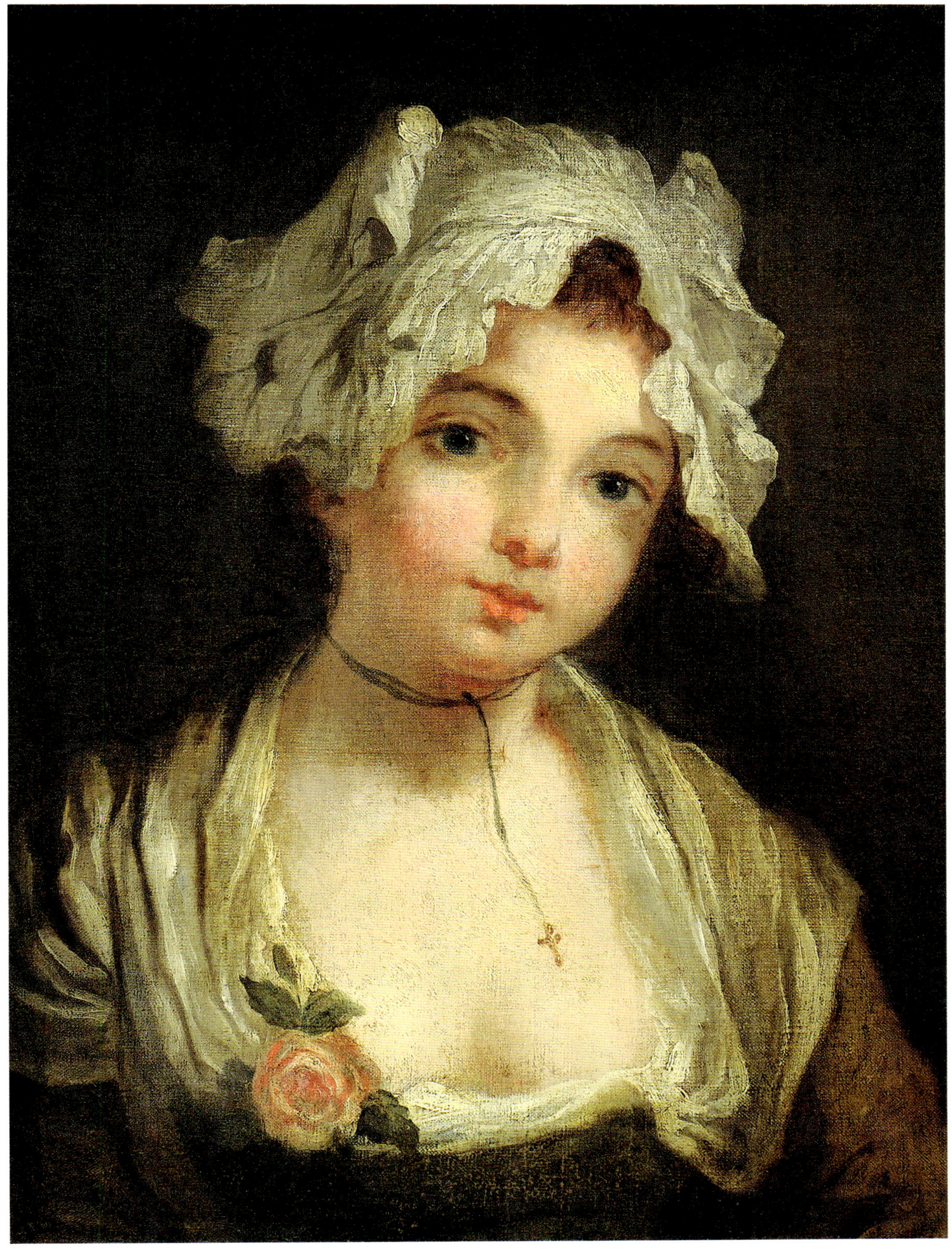

CAT. 46. JEANNE PHILIBERTE LEDOUX (1767–1840), *Portrait of a Young Girl*, 1st half of 19th century.
Oil on canvas. Musée des beaux-arts, Pau

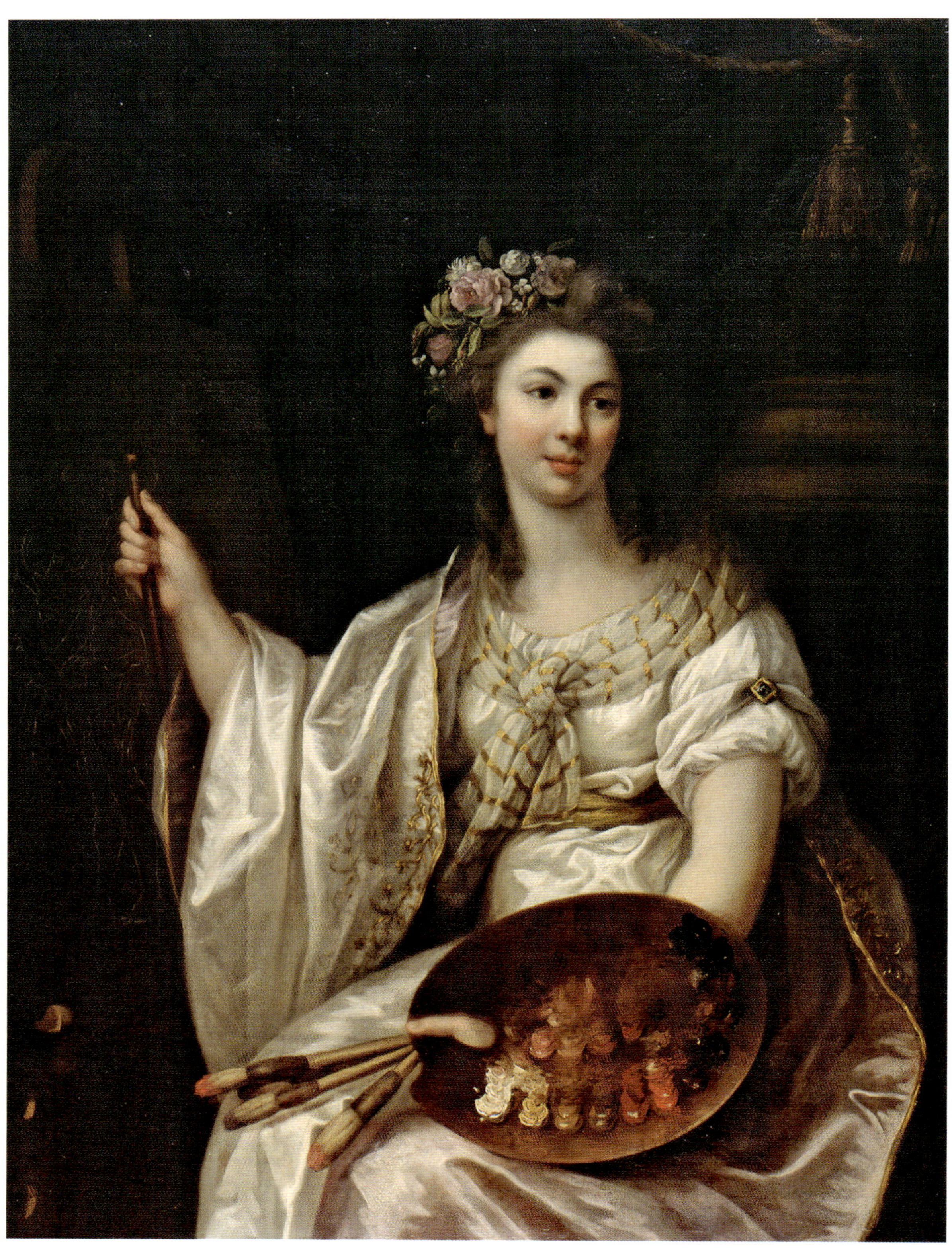

CAT. 47. MARIE VICTOIRE LEMOINE (1754–1820), *Portrait of the Artist*, ca. 1780/1790.
Oil on canvas. Musée des beaux-arts, Orléans

Marie Victoire Lemoine

(Paris, 1754 – Paris, 1820)

MARIE VICTOIRE LEMOINE led a remarkably quiet existence in one of history's most tumultuous eras. Born into the middle-class home of Charles Lemoine and Marie Anne Rousselle, Lemoine never married, living with family throughout her life.[1] She was the eldest of four daughters, three of whom were practicing artists (including Nisa Villers, née Marie-Denise Lemoine, 1774–1821).[2] She exhibited sporadically and attracted only occasional notice. Yet she produced a stunning, if enigmatic, oeuvre that is still being pieced together.

Lemoine studied with the history painter François Guillaume Ménageot (1744–1816), a member of the Académie royale de peinture et de sculpture.[3] She is also said to have taken lessons from Élisabeth Louise Vigée-LeBrun (see cats. 11, 23, 63), who with her husband owned the home where Ménageot lived.[4] Indeed, Joseph Baillio, who has compiled a catalogue of Lemoine's work, observes that Lemoine's portraits and allegories are closer in spirit to those of Vigée-LeBrun than to the more dramatic canvases of Ménageot.[5]

That the first painting Lemoine exhibited was a portrait (untraced) of the princesse de Lamballe — a favorite of Queen Marie-Antoinette — suggests connections at court; Lemoine sent the work to Pahin de la Blancherie's Salon de la Correspondance in 1779.[6] Commissions also came from the circle of the duc de Chartres (who later became the duc d'Orléans); Lemoine's portrait of the young Mademoiselle de Chartres (untraced) appeared in Pahin's rooms in 1785. Lemoine is represented in the current exhibition by another work from the 1780s, an allegory of painting presumed to be a self-portrait (cat. 47). Here a youthful female figure dressed in a white, classically inspired robe and wearing violets in her hair appears seated at, but turning away from, an easel. The attributes of painting are all present, but none is in use: the figure's right hand rests on an upright maulstick, and her left hand steadies a palette that rests on her lap along with a group of large paintbrushes.

Lemoine made her Salon debut in 1796, exhibiting three genre paintings and a selection of miniatures. One of these, her best-remembered work, is now in the collection of New York's Metropolitan Museum of Art, which gives it the title *Atelier of a Painter, Probably Madame Vigée Le Brun (1755–1842), and Her Pupil.*[7] She would go on to display portraits and genre scenes at the Salons of 1798, 1799, 1802, 1804, and 1814.

Notes

1. The biographical information included here is based on Joseph Baillio, "Vie et œuvre de Marie Victoire Lemoine (1754–1820)," *Gazette des beaux-arts*, 6th ser., 127 (January 1996), pp. 125–64; Margaret A. Oppenheimer, "Women Artists in Paris, 1791–1841" (PhD diss., New York University, 1996), pp. 222–24; and Mary D. Sheriff, "Lemoine, Marie-Victoire," in *Dictionary of Women Artists*, ed. Delia Gaze (London, 1997), vol. 2, pp. 836–39.

2. On Villers, see Margaret A. Oppenheimer, "Nisa Villers, née Lemoine (1774–1821)," *Gazette des beaux-arts*, 6th ser., 127 (January 1996), pp. 165–80.

3. On Ménageot, see Nicole Willk-Brocard, *François-Guillaume Ménageot, 1744–1816: Peintre d'histoire, directeur de l'Académie de France à Rome* (Paris, 1978).

4. On Lemoine's studying with Vigée-LeBrun, see Ulrich Thieme and Felix Becker, eds., *Allgemeines Lexikon der bildenden Künstler von der Antike bis zur Gegenwart* (Leipzig, 1929), vol. 23, p. 34.

5. Baillio, "Marie Victoire Lemoine," p. 126.

6. The portraits of the princesse de Lamballe and Mademoiselle de Chartres are listed as untraced in Mary D. Sheriff, "Marie-Victoire Lemoine," 2005 entry in *Dictionnaire des femmes de l'ancienne France*, http://www.siefar.org/dictionnaire/fr/Marie-Victoire_Lemoine.

7. Illustrated, with the title *Interior of the Atelier of a Woman Painter,* in Ann Sutherland Harris and Linda Nochlin, *Women Artists, 1550–1950,* exh. cat. (New York, 1976), p. 188, no. 57.

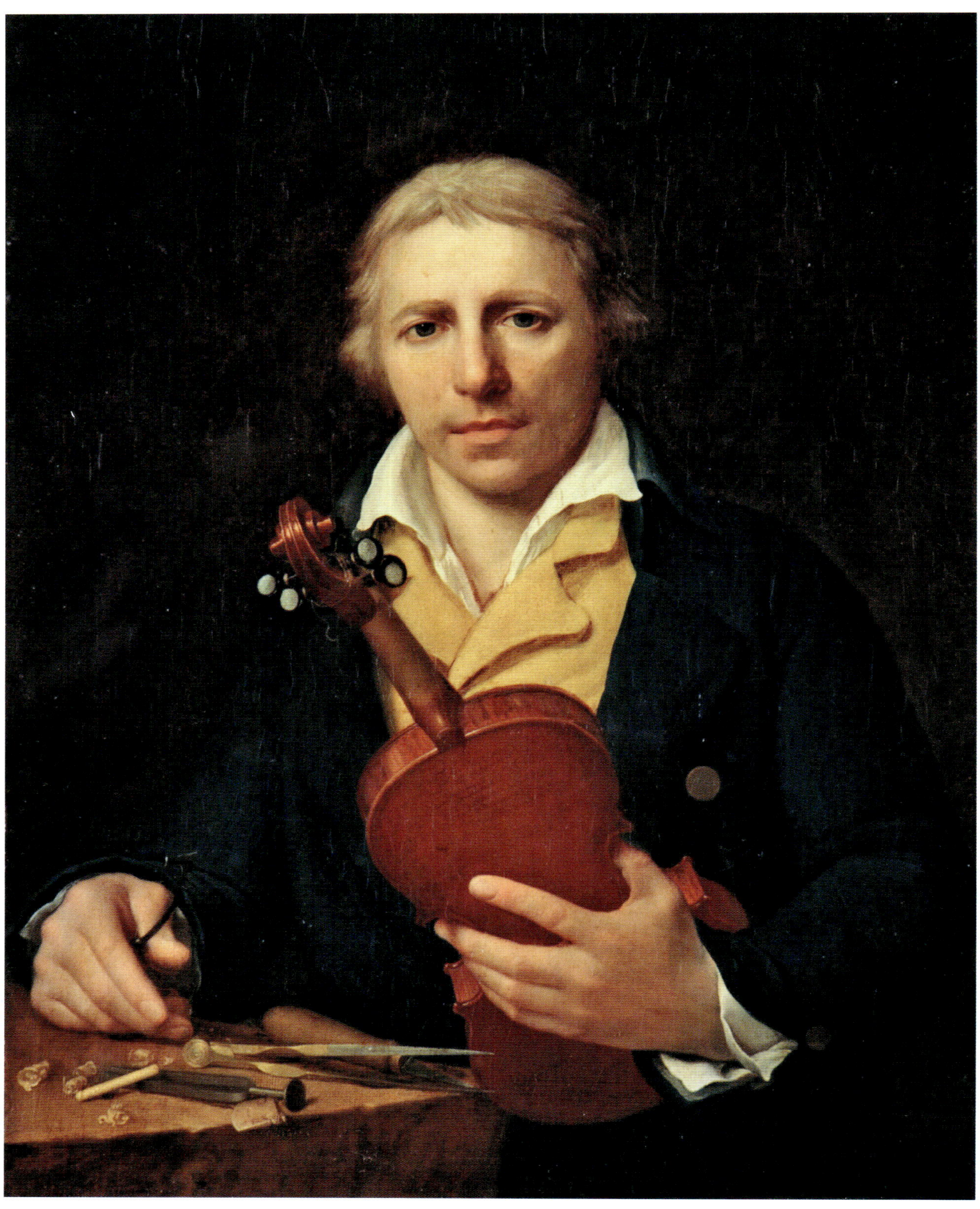

CAT. 48. HENRIETTE LORIMIER (1775–1854), *Portrait of Nicolas Lupot*, 1805. Oil on canvas.
Musée de la lutherie et de l'archèterie française, Mirecourt

Henriette Lorimier

(Paris, 1775 – Paris, 1854)

HENRIETTE LORIMIER was a highly successful painter of portraits, genre scenes, and sentimental history paintings in the Troubadour style. Born out of wedlock to Marguerite Gagnat and Antoine-Jean Lorimier, an officer in the French army, Lorimier was accepted by her paternal family.[1] In the 1790s she joined the household of an uncle, Étienne-François Lorimier, a painter who applied for admission to the Commune générale des arts, successor to the Académie royale de peinture et de sculpture, just a few weeks after it was founded.[2] Henriette was a student of Jean-Baptiste Regnault (1754 – 1829), and may also have studied with her uncle.

Between 1800 and 1814 Lorimier was a frequent participant in the Paris Salons. She attracted widespread approbation for the tender emotions that imbue her narrative paintings — a trait deemed particularly desirable in the work of female artists.[3] Her first such painting, shown in 1802, depicts a young woman crying while reading Chateaubriand's popular novel *Atala* (1801), a tale of doomed love among Native Americans. Her 1804 scene of a goat nursing a human infant while the child's mother (whose milk, presumably, has failed) looks on was purchased by Napoléon's sister Caroline Murat. Lorimier received a gold medal in 1806 for her painting, set in medieval France, depicting Joan of Navarre instructing her son before the tomb of her fallen husband, John V, Duke of Brittany. The empress Joséphine purchased this work, which still hangs in her home, the château of Malmaison.[4]

Lorimier was also sought after as a portraitist. The present exhibition includes three works in this genre (cats. 2, 4, 48). They depict Nicolas Lupot (1758 – 1824), one of the most skilled luthiers of the era, seen in his workshop completing a violin; Madame de Marjolin, née Marie Duval, the wife of a noted surgeon whose son married the daughter of Romantic painter Ary Scheffer (1795 – 1858);[5] and François Pouqueville (1770 – 1838), a diplomat and member of the Institut de France who wrote extensively of his travels throughout the Ottoman Empire. Lorimier was Pouqueville's companion; although they never married, they lived together for the last twenty years of Pouqueville's life, and appear to have been accepted as a couple throughout Parisian society.

Notes

1. Except where noted, the biographical information presented here is based on Margaret A. Oppenheimer, "Women Artists in Paris, 1791 – 1814" (PhD diss., New York University, 1996), pp. 228 – 30. See also E. Bénézit, *Dictionnaire critique et documentaire des peintres, sculpteurs, dessinateurs, et graveurs de tous les temps et de tous les pays par un groupe d'écrivains spécialistes français et étrangers*, new ed. (Paris, 1999), vol. 8, p. 1247, and Charles Gabet, *Dictionnaire des artistes de l'école française, au XIXe siècle* (Paris, 1831), p. 470.

2. Henri Lapauze, ed., *Procès-verbaux de la Commune générale des arts de peinture, sculpture, architecture et gravure de la Société populaire et républicaine des arts* (Paris, 1903), p. 212. His admission is recorded in the minutes of 6 plûviose Year 2 (January 25, 1794). As a woman, Henriette Lorimier was not permitted to enter the Commune.

3. On Lorimier's Troubadour paintings as gender-appropriate, see Margaret Fields Denton, "A Woman's Place: The Gendering of Genres in Post-Revolutionary French Painting," *Art History* 21, no. 2 (June 1998), pp. 234 – 36, 239 – 41; Gen Doy, *Women and Visual Culture in Nineteenth-Century France, 1800 – 1852* (London and New York, 1998), pp. 91 – 95; and Charlotte Yeldham, *Women Artists in Nineteenth-Century France and England* (New York, 1984), vol. 1, p. 176.

4. Reproduced in Doy, *Women and Visual Culture*, p. 43, pl. 5.

5. On this family, see Pierre Baron, "Une famille de dentistes au XVIIIème siècle: Les Leroy de la Faudignère," *Histoire des sciences médicales* 36, no. 1 (January-March 2002), pp. 55 – 73.

Catherine Lusurier

(Paris, 1752 – Paris, 1781)

THE PORTRAITIST Catherine Lusurier lived most of her brief life among artists and artisans. Born to Jeanne Callot, a dressmaker, and Pierre Lusurier, who hailed from a family of milliners, Lusurier was apprenticed to her uncle, the portraitist and miniaturist Hubert Drouais, *père* (1699 – 1757), by the time of his death.[1] She continued to live with his widow, Marie-Marguerite Lusurier, on the rue des Orties, in the parish of Saint-Roch, and likely worked alongside their son, François-Hubert Drouais, *fils* (1727 – 1775), and grandson Jean-Germain Drouais (1763 – 1788).[2]

The Lusurier scholar Helen Ashmore places twenty-one paintings in the artist's oeuvre. The current exhibition features her best-known works: *The Painter Germain-Jean Drouais at Age Fifteen* (1778; cat. 49) and *Portrait of Jean Le Rond d'Alembert* (1777; cat. 22). The portrait of Drouais depicts her fifteen-year-old cousin, who studied history painting with Jacques-Louis David (1748 – 1825), in the process of sketching, using a portfolio as a makeshift support.[3] The portrait of d'Alembert (1717 – 1783) offers a more formal vision of the philosopher, mathematician, and physicist who may be best remembered today for co-editing the *Encylopédie* (1751 – 72) with Denis Diderot; he sits at an ornate desk, pen in hand, surrounded by attributes of learning and taste.[4]

Lusurier was only twenty-eight when she died. An obituary published in the newsletter known as the *Mémoires secrets* lamented that "the arts have had a true loss" and predicted that, had she lived, Lusurier would have developed skills to rival those of Anne Rosalie Filleul, Anne Vallayer-Coster, and Élisabeth Louise Vigée-LeBrun — all of whom feature in this exhibition.[5]

Notes

1. This biography is based primarily on Helen Ashmore, "Catherine Lusurier (1752 – 81): A Woman Painter in Eighteenth-Century Paris," *Apollo* 153, no. 471 (May 2011), pp. 34 – 40. Prior to the publication of Ashmore's article, the most extensive discussion of Lusurier was found in M.-E. Sainte-Beuve, "Une portraitiste du XVIIIe siècle Catherine Lusurier," *Gazette des beaux-arts*, 5th ser., 16, no. 779 (July-August 1927), pp. 80 – 86. Ashmore corrects multiple errors found in Sainte-Beuve.

2. The rue des Orties was destroyed during the Second Empire to make way for the avenue de l'Opéra. See C. Gabillot, "Les trois Drouais (1er article)," *Gazette des beaux-arts*, 3rd ser., 34, no. 579 (September 1905), p. 190.

3. See Christine Kayser, Xavier Salmon, and Laurent Hugues, *L'enfant chéri au siècle des lumières: Après l'Émile*, exh. cat. (Marly-le-Roi, 2003), pp. 102, 105, cat. no. 41.

4. For decades a different painting in the Musée Carnavalet, prominently signed by Lusurier and now understood to depict an as yet unidentified sitter, was believed to be her portrait of d'Alembert. When the true portrait of d'Alembert surfaced in 1986, it was promptly acquired for the Carnavalet. See Ashmore, "Catherine Lusurier," p. 36.

5. Obituary notice as excerpted and translated by Ashmore, "Catherine Lusurier," p. 35. Ashmore (ibid., p. 40, n. 16) cites *Mémoires secrets* 17 (February 5, 1781), pp. 60 – 61. However, I located the text on page 55 of the same volume.

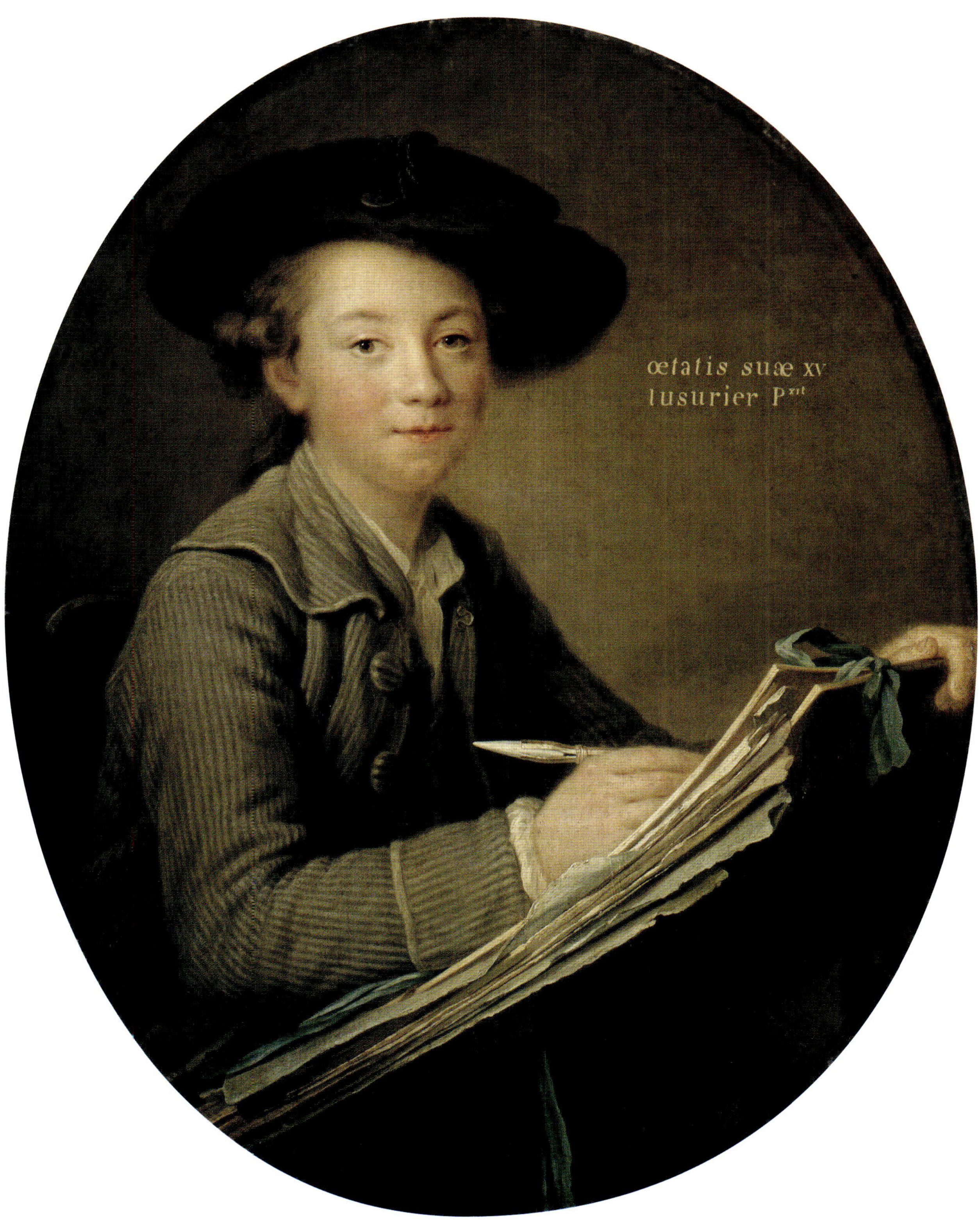

CAT. 49. CATHERINE LUSURIER (1752–1781), *The Painter Germain-Jean Drouais at Age Fifteen*, 1778.
Oil on canvas. Musée du Louvre, Département des peintures, Paris

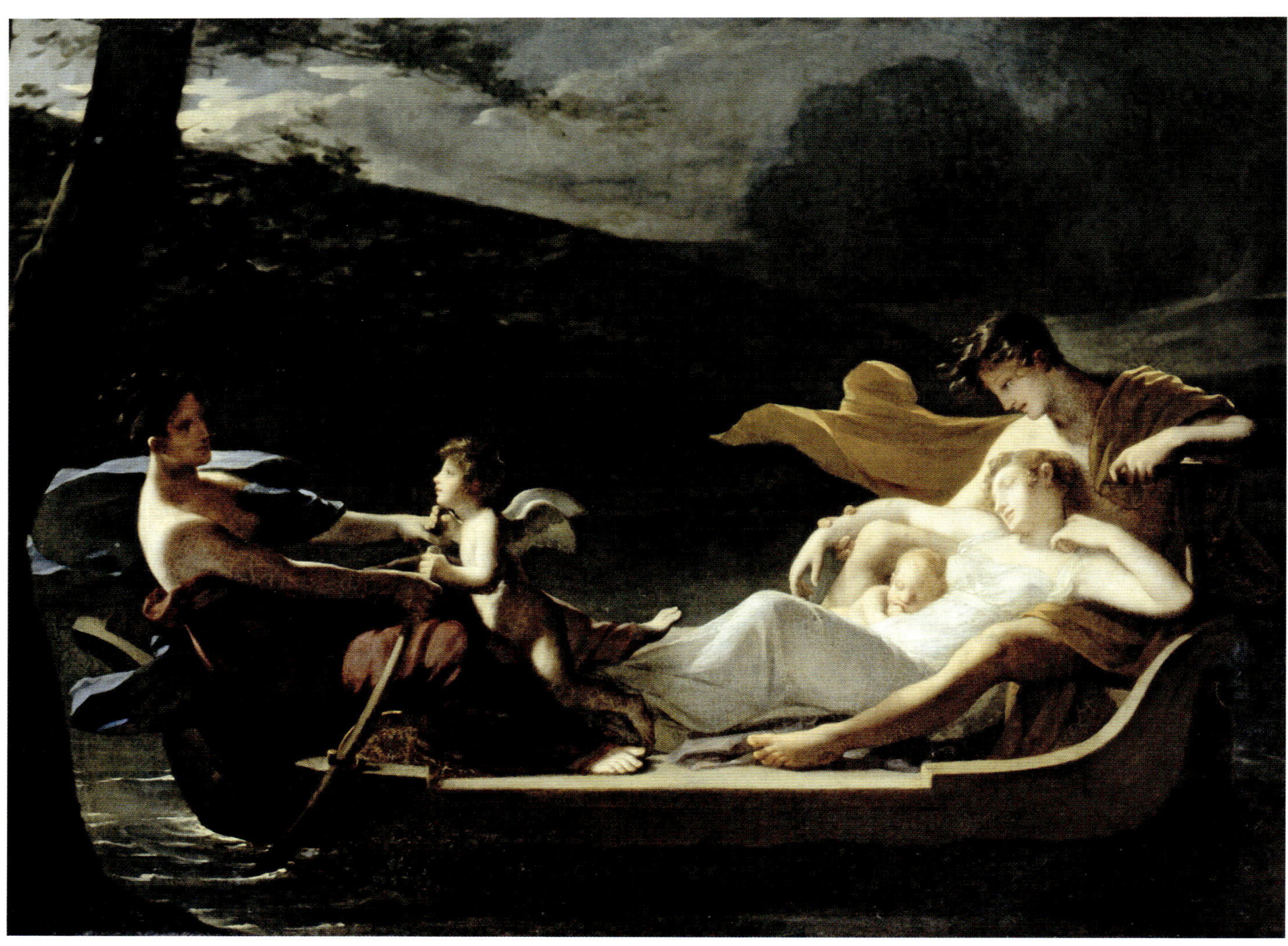

CAT. 50. CONSTANCE MAYER (1775–1821), *The Dream of Happiness*, 1st quarter of 19th century. Oil on canvas. Musée du Louvre, Département des peintures, Paris

Constance Mayer

(Paris, 1775 – Paris, 1821)

CONSTANCE MAYER worked with several teachers in various styles before her life and art became inextricably entwined with those of the history painter Pierre-Paul Prud'hon (1758 – 1823). She first exhibited in 1791, when she sent four portraits to the Exposition de la jeunesse, held in the gallery of Jean-Baptiste-Pierre Le Brun.[1] The *livret* for that exhibition includes her twice — once as Mademoiselle Mayer (the name of her natural father, a well-off German linen dealer living in Paris) and once as Mademoiselle La Martinière (the name of her mother's first husband, Constance's putative father). At her 1796 Salon debut she was listed as a student of Joseph-Benoît Suvée (1743 – 1807), and at the 1801 Louvre exhibition she appeared as a student of both Suvée and Jean-Baptiste Greuze (1725 – 1805).[2]

In 1803 Mayer became Prud'hon's first painting student. When Prud'hon's wife was institutionalized for insanity in the same year, Mayer took on the domestic management of Prud'hon's household in the Sorbonne, where he lived with his five children in government-appointed rooms. Mayer maintained a separate apartment, but went daily to Prud'hon's studio, and the pair developed a fully collaborative working method. Prud'hon, a consummate draftsman, would generate multiple compositional and figural studies which Mayer would work up into finished paintings on canvas. *The Dream of Happiness*, exhibited at the 1819 Salon and included in the present exhibition (cat. 50), resulted from such a process, as did the other eight allegories and genre scenes that Mayer displayed at the Louvre between 1804 and 1821.[3] These large narrative paintings dealing with themes of love and family present gracefully attenuated figures in dreamlike settings. Although Mayer sent the canvases to the Salons under her own name, dealers later sold many of them as Prud'hon's, thereby fetching higher prices while generating considerable confusion concerning Mayer's oeuvre.[4]

Around 1818 financial strains began to burden the formerly wealthy Mayer, who now struggled with bouts of depression. On May 26, 1821, she removed a straight razor from Prud'hon's drawer and slit her throat. The proximate cause of the suicide appears to have been Prud'hon's declaration that, were his institutionalized wife to die, he would never remarry. In a final reversal of roles, Prud'hon took his brush to an unfinished painting begun by Mayer; *The Unfortunate Family* appeared under Prud'hon's name at the 1822 Salon.

Notes

1. The first scholar to mention Mayer's 1791 exhibition was Margaret A. Oppenheimer, "Women Artists in Paris, 1791 – 1814" (PhD diss., New York University, 1996), p. 232.

2. Elizabeth E. Guffey, *Drawing an Elusive Line: The Art of Pierre-Paul Prud'hon* (Newark, DE, 2001), p. 170. This biography is based primarily on Guffey, *Drawing an Elusive Line*, pp. 166 – 233. See also Helen Weston, "Mayer, Constance," in *Dictionary of Women Artists*, ed. Delia Gaze (London, 1997), vol. 2, pp. 928 – 38.

3. See also Elizabeth E. Guffey, "Pierre-Paul Prud'hon, Constance Mayer, and *The Dream of Happiness*," *Master Drawings* 34, no. 4 (December 1996), pp. 390 – 99, and Ann Sutherland Harris and Linda Nochlin, *Women Artists, 1550 – 1950*, exh. cat. (New York, 1976), pp. 212 – 14.

4. See Helen Weston, "The Case for Constance Mayer," *Oxford Art Journal* 3, no. 1 (April 1980), pp. 14 – 19.

Angélique Mongez

(Conflans-l'Archevêque, 1776–Paris, 1855)

ANGÉLIQUE MONGEZ was the first Frenchwoman to lay full claim to the title of history painter.[1] She entered the studio for women of Jean-Baptiste Regnault (1754–1829) in the early 1790s; she later became a student of Jacques-Louis David (1748–1825), and remained closely linked to him throughout her career.[2] Mongez produced copies of his works (at his request), included the phrase "student of David" (*élève de M David*) in a painted signature in 1806, and is said to have been responsible for the underpainting on his 1809 *Sappho and Phaon* (State Hermitage Museum, Saint Petersburg). David's 1812 double portrait (Musée du Louvre, Paris) of Angélique and her husband, the antiquarian and director of the Mint, Antoine Mongez, testifies to their friendship, as does David's apparent placement of the couple among his own family in the audience of his *Coronation of Napoléon and Joséphine* (1807) (Musée du Louvre, Paris).[3] When David suffered financial hardships, the Mongez family lent him money. And in 1824, during David's exile, Mongez joined with two of his male students to orchestrate an exhibition of David's *Mars Disarmed by Venus* (Musées royaux des beaux-arts, Brussels), completed that year.

Mongez exhibited at the Salons regularly from 1802 until 1819, and participated in one final Salon in 1827. For her 1802 debut she presented a painting of *Astyanax Torn from the Arms of His Mother*. The tragic episode, from Euripides' *The Trojan Women*, ends with the child Astyanax being hurled to his death from the walls of Troy. At the next Salon, in 1804, Mongez was awarded a gold medal for her painting of *Alexander Mourning the Death of the Wife of Darius*. The work included in the current exhibition, *Mars and Venus* (1841; cat. 51), is generally believed to be an autograph copy of a painting sent to the Salon in 1814. However, Margaret A. Oppenheimer speculates that it may be the same canvas with a tunic added to the figure of Mars, who was nude in the 1814 version.[4]

Mongez's paintings enjoyed mixed receptions: some critics compared them unfavorably to those of David, whereas others saw them as evidence that women could succeed in the most masculine of genres. In either case, Mongez's reputation was inextricably tied to the rarity of her position as a female history painter working in the idiom of Davidian classicism.

Notes

1. This biography is based on Margaret Fields Denton, "A Woman's Place: The Gendering of Genres in Post-Revolutionary French Painting," *Art History* 21, no. 2 (June 1998), pp. 219–46; Gen Doy, "Hidden from Histories: Women History Painters in Early Nineteenth-Century France," in *Art and the Academy in the Nineteenth Century*, ed. Rafael Cardoso Denis and Colin Trodd (Manchester, 2000), pp. 71–85; Gen Doy, *Women and Visual Culture in Nineteenth-Century France, 1800–1852* (London and New York, 1998), pp. 95–129; and Margaret A. Oppenheimer, "Women Artists in Paris, 1791–1814" (PhD diss., New York University, 1996), pp. 238–42.

2. In addition to the sources cited above, see also Mary D. Sheriff, "Jacques-Louis David and the Ladies," in *Jacques-Louis David: New Perspectives*, ed. Dorothy Johnson (Newark, DE, 2006), p. 105.

3. Philippe Bordes, *Jacques-Louis David: Empire to Exile*, exh. cat. (New Haven, 2005), p. 156.

4. Oppenheimer, "Women Artists," p. 242, n. 430.

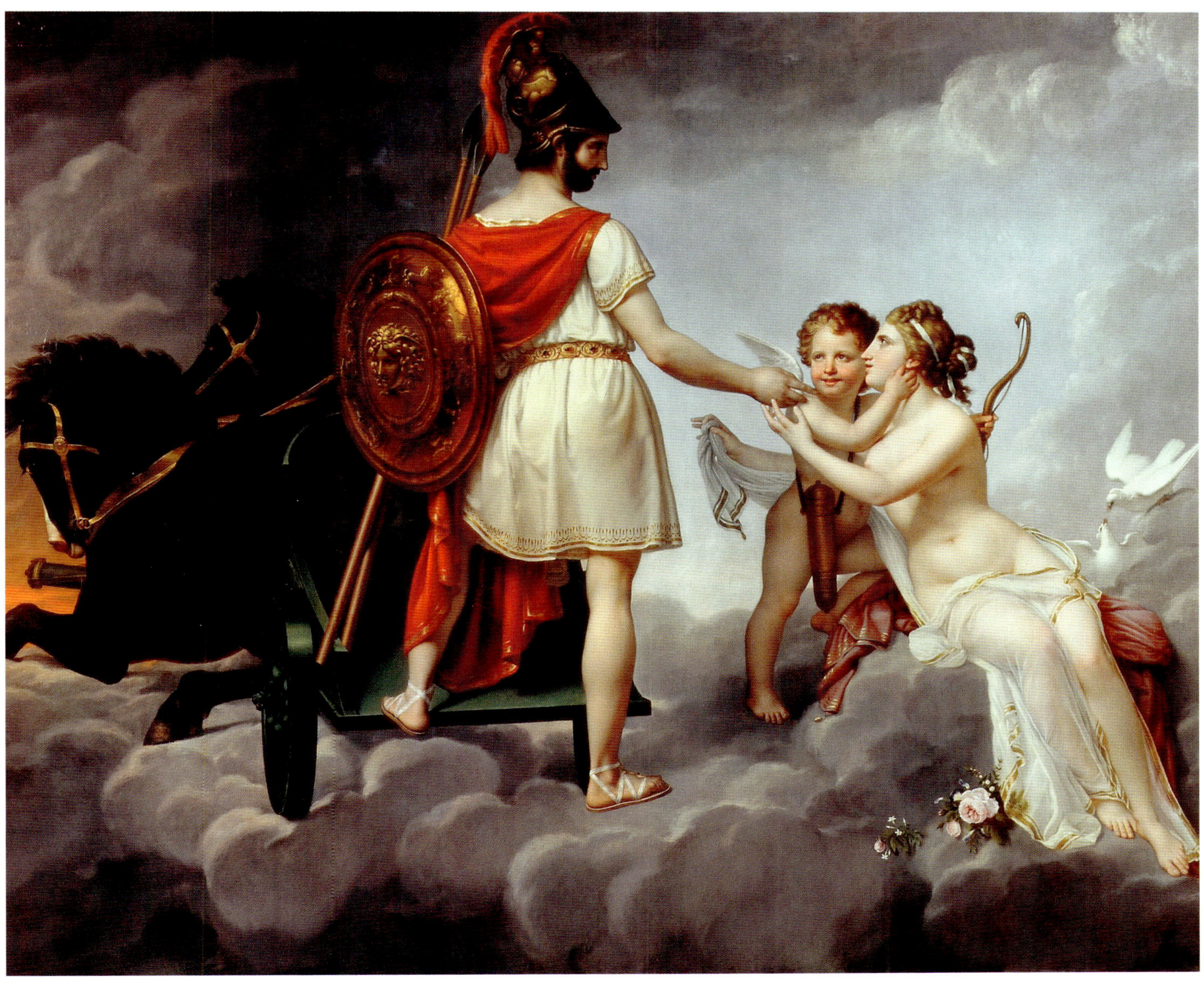

CAT. 51. ANGÉLIQUE MONGEZ (1776–1855), *Mars and Venus*, 1841. Oil on canvas. Musées d'Angers

Eulalie Morin, née Cornillaud

(Nantes, 1765 – ?, 1837)

EULALIE MORIN WAS A painter of portraits and miniatures who enjoyed a brief exhibiting career. We know little about her background beyond the names of family members: her parents were Jacques Cornillaud and Eulalie Barbaux, and her husband was Nicolas-Jean-Baptiste-Joseph Morin.[1] The art historian Margaret A. Oppenheimer has discovered that Eulalie Morin owned a partial interest in a Caribbean coffee plantation.

One of the many female students of Guillaume Lethière (1760–1832), Morin seems also to have taken lessons with Jean-Baptiste Isabey (1767–1855) and to have received advice, if not instruction, from Jean-Jacques Bachelier (1724–1806). Bachelier, a member of the Académie royale and founder of the École gratuite de dessin, apparently encouraged her to work in encaustic, a medium which suspends pigment in hot wax.[2]

Morin appeared at the Paris Salons between 1798 and 1804, showing portraits in oil as well as miniatures, drawings, and encaustics. Her best-known painting, *Portrait of Madame Récamier,* was on view at the 1799 Salon and is included in the current exhibition (cat. 52). It is the earliest identified portrait of the renowned beauty, who was only twenty-one years old when Morin portrayed her in the simple white dress *à l'antique* that Récamier (1777–1849) had helped to popularize.[3] This painting must have been favored by the sitter, for her dear friend the celebrated author Madame de Staël (1766–1817) possessed a copy in her collection at Coppet, Switzerland.

Morin is said to have taught art to the daughters of Élisa Bonaparte, younger sister of Napoléon.[4] Perhaps the archives of the princess will yield more information about this enigmatic artist.

Notes

1. The most complete discussion of Morin's biography is Margaret A. Oppenheimer, "Women Artists in Paris, 1791–1814" (PhD diss., New York University, 1996), pp. 242–43. Other sources consulted include Émile Bellier de la Chavignerie, *Dictionnaire général des artistes de l'école française depuis l'origine des arts du dessin jusqu'à nos jours: Architectes, peintres, sculpteurs, graveurs et lithographes* (Paris, 1882), p. 129; E. Bénézit, *Dictionnaire critique et documentaire des peintres, sculpteurs, dessinateurs, et graveurs de tous les temps et de tous les pays par un groupe d'écrivains spécialistes français et étrangers,* new ed. (Paris, 1999), vol. 9, p. 1327; Germaine Greer, *The Obstacle Race: The Fortunes of Women Painters and Their Work* (New York, 2001), pp. 276–77; and Jean-François Heim, Claire Béraud, and Philippe Heim, *Les salons de peinture de la Révolution française, 1789–1799* (Paris, 1989), p. 294.

2. *Jean-Jacques Bachelier, 1724–1806: Peintre du roi et de Madame de Pompadour,* exh. cat. (Paris, 1999), p. 73.

3. Stéphane Paccoud and Sylvie Ramond, eds., *Juliette Récamier, muse et mécène,* exh. cat. (Paris, 2009), pp. 62–63.

4. Bénézit, *Dictionnaire,* vol. 9, p. 1327.

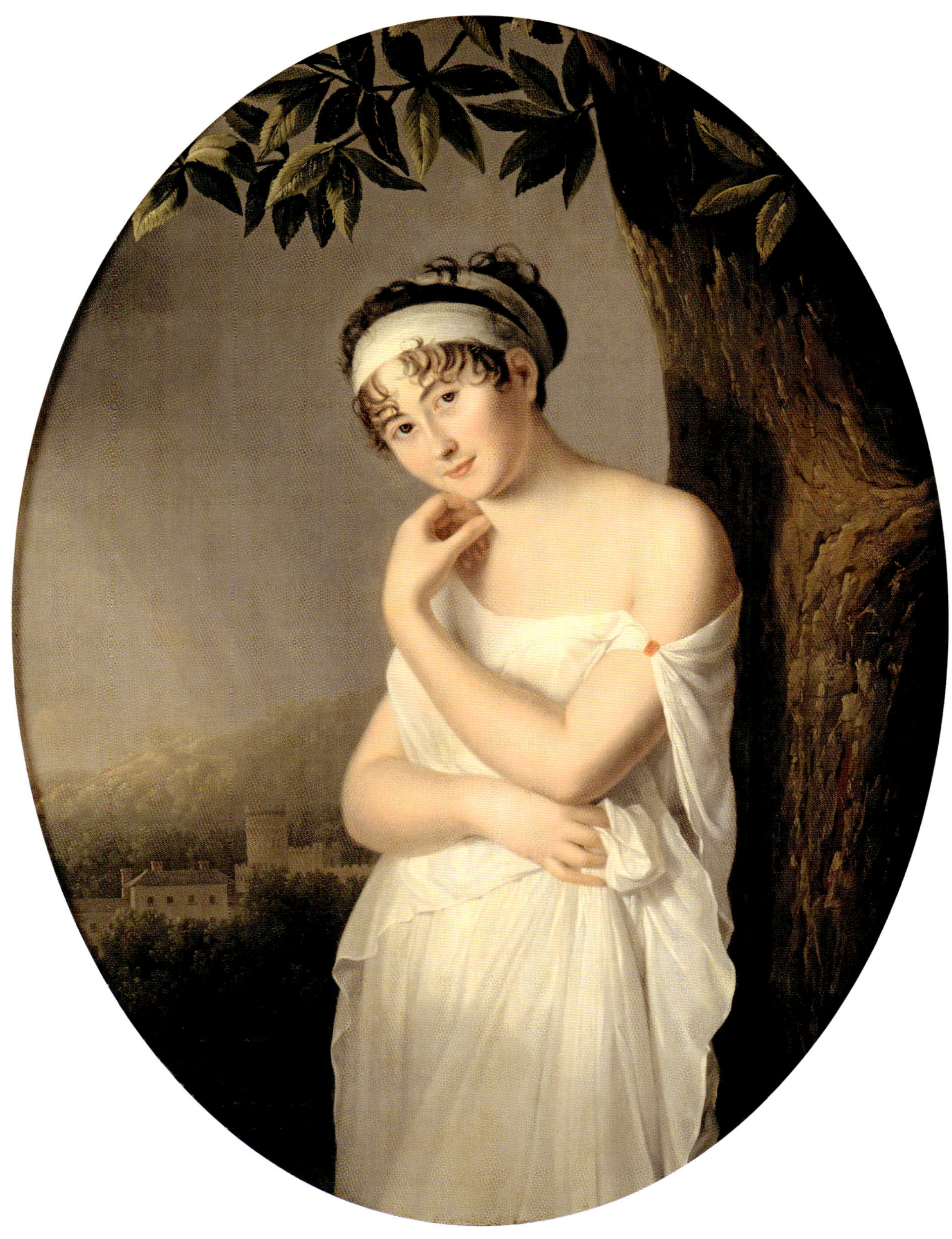

CAT. 52. EULALIE MORIN (1765–1837), *Portrait of Madame Récamier (1777–1849)*, 4th quarter of 18th century.
Oil on canvas. Musée national des châteaux de Versailles et de Trianon

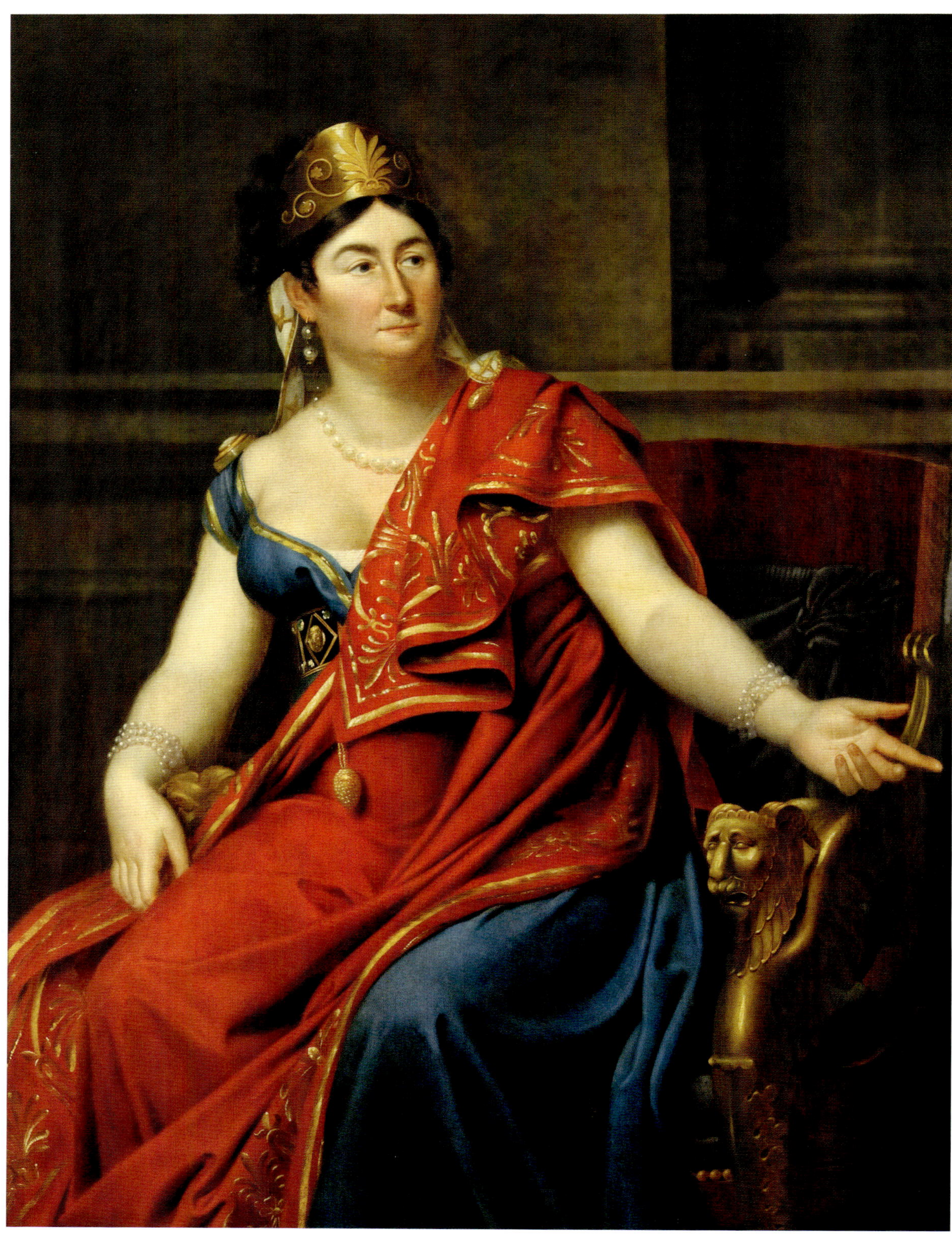

CAT. 53. ADÈLE ROMANY (1769–1846), *Portrait of Mademoiselle Raucourt, of the Opéra-Comique*, 1812.
Oil on canvas. Collections de la Comédie-Française, Paris

Adèle Romany

(Paris, 1769 – Paris, 1846)

ADÈLE ROMANY (known also as Adèle de Romance and Adèle Romanée) lived an unconventional life.[1] She was born to Jeanne-Marie-Bernadine Mercier, who gave her daughter her own last name and baptized her Marie-Jeanne. Although Mercier was married, her husband had not fathered the child. The father was the marquis de Romance-Mesmon, the subject of one of the paintings on view (cat. 6). A former captain of the guard and chevalier of Saint-Louis, the marquis asked the king to legitimize his daughter; she became known as Marie-Jeanne de Romance in 1778. Ten years later, when her first child was born, she may or may not have been wed to the acknowledged father, the miniaturist François-Antoine Romany (ca. 1756 – 1839). She was married to him by 1790, having brought to the union a substantial dowry of 40,000 livres plus additional income. It was not a happy marriage, with at least part of the friction arising from conflicts between Romany's liberal politics and the royalist leanings of his wife's family. The pair divorced in 1793, and Adèle (as she was now called) later bore children, one in 1797 and one in 1806, to two different fathers.

Having studied with Jean-Baptiste Regnault (1754 – 1829), the artist made her Salon debut in 1793, exhibiting several portraits under the names "Citizen Romany (Adèle)" and "Citizen Adel-Romany."[2] She would ultimately display some seventy-eight canvases at the Paris Salons between 1793 and 1833, identifying herself as Romany until 1808, and as Romance in later exhibitions. She occasionally exhibited allegories or genre scenes, but her best-known paintings are portraits of artists and actors, with the latter often portrayed in costume. The *Portrait of Mademoiselle Raucourt, of the Opéra-Comique*, included in the current exhibition (cat. 53), presents the popular actress (1756 – 1815) in the costume associated with one of her roles. Indeed, Romany's family was closely associated with the theaters of Paris; her daughter became an actress and, like her mother and grandmother, bore at least one illegitimate child (whom Romany raised).

The enterprising artist supplemented her income through a variety of investment schemes. Most notably, she speculated on *assignats* (paper currency introduced during the Revolution). With impeccable timing, she sold her holdings just days before the fall of Robespierre burst the speculative bubble.

Notes

1. For biographical entries, see Émile Bellier de la Chavignerie, *Dictionnaire général des artistes de l'école française depuis l'origine des arts du dessin jusqu'à nos jours: Architectes, peintres, sculpteurs, graveurs et lithographes* (Paris, 1882), vol. 2, p. 413, and E. Bénézit, *Dictionnaire critique et documentaire des peintres, sculpteurs, dessinateurs, et graveurs de tous les temps et de tous les pays par un groupe d'écrivains spécialistes français et étrangers*, new ed. (Paris, 1999), vol. 11, p. 1309. The present biography is indebted to the detailed research presented in Carlo Jeannerat, "L'auteur du portrait de Vestris 11, Adèle de Romance, et son mari, le miniaturiste François-Antoine Romany," *Bulletin de la Société de l'histoire de l'art français* (1923), pp. 52 – 63, and Margaret A. Oppenheimer, "Women Artists in Paris, 1791 – 1814" (PhD diss., New York University, 1996), pp. 55 – 60.

2. *Explication des ouvrages de peinture, sculpture, architecture et gravure exposés au salon du Louvre* (Paris, 1793), pp. 184, 374.

Sophie Rude, née Frémiet

(Dijon, 1797 – Paris, 1867)

ALTHOUGH SOPHIE RUDE began studying painting with Anatole Devosge (1770–1850) in her native Dijon, she first exhibited in Flanders.[1] Her father, Louis Frémiet, was a staunch supporter of Napoléon Bonaparte and fled France when the Bourbon monarchy was restored; his wife and children joined him in Brussels in 1816. By the time that Rude sent two portraits of women to the Brussels Salon in October 1818, she and her sister Victorine were students of Jacques-Louis David (1748–1825), who, as both a Bonapartist and a regicide, shared their exile.

Relations between David and the Frémiets quickly grew both close and complicated. In July 1818 a local newspaper announced that David had commissioned Rude to copy his just-finished painting *The Farewell of Telemachus and Eucharis* (J. Paul Getty Museum, Los Angeles).[2] David had explained that, wanting a version for his own collection, he had selected Rude not only because her sensibilities were close to his own but also because the commission would help his friend Louis Frémiet (who had boosted David in 1817 by writing, and publishing anonymously, two glowing reviews of David's controversial *Cupid and Psyche*). Difficulties began to arise in 1823, when the actor Bernard Wolf displayed a portrait by Rude (cat. 54) as a work of David.[3] This episode is presumed to have initiated the 1823 break between David and the Frémiet family. In 1825 David sold Rude's copy of *Telemachus and Eucharis* (private collection) to the dealer Firmin Didot, after having signed and backdated the canvas.[4]

Rude continued to thrive without David. She had begun teaching in Brussels in 1819, and the works that she sent to the Salons in Antwerp in 1819, Brussels in 1821, Ghent in 1820 (awarded a medal of honor), 1824 (awarded a medal of honor), and 1826, and Lille in 1825 (awarded a bronze medal) were well received. In 1821 she married the French sculptor François Rude (1784–1855), who had been allied with her family in both Dijon and Brussels.[5] The couple returned to France in 1830, the same year that their only child died. François would go on to carve much of the relief work on the Arc de Triomphe (1833–36), while Sophie exhibited at the Salons in both Dijon and Paris, where she won a second-class medal in 1833.

Notes

1. The most complete source on Sophie Rude is Monique Geiger, *Sophie Rude, peintre et femme de sculpteur: Une vie d'artiste au XIXe siècle (Dijon–Bruxelles–Paris)*, exh. cat. (Dijon, 2004). See also Martin Rosenberg, "Rude, Sophie," in *Dictionary of Women Artists*, ed. Delia Gaze (London, 1997), vol. 2, pp. 1206–8, and Mary Vidal, "The 'Other Atelier': Jacques-Louis David's Female Students," in *Women, Art and the Politics of Identity in Eighteenth-Century Europe*, ed. Melissa Lee Hyde and Jennifer Milam (Aldershot, 2003), pp. 254–56, 258.

2. On the episode involving *The Farewell of Telemachus and Eucharis*, see Geiger, *Sophie Rude*, pp. 147–50. See also Helmut Engelhart, "The Early History of Jacques-Louis David's 'The Farewell of Telemachus and Eucharis,'" *The J. Paul Getty Museum Journal* 24 (1996), pp. 21–43, which reproduces the David on p. 22, fig. 1, and the Rude copy on p. 32, fig. 11.

3. The false attribution was first noted in 1825, when an article in a Brussels newspaper objected that a lithographic reproduction had incorrectly identified the portrait as the work of David. Nevertheless, the *Portrait of Wolf* was exhibited throughout most of the twentieth century as a David. The painting was reattributed to Rude with the publication of Antoine Schnapper, "Portrait de Wolf, dit Bernard," in *1770–1830: Autour du néo-classicisme en Belgique*, ed. Denis Coekelberghs and Pierre Loze, exh. cat. (Ixelles, 1985), p. 421, cat. no. 415. I was directed to this source by Geiger, *Sophie Rude*, pp. 61 and 154. See also Philippe Bordes, *Jacques-Louis David: Empire to Exile*, exh. cat. (New Haven, 2005), pp. 352–53, n. 6.

4. The location of the Rude painting is given as "private collection" in Engelhart, "Early History," p. 132.

5. See Louis de Fourcaud, *François Rude, sculpteur: Ses œuvres et son temps (1784–1855)* (Paris, 1904).

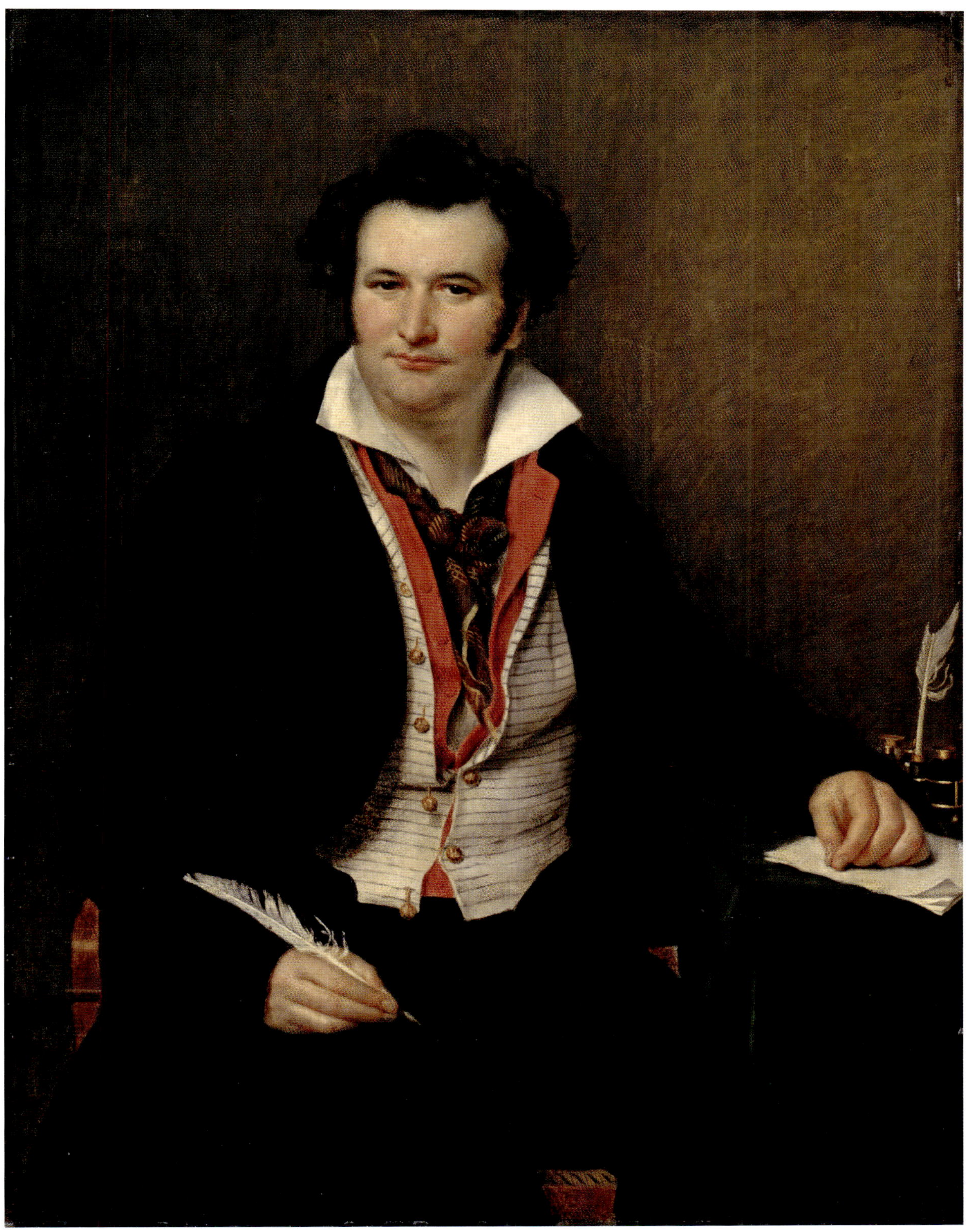

CAT. 54. SOPHIE RUDE (1797–1867), *Bernard Wolf (1778–1850), Author, Actor, and Director of the Théâtre de la Monnaie, Brussels*, before 1823. Oil on canvas. Musée du Louvre, Département des peintures, Paris

Louise Joséphine Sarazin de Belmont

(Versailles, 1790 – Paris, 1870)

LOUISE JOSÉPHINE SARAZIN DE BELMONT was one of a number of women who established careers as landscape painters in the early and middle years of the nineteenth century.[1] Sarazin de Belmont was born in Versailles in the early months of the French Revolution to Amable-Joseph Prevost, wife of Claude-François Sarazin de Belmont, a commissioner in the War Administration.[2] We do not know how the artist's family fared during the Revolution, but her father apparently lived long enough to receive a pension from Napoléon.[3]

Sarazin de Belmont's teacher was Pierre-Henri Valenciennes (1750–1819), whose influential treatise on landscape painting was first published in 1800.[4] Her paintings follow the precepts outlined by Valenciennes, who urged students to create "landscape portraits" by studying nature on-site and faithfully recording its appearance before returning to the studio to ennoble their firsthand observations through a process of selection and idealization. Evidence of both stages of this process are on view in the present exhibition, which includes two marine studies by Sarazin de Belmont (cats. 56, 57), seemingly completed on-site, and two finished paintings that nonetheless retain the flavor of their locales: *View of Saint-Pol-de-Léon* (cat. 55), on France's northwest coast, and *Naples, View from Posilipo* (cat. 10).

Although many women who painted landscapes captured views close to home, Sarazin de Belmont was a frequent traveler. In the course of her eighty years she journeyed to Italy, Sicily, Switzerland, the Pyrenees, Brittany, Fontainebleau, and elsewhere. These trips yielded a prodigious number of sketches that served as the basis for the paintings, drawings, and lithographs that she exhibited at Salons in Paris, Lille, Douai, Cambrai, and Valenciennes between 1812 and 1868, and at the Exposition universelle held in Paris in 1867. In addition, her work was seen at three or more public sales during her lifetime, held in 1829, 1839, and 1859.[5] Her 1831 and 1834 Salon offerings received medals, and her work was well received by the critics of the era.

Notes

1. On the female landscapists of the early- and mid-nineteenth century, including Sarazin de Belmont, see Gen Doy, *Women and Visual Culture in Nineteenth-Century France, 1800–1852* (London and New York, 1998), pp. 85–91. Other sources consulted for this biography include Émile Bellier de la Chavignerie, *Dictionnaire général des artistes de l'école française depuis l'origine des arts du dessin jusqu'à nos jours* (1882–85; rpr., Paris, 1997), vol. 2, pp. 463–64; E. Bénézit, *Dictionnaire critique et documentaire des peintres, sculpteurs, dessinateurs, et graveurs de tous les temps et de tous les pays par un groupe d'écrivains spécialistes français et étrangers*, new ed. (Paris, 1999), vol. 12, pp. 415–16; *La femme artiste: D'Élisabeth Vigée-Lebrun à Rosa Bonheur*, exh. cat. (Mont-de-Marsan, 1981), p. 53; Charles Gabet, *Dictionnaire des artistes de l'école française, au XIXᵉ siècle* (Paris, 1831), p. 623; *The Lure of Rome: Some Northern Artists in Italy in the Nineteenth Century* (London, 1979), p. 20; and Margaret A. Oppenheimer, "Women Artists in Paris, 1791–1814" (PhD diss., New York University, 1996), pp. 262–64.

2. Oppenheimer ("Women Artists," p. 262) identifies the parents.

3. Monsieur Sarazin de Belmont evidently retired on May 1, 1809, from a post as "first checker in the bureau of forage in the War Administration" and received a pension approved by Napoléon. Ernest Picard and Louis Tuetey, eds., *Unpublished Correspondence of Napoleon I Preserved in the War Archives*, trans. Louise Seymour Houghton (New York, 1913), vol. 3, p. 68.

4. *Lure of Rome*, p. 8. See also Joshua C. Taylor, ed., *Nineteenth-Century Theories of Art* (Berkeley, 1987), pp. 246–59, for a discussion and translated excerpt.

5. *Lure of Rome*, p. 22, mentions the 1829 and 1839 sales. The Frick Art Reference Library (The Frick Collection, New York) houses the catalogue of two sales of her work: "120 Études, en italie, en sicile, en suisse," held by Madame Bataillard on February 25, 1839, and "240 tableaux, dessins, croquis," offered at the Hôtel Drouot on May 2, 1859.

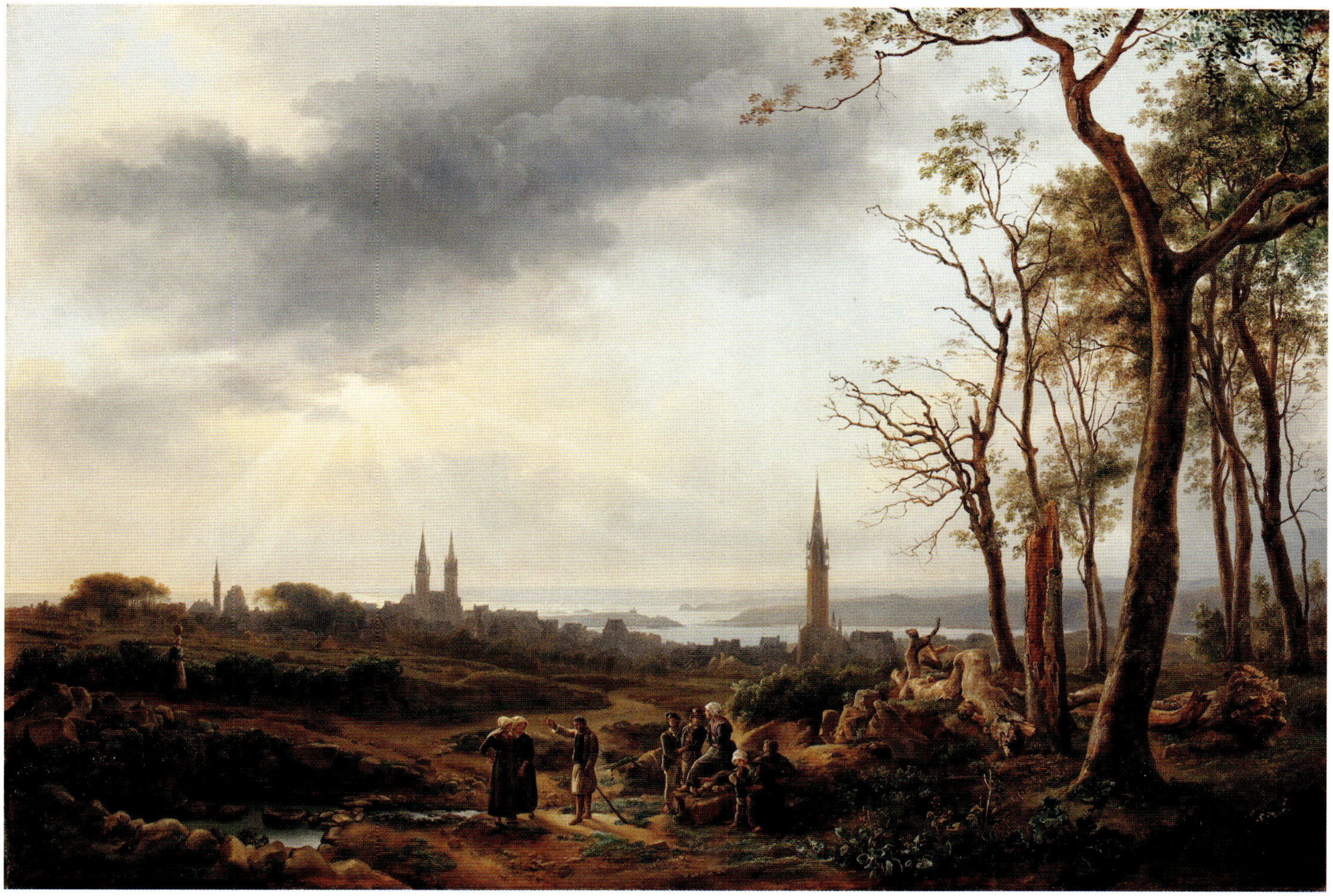

CAT. 55. LOUISE JOSÉPHINE SARAZIN DE BELMONT (1790–1870), *View of Saint-Pol-de-Léon*, 1837.
Oil on canvas. Musée des beaux-arts, Quimper

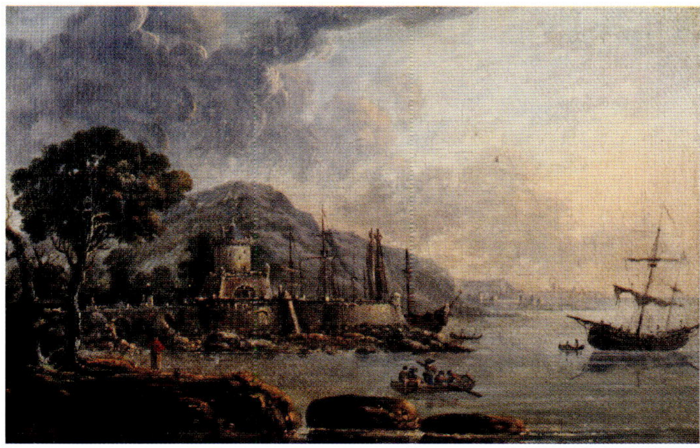

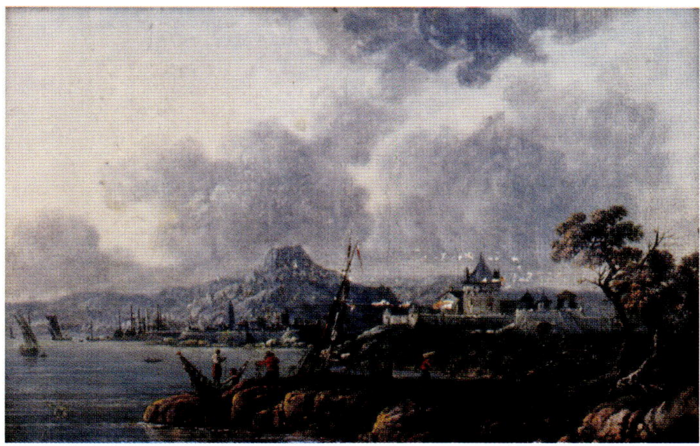

CAT. 56. LOUISE JOSÉPHINE SARAZIN DE BELMONT (1790–1870),
Marine Study, 1815/1850. Oil on canvas pasted on wood. Musée des
beaux-arts, Quimper

CAT. 57. LOUISE JOSÉPHINE SARAZIN DE BELMONT
(1790–1870), *Marine Study*, 1815/1850. Oil on canvas pasted
on wood. Musée des beaux-arts, Quimper

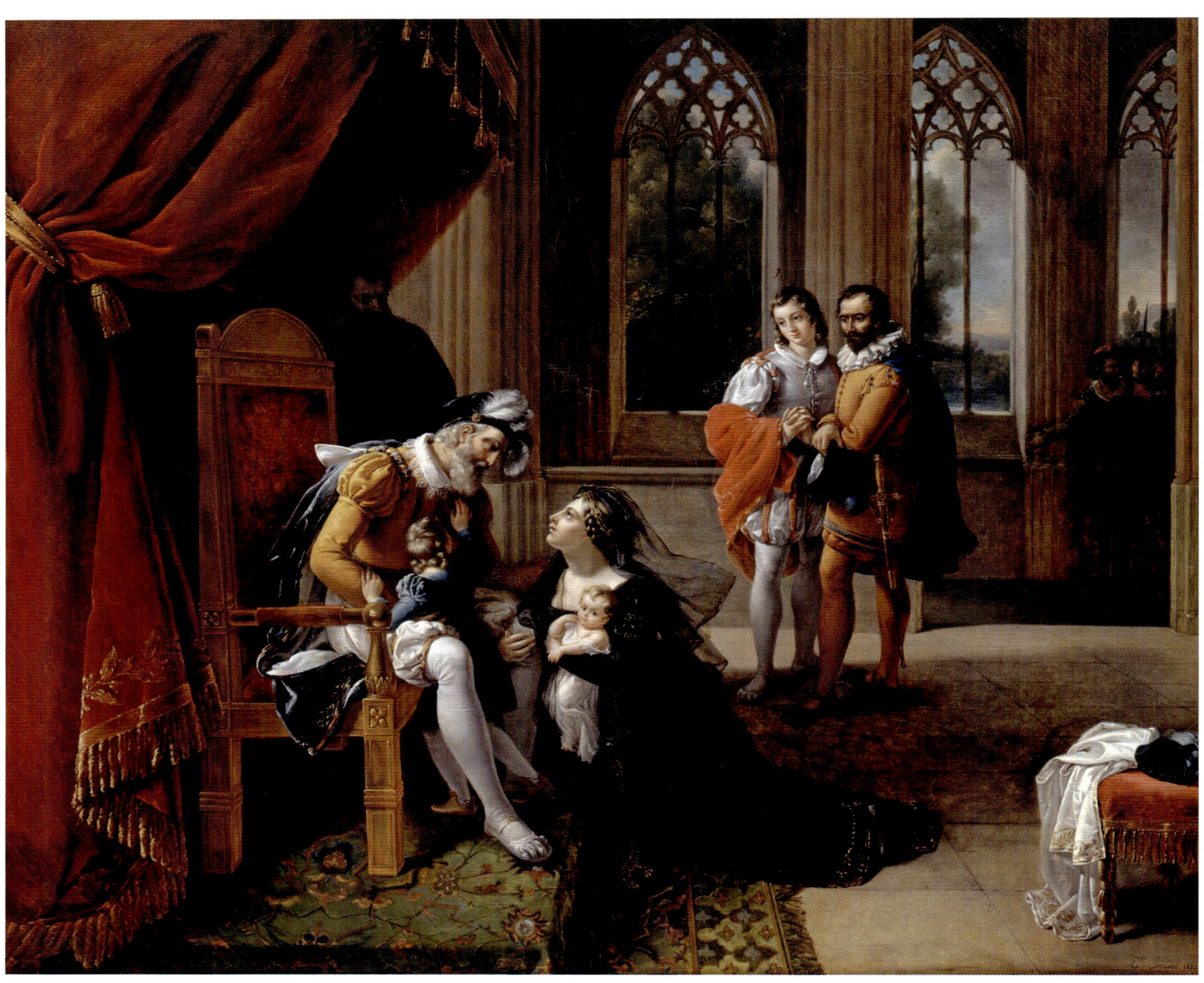

CAT. 58. EUGÉNIE SERVIÈRES (1784–1832), *Inês de Castro with Her Children at the Feet of Afonso IV, King of Portugal, Seeking Clemency for Her Husband, Don Pedro, 1335*, 1822. Oil on canvas. Musée national des châteaux de Versailles et de Trianon

Eugénie Servières, née Lethière(?)

(Paris, 1784–Paris, 1832)

EUGÉNIE SERVIÈRES was one of the many female artists who adopted the subjects and styles of Troubadour painting in the first half of the nineteenth century.[1] A student of Guillaume Lethière (1760–1832), Servières may also have been his daughter, as indicated in the Salon *livrets* of 1806 and 1808.[2] When she debuted at the 1806 Paris Salon, both she and Lethière were living in the building that before the Revolution housed the Collège des quatre-nations and that is known today as the Palais de l'Institut de France.

Servières sent only a *Portrait of a Woman at Her Piano* (Musée national des châteaux de Versailles et de Trianon) to the 1806 exhibition, but began to make her name as a painter of historical episodes at the Salon of 1808, when she displayed *Hagar in the Desert* and received a gold medal.[3] She went on to participate in every Salon held in Paris from 1812 to 1824, winning a second gold medal in 1817. She also exhibited at the Douai Salons of 1823 and 1825, and at the Lille Salon in 1825.

The present exhibition features a prime example of Servières's history paintings: *Inês de Castro with Her Children at the Feet of Afonso IV, King of Portugal, Seeking Clemency for Her Husband, Don Pedro, 1335* (1822 Salon; cat. 58). Set in a stone interior illuminated by three windows decorated with Gothic tracery, the sentimental scene depicts a tender moment in a tragic love story taken from medieval history. Inês de Castro was the beloved mistress of Don Pedro, heir to the throne of Portugal. After the death of his wife, Don Pedro angered his father, Afonso IV, by refusing to marry anyone but the Castilian Inês. Here we see Inês imploring the king to reconsider his stance, presenting him with the children she had borne to Don Pedro. As one child embraces him, Afonso bends toward the kneeling woman as though in sympathy. But Salon-goers who remembered previous written or painted versions of the tale would have known that Afonso went on to order the murder of Inês. When Don Pedro ascended to the throne, he revealed that the pair had been secretly married, and crowned her posthumously as his queen. The painting was purchased by the French government in 1825.

Notes

1. François Pupil, *Le style troubadour, ou, La nostalgie du bon vieux temps* (Nancy, 1985), pp. 501–2, discusses Servières's *Inês de Castro* as an example of the "feminine orientation" of Troubadour painting. Other sources consulted for this entry include Émile Bellier de la Chavignerie, *Dictionnaire général des artistes de l'école française depuis l'origine des arts du dessin jusqu'à nos jours* (1882–85; rpt., Paris, 1997), vol. 2, p. 498; Charles Gabet, *Dictionnaire des artistes de l'école française, au XIXe siècle* (Paris, 1831), pp. 631–32; Margaret A. Oppenheimer, "Women Artists in Paris, 1791–1814" (PhD diss., New York University, 1996), pp. 264–66; and Charlotte Yeldham, *Women Artists in Nineteenth-Century France and England* (New York, 1984), vol. 1, pp. 181–85, vol. 2, pp. 179–85.

2. We have conflicting accounts of Servières's paternity. Servières's maiden name is given as Charen in Gabet, *Dictionnaire*, p. 631, and Oppenheimer, "Women Artists," p. 264. The latter, however, notes that Servières exhibited in 1806 as "Eugénie Lethiers," and writes that "her contemporaries spoke of her as the daughter of Guillaume Guillon-Lethière.... [S]he was probably his natural daughter or stepdaughter" (p. 264). Bellier de la Chavignerie (*Dictionnaire*, vol. 2, p. 498) and Yeldham (*Women Artists*, vol. 2, p. 179) give her maiden name as Lethières. The 1806 Salon *livret* seems clear on this point, listing the artist as "Lethiers (Eugénie), student of her father." *Explication des ouvrages de peinture, sculpture, architecture et gravure, des artistes vivans, exposés au Musée Napoléon, 15 septembre 1806* (Paris, 1806), p. 69. And the 1808 *livret* presents her as "Madame Servières, née Le Thi[?]." *Explication des ouvrages de peinture, sculpture, architecture et gravure, des artistes vivans, exposés au Musée Napoléon, le 14 octobre 1808, second anniversaire de la bataille d'Iéna* (Paris, 1808), p. 84.

3. Long untraced, the painting in Versailles was attributed to Servières by Oppenheimer, "Women Artists," p. 266. It had previously been attributed to Jean-Baptiste Regnault.

Arsène Trouvé

(act. 1830s)

MADEMOISELLE ARSÈNE TROUVÉ lived at 43, rue
Hauteville, in what is now the tenth arrondissement of
Paris, where she specialized in painting on porcelain
plaques.[1] She debuted at the Paris Salon of 1831 with
a *Portrait of Élisabeth de France*, on porcelain, after an
original by Peter Paul Rubens (untraced).[2] She participated in just three more Salons, in 1833, 1834, and 1835,
showing copies of oil paintings at all of them.[3] In addition, her 1834 Salon offerings included a watercolor
rendering of a vegetable seller, which may have been an
original composition.[4]

Trouvé is represented in the current exhibition
by her *Portrait of Jean-Baptiste Deburau* (1832; cat. 59),
a painting on porcelain shown at the Salon of 1835.[5]
Based on an original by Auguste Bouquet (1810–1846),
the portrait depicts the beloved mime Jean-Gaspard
Deburau (1796–1846) in the costume of the commedia
dell'arte character Pierrot. The actor, who under the
stage name Jean-Baptiste Deburau had been performing
Pierrot at the Parisian Théâtre des Funambules for more
than a decade, was catapulted to fame in 1832 by the appearance of a book about him by the writer and critic
Jules Janin. A lithograph after the Bouquet portrait was
featured in that wildly popular book, and according to
Janin, its publication "made [Bouquet's] name." Major
figures of the Romantic movement were among those
captivated by Deburau, who is praised in the writings
of authors from Champfleury to Théophile Gautier to
Georges Sand. When Deburau died, his son donned
the white costume and was himself immortalized in a
famous series of photographs by Nadar, first exhibited
at the Exposition universelle of 1855.[6]

Notes

1. *Explication des ouvrages de peinture, sculpture, architecture,
gravure, et lithographie des artistes vivans, exposés au Musée royal,
le 1ᵉʳ mars 1834* (Paris, 1834), p. 171.

2. This work is listed as untraced in Émile Bellier de la
Chavignerie, *Dictionnaire général des artistes de l'école française
depuis l'origine des arts du dessin jusqu'à nos jours: Architectes,
peintres, sculpteurs, graveurs, et lithographes* (1882–85; rpr., Paris,
1997), vol. 2, p. 596.

3. For the list of works exhibited by Trouvé, see Bellier de
la Chavignerie, *Dictionnaire*, vol. 2, p. 596. Note, however, that
the address given by Bellier de la Chavignerie differs from that
listed in the Salon *livrets*.

4. *Explication*, p. 171.

5. Information and quote concerning the portraits of Deburau
by Trouvé and Bouquet are from Jules Gabriel Janin, *Deburau:
Histoire du théâtre à quatre sous, pour faire suite à l'histoire du
théâtre-français*, 3rd ed. (Paris, 1833), vol. 1, p. 153.

6. Nadar's photographs of Charles Deburau have received
considerable scholarly attention. See, most recently, Rebecca
Schneider, *Performing Remains: Art and War in Times of
Theatrical Reenactment* (New York, 2011), p. 150.

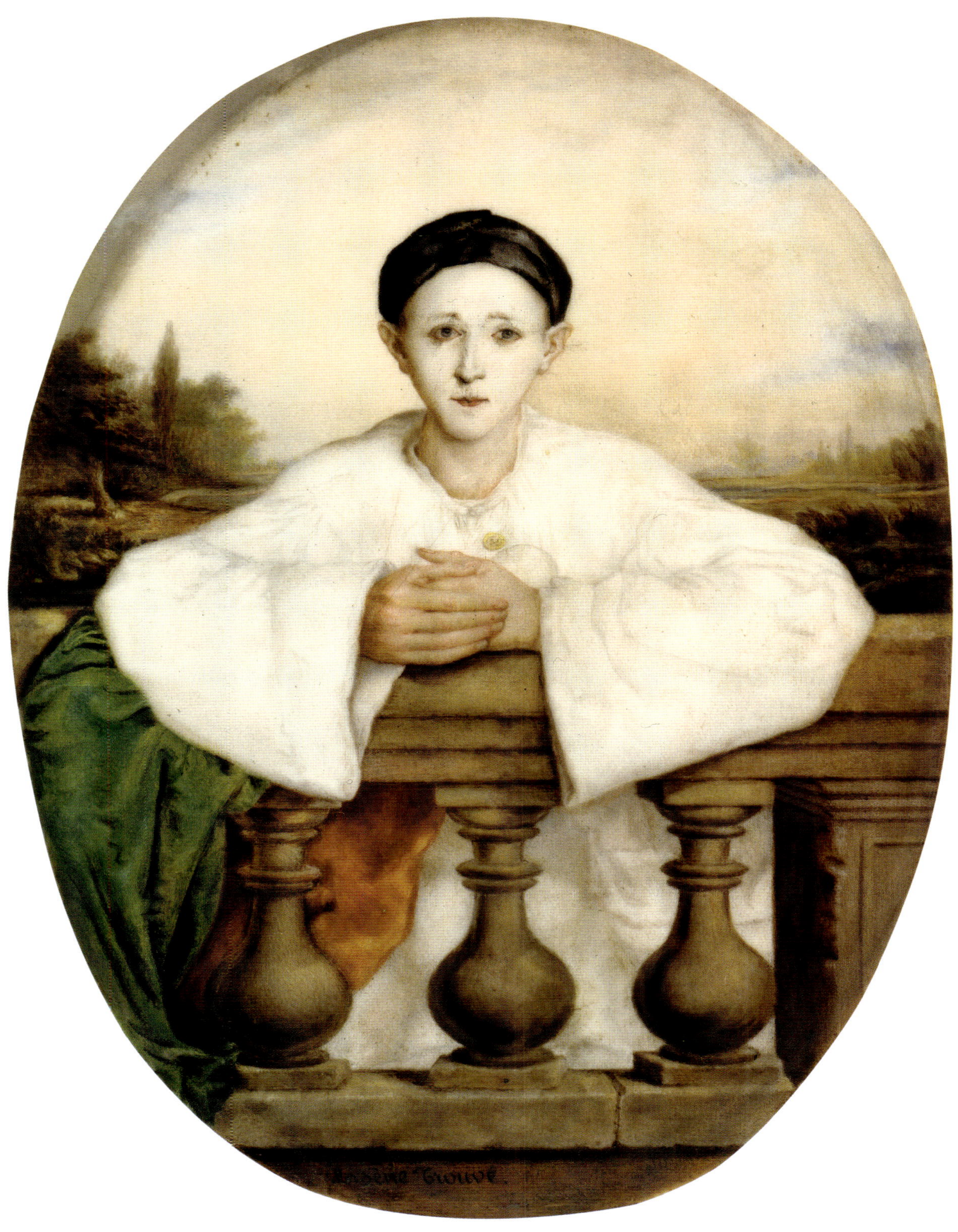

CAT. 59. ARSÈNE TROUVÉ (act. 1830s), *Portrait of Jean-Baptiste Deburau*, 1832.
Oil on porcelain. Musée Carnavalet – Histoire de Paris

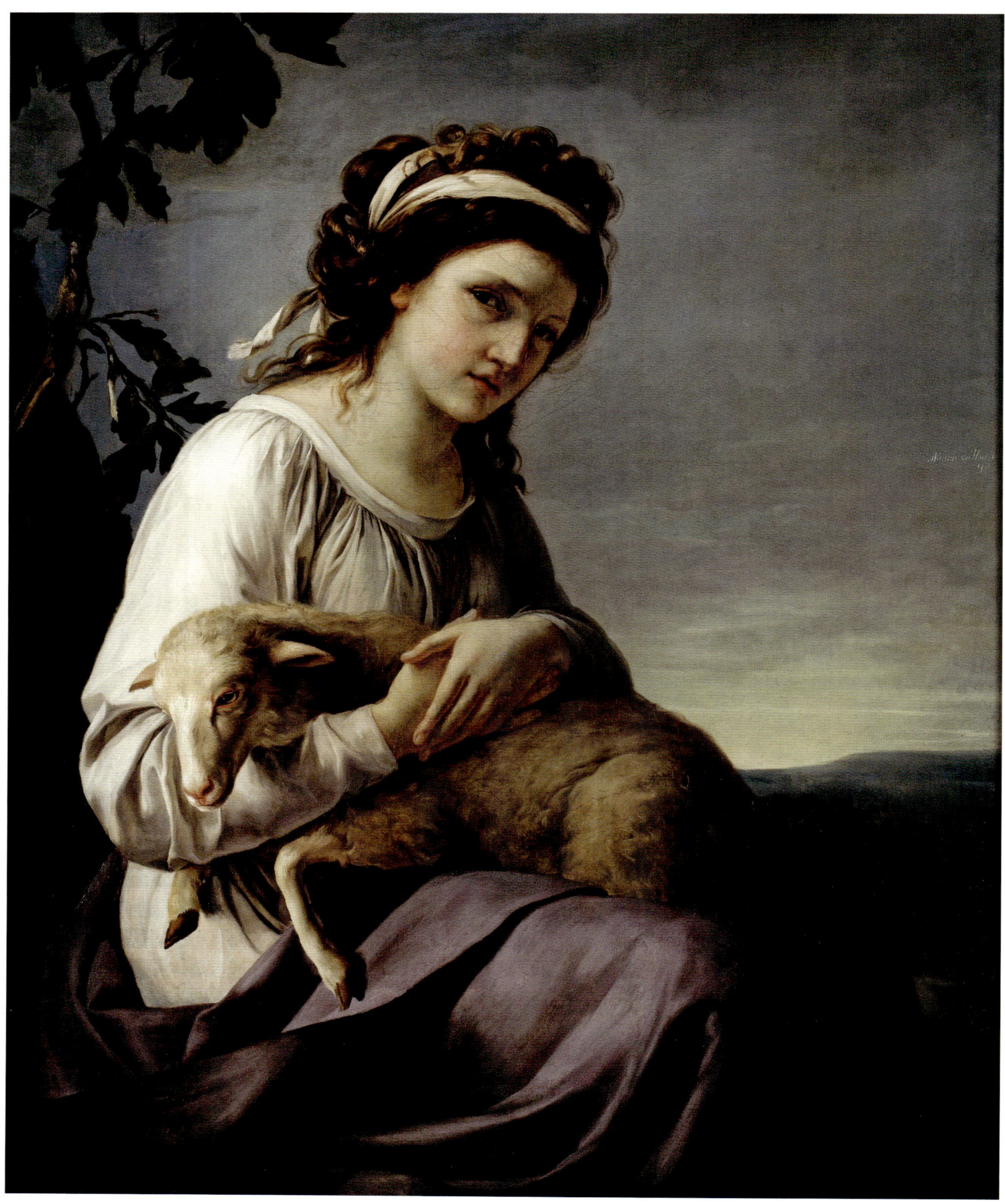

CAT. 60. NANINE VALLAIN (1767–1815), *Portrait of a Young Girl with a Lamb*, 1788.
Oil on canvas. Musée Cognacq-Jay, Paris

Nanine Vallain

(Paris, 1767–Paris, 1815)

BORN IN PARIS TO THE family of a master scribe, Nanine Vallain (sometimes called Jeanne-Louise Vallain and Madame Piètre) studied painting and drawing with Jacques-Louis David (1748–1825) and Joseph-Benoit Suvée (1743–1807).[1] Portraits, such as the *Portrait of a Young Girl with a Lamb* (1788) included in the current exhibition (cat. 60), were a mainstay of her output. She also produced genre scenes, paintings of biblical and classical history, and allegories.

Like many women artists of the late eighteenth century, Vallain first exhibited at the annual outdoor exhibition held at the place Dauphine. She debuted in 1785 with a drawing of a young draftsman (untraced), which a writer for the *Mercure de France* praised for its "spirit and truth."[2] Having few alternatives, she continued to exhibit at the place Dauphine in 1787 and 1788, and sent four paintings to the final Exposition de la jeunesse, held in the gallery of Jean-Baptiste-Pierre Le Brun (husband of Élisabeth Louise Vigée-LeBrun) in 1791.

Vallain was politically and professionally active during the Revolution. In 1793, the same year that she married Barthèlemy Piètre, she joined the short-lived Commune générale des arts, which briefly permitted female members. Her best-known work is an allegory of *Liberty* (1793–94) (Musée de la Révolution française, Vizille) featuring a seated female figure, dressed in classical attire, with her raised left arm supporting a pike topped with a liberty cap, and with a scroll of papers containing the Declaration of the Rights of Man spilling open from her right hand.[3] Although women's political activities were banned in the fall of 1793, Vallain's *Liberty* decorated the Jacobin headquarters until the club was shuttered in 1794.

From 1793 to 1810 Vallain participated regularly in the Louvre Salons. However, her work received little favorable attention from the critics of the day, and her name is absent from Charles Gabet's 1832 dictionary of nineteenth-century French artists.

Notes

1. This bibliography is based on Vivian P. Cameron, "Nanine Vallain," 2004 entry in *Dictionnaire des femmes de l'ancienne France*, http://www.siefar.org/dictionnaire/fr/Nanine_Vallain; Ute Krebs and Esmé Ward, "Vallain, Nanine," in *Dictionary of Women Artists*, ed. Delia Gaze (London, 1997), vol. 2, pp. 1387–89; and Margaret A. Oppenheimer, "Women Artists in Paris, 1791–1814" (PhD diss., New York University, 1996), pp. 270–71.

2. As quoted and translated by Krebs and Ward, "Vallain," p. 1387. Cameron, "Nanine Vallain," indicates that the work is untraced.

3. Reproduced in Philippe Bordes and Régis Michel, eds., *Aux armes et aux arts!: Les arts de la Révolution 1789–1799* (Paris, 1988), p. 124.

Anne Vallayer-Coster

(Paris, 1744 – Paris, 1818)

VALLAYER-COSTER, one of the foremost still-life painters of her day, was raised among artists and craftsmen.[1] Her father, Louis-Joseph Vallayer, was a goldsmith to the king. He apprenticed at the Gobelins manufactory, where the family lived until 1754. That Vallayer and his wife selected Madeleine Françoise Basseporte (included in this exhibition) as godmother to one of their four daughters suggests ties to a wider artistic community. Basseporte may also have instructed Anne Vallayer in the study of nature, as the landscape painter Joseph Vernet (1714 – 1789) certainly did.

Success came early. In recognition of the merit of her "paintings in the genre of flowers, fruit, bas-reliefs, [and] animals," Vallayer was admitted to the Académie royale de peinture et de sculpture in 1770.[2] Granted an apartment in the Louvre in 1779, thanks in part to the intervention of Queen Marie-Antoinette, she took up residency there in 1780. Indeed, Marie-Antoinette was one of several royal women who supported the artist. In 1779 and 1780 three aunts of Louis XVI, known as Mesdames Adélaïde, Sophie, and Victoire, sat for portraits, as did the queen herself. In 1781 Marie-Antoinette further indicated her favor when she signed the marriage contract uniting Vallayer with the attorney Jean-Pierre-Silvestre Coster.

From 1771 to 1789 Vallayer-Coster participated in every Salon, and her still lifes won consistent praise. The two examples included here typify her approach to flowers and game, respectively. *Flowers in a Glass* (cat. 16) features a vibrant array of colors and blossoms, with roses in full bloom, bending under their own weight, set against papery wildflowers in bold shades of white and red. *A Rooster and a White Chicken on a Stone Ledge* (cat. 61), exhibited in 1787 and owned by the comte d'Angiviller, offers a simpler composition, with the mir-

rored curves of the two birds' limp bodies splayed across a stone ledge in a study of light and dark.

Vallayer-Coster remained loyal to the monarchy throughout the Revolution. She was absent from the Louvre Salons from 1791 to 1795, and then exhibited only sporadically until her death. At the 1817 Salon, which was both her final exhibition and the first Salon of the Bourbon Restoration, she displayed her masterful *Still Life with Lobster* (Musée du Louvre, Paris), measuring seventy inches wide and filled with quotations from a lifetime of work. The late Marianne Roland Michel, the preeminent scholar of Vallayer-Coster, surmised that the painting may have been a gift from the artist to its owner — King Louis XVIII.[3]

Notes

1. This biography is based on the two definitive texts on the artist: Eik Kahng et al., *Anne Vallayer-Coster, Painter to the Court of Marie-Antoinette*, exh. cat. (New Haven, 2002), and Marianne Roland Michel, *Anne Vallayer-Coster (1744 – 1818)* (Paris, 1970).

2. This quote, from the *Mercure de France* of September 1770, is translated in Marianne Roland Michel, "Vallayer in Her Time," in Kahng, *Vallayer-Coster*, p. 17.

3. The work is illustrated, with provenance, exhibition history, and bibliography, in Kahng, *Vallayer-Coster*, p. 213, no. 99.

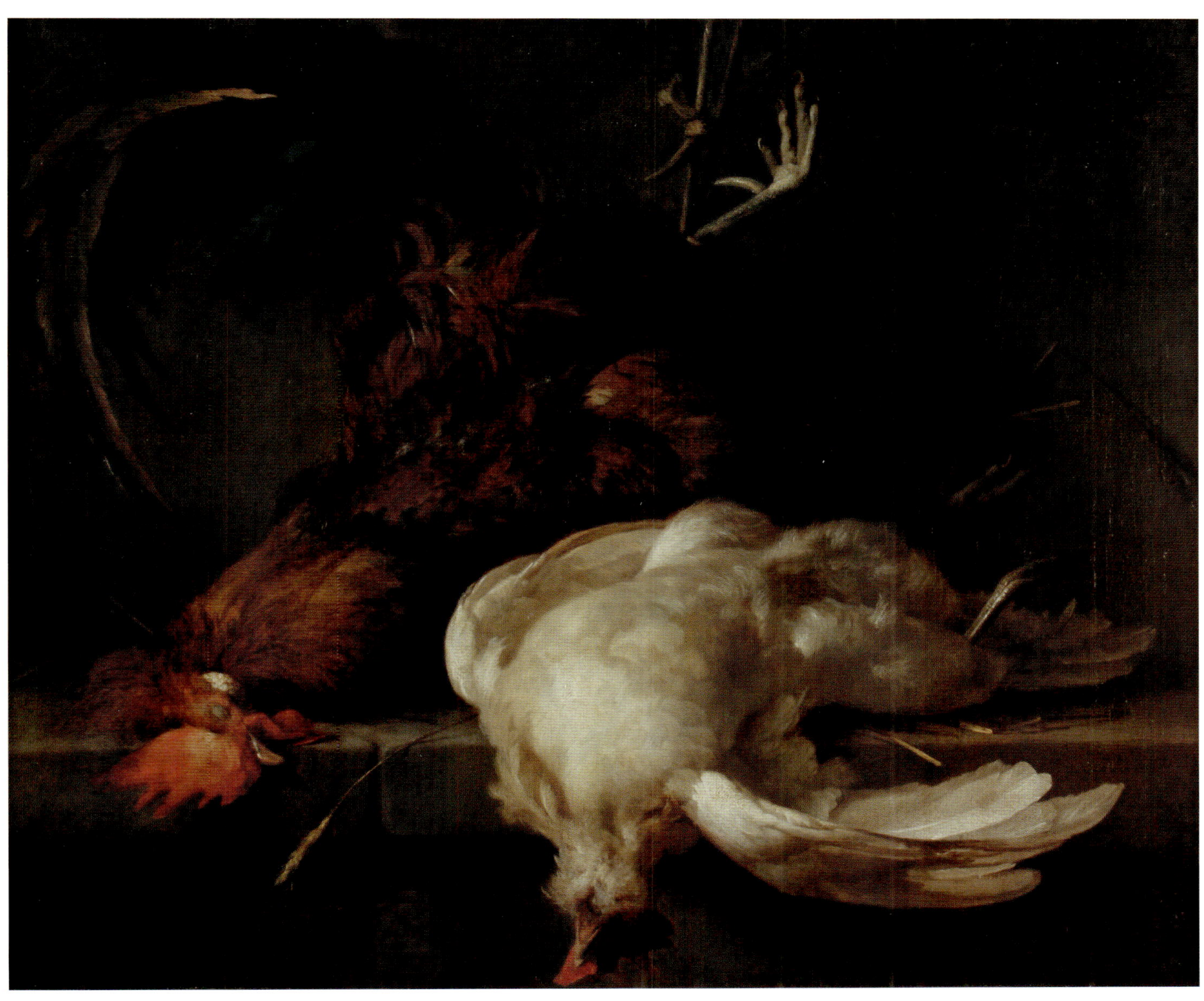

Cat. 61. Anne Vallayer-Coster (1744–1818), *A Rooster and a White Chicken on a Stone Ledge*, 1787.
Oil on canvas. Musée de Tessé, Ville du Mans

Marie Thérèse Vien

(Paris, 1728 – Paris, 1805)

A PAINTER OF NATURAL HISTORY, Marie Thérèse Vien (known also as Marie Thérèse Reboul and Madame Vien) appears to have been a student of Madeleine Françoise Basseporte, whose works accompany hers in the current exhibition (see cats. 25, 26).[1] She also learned from the history painter Joseph-Marie Vien (1716 – 1809), whom she married in 1757, and studied from 1775 to 1781 at the Accademia di San Luca, in Rome, while her husband served as the director of the Académie de France in that city.

Madame Vien was admitted to the Académie royale de peinture et de sculpture on July 30, 1757, as a "painter of miniatures and gouaches specializing in flowers, butterflies and birds."[2] Much of our information about her remains speculative, as most of her paintings are lost and few documents have come to light. We know that she exhibited small works on paper depicting birds, flowers, and butterflies at the Paris Salons of 1757, 1759, 1763, and 1767. The gouache depicting *Two Pigeons on a Tree Branch* (1762), seen in the present exhibition (cat. 62), may have been presented at the 1763 Salon.

Madame Vien's paintings, with their careful rendering of detail, were said to evince her close observation of nature. But her skill was not enough to satisfy the philosopher Denis Diderot (1713 – 1784), who granted Madame Vien only the faintest praise in the Salon reviews that he circulated to a select readership of European elites. Referring to her work, Diderot opined in 1765: "You might think that, in view of strengthening one's color skills, some study of birds and flowers wouldn't hurt. Wrong, my friend. Such imitation will never enhance one's feeling for flesh."[3] In 1767 he perceived a discrepancy between her painting of a crested hen, which he liked, and another of a pair of birds, which he found to be "like little bits of shrubbery trimmed into the shapes of canaries."[4] He concluded: "Madame Vien, you made these canaries all by yourself; as for your hen, I suspect your husband flirted with her a bit."[5]

In contrast, the engraver Charles-Nicolas Cochin (1715 – 1790) believed that Madame Vien could have earned a substantial living as a portraitist.[6] It was not lack of skill, he wrote, but the prohibition of the influential antiquarian the comte de Caylus (1692 – 1765), who protected both of the Viens, that prevented her from undertaking the more lucrative genre. As Cochin saw it, Caylus "absolutely wished that she paint only natural history."[7]

Notes

1. This biography is based largely on Émile Bellier de la Chavignerie, *Dictionnaire général des artistes de l'école française depuis l'origine des arts du dessin jusqu'à nos jours: Architectes, peintres, sculpteurs, graveurs et lithographes* (Paris, 1882), vol. 2, p. 674; Octave Fidière, *Les femmes artistes à l'Académie royale de peinture et de sculpture* (Paris, 1885), pp. 28 – 31; Melissa Lee Hyde, "Women and the Visual Arts in the Age of Marie-Antoinette," in Eik Kahng et al., *Anne Vallayer-Coster, Painter to the Court of Marie-Antoinette*, exh. cat. (New Haven, 2002), p. 310; and Charles Oulmont, *Les femmes peintres du XVIIIᵉ siècle* (Paris, 1928), pp. 57 – 58.

2. As quoted and translated in Marianne Roland Michel, "Vallayer in Her Time," in Kahng, *Anne Vallayer-Coster*, p. 14. Michel (p. 33, n. 10) gives the original as "peintre en miniature et à la gouache pour les fleurs, les papillons et les oiseaux."

3. Denis Diderot, *The Salon of 1765 and Notes on Painting*, vol. 1 of *Diderot on Art*, ed. and trans. John Goodman (New Haven, 1995), pp. 200 – 201. "Vous pourriez croire que pour se fortifier dans la couleur un peu d'étude des oiseaux et des fleurs ne nuiroit pas. Non, mon ami; jamais cette imitation ne donnera le sentiment de la chair." *Œuvres de Denis Diderot*, ed. Jacques-André Naigeon (Paris, 1798), vol. 13, p. 396.

4. Denis Diderot, *The Salon of 1767*, vol. 2 of *Diderot on Art*, ed. and trans. John Goodman (New Haven, 1995), p. 137. "Ces serins sont comme des petits morceaux de buis taillés en canaris." *Œuvres de Denis Diderot*, vol. 14, p. 278.

5. As translated by Goodman in Diderot, *Salon of 1767*, p. 137. "Madame Vien, vous avez fait ces serins-là toute seule; pour

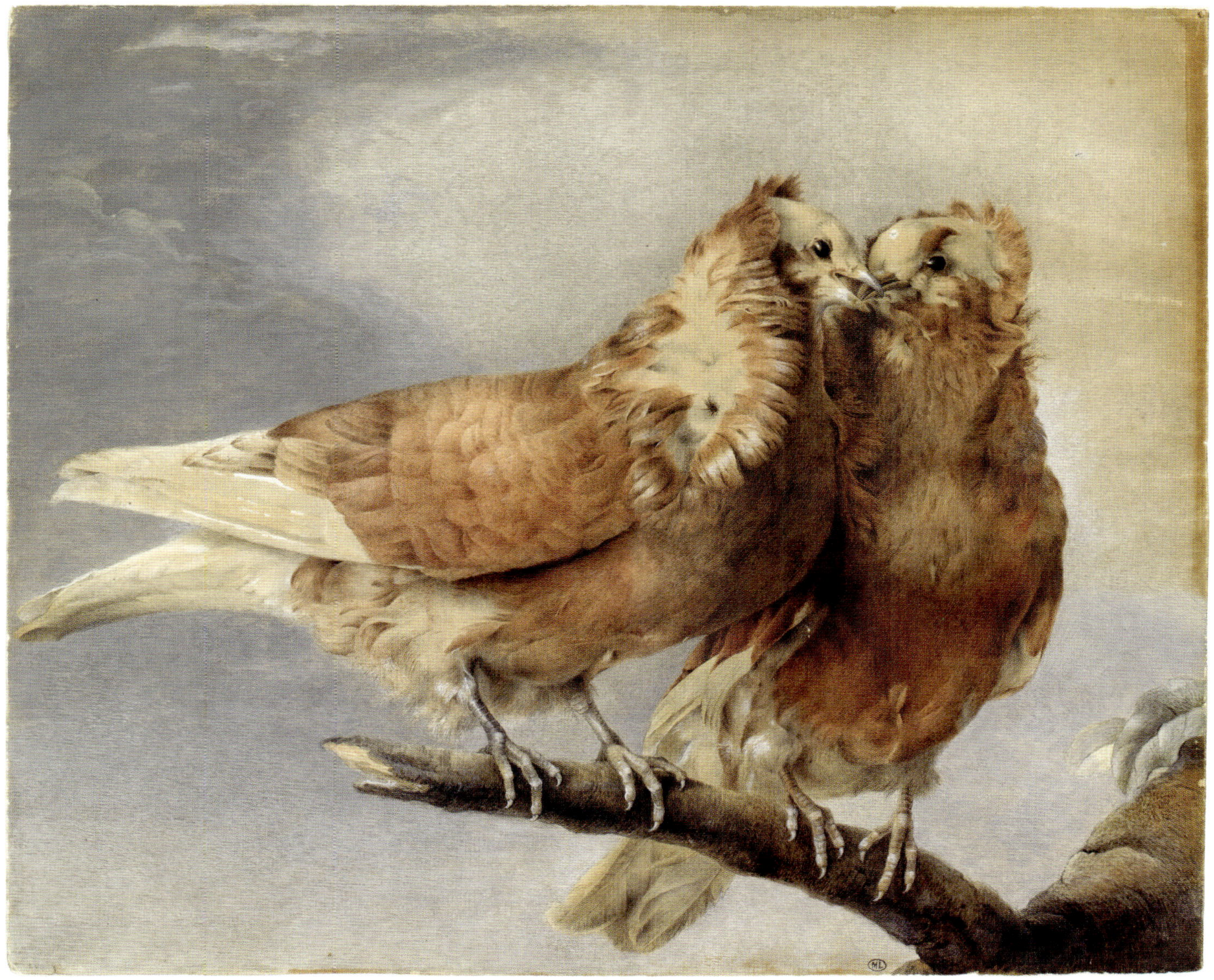

votre poule, votre mari pourroit bien l'avoir un peu coquetée." *Œuvres de Denis Diderot*, vol. 14, p. 278.

6. Charles Henry, ed., *Mémoires inédits de Charles-Nicolas Cochin sur le comte de Caylus, Bouchardon, les Slodtz* (Paris, 1880), p. 67. I was directed to this source by Hyde. "Women and the Visual Arts," p. 10.

7. Henry, *Mémoires inédits de Cochin*, p. 67: "Mme Vien…n'osa jamais entreprendre de s'attacher à peindre des têtes, ce qui lui auroit pu valoir beaucoup d'argent, dans la crainte d'irriter M. de Caylus, qui vouloit absolument qu'elle ne fît que de l'histoire naturelle."

Élisabeth Louise Vigée-LeBrun

(Paris, 1755 – Paris, 1842)

ÉLISABETH LOUISE VIGÉE-LEBRUN was one of the most celebrated painters of pre-Revolutionary Paris and is today the best-known female artist of her generation.[1] Her first instructor was her father, Louis Vigée (1715 – 1767), who specialized in pastel portraits and taught in the Académie de Saint-Luc. Famously precocious, she had established her own studio by 1770 — the year she turned fifteen — and joined the Académie de Saint-Luc in 1774, sending works in both pastels and oils to the organization's exhibition that year.

A 1776 marriage to the painter and prominent art dealer Jean Baptiste Pierre Le Brun (1748 – 1813) yielded both opportunities and complications. Through her husband, Vigée-LeBrun enjoyed access to important art collections in France and abroad; her painting style particularly reflects exposure to such seventeenth-century Flemish masters as Anthony Van Dyck and Peter Paul Rubens. That she had married into the art market would be held against her, however, when she sought membership in the Académie royale de peinture et de sculpture in 1783: academicians were prohibited from engaging in commerce. In the end, the support of Queen Marie-Antoinette trumped such concerns. Vigée-LeBrun was admitted to the Académie on May 31, 1783, the same day as Adélaïde Labille-Guiard, who is also included in this exhibition.

Vigée-LeBrun first painted Marie-Antoinette in 1778, the same year that she produced the portrait of the landscape painter and academician Joseph Vernet (1714 – 1789) on view in the present exhibition (cat. 23). Images of the queen regularly featured among the portraits and allegorical paintings that Vigée-LeBrun sent to the Louvre Salons of the 1780s. A staunch monarchist, Vigée-LeBrun wisely fled France with her daughter, Julie, shortly after the outbreak of Revolutionary violence in 1789. Her husband remained in France and divorced her in absentia in 1794, gaining control of her sizable assets.

For the next sixteen years Vigée-LeBrun would tour the courts of Europe. Feted in Florence, Rome, Naples, Vienna, Saint Petersburg, London, and other cities throughout the Continent, she returned to France in 1805 having painted a vast number of stunning portraits of the international aristocracy. Her travels constitute some of the most compelling moments in her unreliable but charming *Souvenirs*, first published between 1835 and 1837 and reprinted in many editions and translations since her death in 1842.

Note

1. Vigée-LeBrun has received more scholarly attention than any other artist included in this exhibition. For three very different approaches, see Joseph Baillio, *Elisabeth Louise Vigée Le Brun, 1755 – 1842*, exh. cat. (Fort Worth, 1982); Gita May, *Elisabeth Vigée Le Brun: The Odyssey of an Artist in an Age of Revolution* (New Haven, 2005); and Mary D. Sheriff, *The Exceptional Woman: Elisabeth Vigée-Lebrun and the Cultural Politics of Art* (Chicago, 1996).

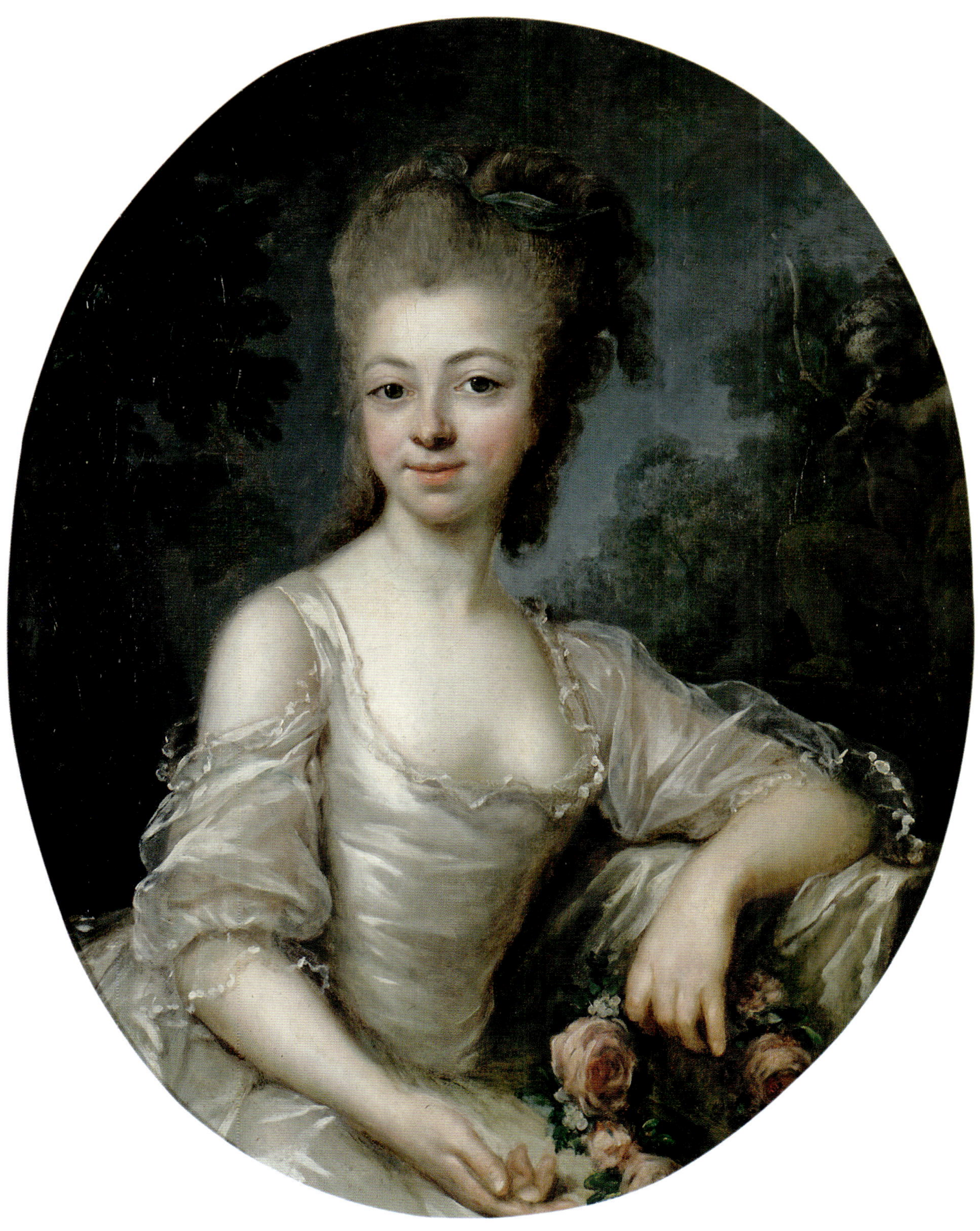

CAT. 63. ÉLISABETH LOUISE VIGÉE-LEBRUN (1755–1842), *Portrait of a Young Girl*, 1775.
Oil on canvas. Musée des beaux-arts, Caen

PAULINE AUZOU (1775–1835)

The Arrival at Compiègne of Empress Marie-Louise, 1810
Oil on canvas
44⅛ × 59⅛ in. (112.2 × 150.2 cm)
Musée national des châteaux de Versailles et de Trianon

MADELEINE FRANÇOISE BASSEPORTE (1701–1780)

Patella, 1747
Red chalk on paper
16½ × 11 in. (42 × 28 cm)
Bibliothèque centrale du Muséum national d'histoire
naturelle, Paris

Pectinidae, 1747
Red chalk on paper
16½ × 11 in. (42 × 28 cm)
Bibliothèque centrale du Muséum national d'histoire
naturelle, Paris

Purpura persica, 1747
Red chalk on paper
16½ × 11 in. (42 × 28 cm)
Bibliothèque centrale du Muséum national d'histoire
naturelle, Paris

Conus, 1749
Red chalk on paper
16½ × 11 in. (42 × 28 cm)
Bibliothèque centrale du Muséum national d'histoire
naturelle, Paris (inv. 3027, fol. 10)

Conus, 1749
Red chalk on paper
16½ × 11 in. (42 × 28 cm)
Bibliothèque centrale du Muséum national d'histoire
naturelle, Paris (inv. 3027, fol. 12)

Cypraea, 1749
Red chalk on paper
16½ × 11 in. (42 × 28 cm)
Bibliothèque centrale du Muséum national d'histoire
naturelle, Paris

Cypraea tigris, 1749
Red chalk on paper
16½ × 11 in. (42 × 28 cm)
Bibliothèque centrale du Muséum national d'histoire
naturelle, Paris

Two Varieties of Queen Scallops, 1749
Red chalk on paper
16½ × 11 in. (42 × 28 cm)
Bibliothèque centrale du Muséum national d'histoire
naturelle, Paris

Cypraea, mid-18th century
Red chalk on paper
16½ × 11 in. (42 × 28 cm)
Bibliothèque centrale du Muséum national d'histoire
naturelle, Paris

Cypraea, 1760
Red chalk on paper
16½ × 11 in. (42 × 28 cm)
Bibliothèque centrale du Muséum national d'histoire
naturelle, Paris

Oliva, 1760
Red chalk on paper
16½ × 11 in. (42 × 28 cm)
Bibliothèque centrale du Muséum national d'histoire
naturelle, Paris

Oliva, 18th century
Red chalk on paper
16½ × 11 in. (42 × 28 cm)
Bibliothèque centrale du Muséum national d'histoire
naturelle, Paris

Spondylus, 18th century
Red chalk on paper
16½ × 11 in. (42 × 28 cm)
Bibliothèque centrale du Muséum national d'histoire
naturelle, Paris

Terebra, 18th century
Red chalk on paper
16½ × 11 in. (42 × 28 cm)
Bibliothèque centrale du Muséum national d'histoire
naturelle, Paris

MARIE GUILHELMINE BENOIST (1768–1826)

Portrait of Napoléon, 1809
Oil on canvas
96 × 67 in. (243.9 × 170.3 cm)
Musées d'Angers

Reading from the Bible, 1810
Oil on canvas
51¼ × 38⅝ in. (130.2 × 98.2 cm)
Musée de Louviers

The Consultation, or The Fortune-Teller, 1812
Oil on canvas
76⅞ × 56¾ in. (195.2 × 144.2 cm)
Musée de la ville, Saintes

MARIE GENEVIÈVE BOULIAR (1763–1825)

*Portrait of Monsieur Olive, Treasurer of the Legislative
Assembly of Brittany, with His Family*, 1791/1792
Oil on canvas
57⅛ × 44½ in. (145.2 × 113.2 cm)
Musée des beaux-arts, Nantes

Aspasia, 1794
Oil on canvas
64 × 50 in. (162.7 × 127 cm)
Musée des beaux-arts, Arras

Portrait of Adélaïde Binard, Wife of Alexandre Lenoir,
ca. 1796
Oil on canvas
32⅜ × 24½ in. (82.2 × 62 cm)
Musée Carnavalet–Histoire de Paris

HENRIETTE JACOTTE CAPPELAERE (act. 1846–59)

Ham, the Dog of Louis-Napoléon, 1850
Oil on canvas
23⅝ × 28¾ in. (60 × 73 cm)
Musée national du château de Compiègne

*Portrait of Elisabeth-Ann Haryett, Called Miss Harriet
Howard, Wife of Trelawny, comtesse de Beauregard*, 1850
Oil on canvas
51½ × 38⅝ in. (130.7 × 98.2 cm)
Musée national du château de Compiègne

CONSTANCE MARIE CHARPENTIER (1767–1849)

Melancholy, 1801
Oil on canvas
51 × 65 in. (129.7 × 165.2 cm)
Musée de Picardie, Amiens

JULIE CHARPENTIER (1770–1843)

Bust of Domenico Zampieri (1581–1641), 1818
Marble
25⅝ × 22½ × 11 in. (65.2 × 57 × 28 cm)
Musée du Louvre, Département des sculptures, Paris

MARIE-AMÉLIE COGNIET (1798–1869)

Studio Interior, 2nd quarter of 19th century
Oil on canvas
12⅝ × 15¾ in. (32.2 × 40 cm)
Palais des beaux-arts, Lille

CÉSARINE HENRIETTE FLORE DAVIN (1773–1844)

Portrait of Askar-Khan, Ambassador from Persia, in 1808,
1808
Oil on canvas
67 × 52½ in. (170 × 133.2 cm)
Musée national des châteaux de Versailles et de Trianon

HERMINIE DEHÉRAIN (1798–1839)

Portrait of Antonin Moine, 1833
Oil on canvas
24⅞ × 21 in. (63 × 53.2 cm)
Musée national des châteaux de Versailles et de Trianon

ROSE ADÉLAÏDE DUCREUX (1761–1802)

Portrait of the Artist, ca. 1799
Oil on canvas
69⅜ × 50⅞ in. (176.2 × 129.2 cm)
Musée des beaux-arts, Rouen

FÉLICIE DE FAUVEAU (1801–1886)

*Letter Opener in the Shape of a Dagger (of the Grand
Duchess Maria Nikolaevna?)*, ca. 1850
Steel, gold, oxidized silver
2 × 13¾ in. (5 × 35 cm)
Musée du Louvre, Département des objets d'art, Paris

ANNE ROSALIE FILLEUL (1752–1794)

Louis-Antoine d'Artois, duc d'Angoulême (1775–1844),
ca. 1785
Oil on canvas
21⅜ × 17⅜ in. (54.2 × 44 cm)
Musée national des châteaux de Versailles et de Trianon

MARGUERITE GÉRARD (1761–1837)

Honoring the Genius of Franklin, 1778
Etching
21⅛ × 15¾ in. (53.7 × 40 cm)
Cliché Bibliothèque nationale de France, Paris

Presumed Portrait of Jean-Jacques Lagrenée, ca. 1787
Oil on zinc
7¼ × 5⅜ in. (18.4 × 13.5 cm)
Musée Cognacq-Jay, Paris

Portrait of Claude-Nicolas Ledoux, 1787–90
Oil on wood
8½ × 6⅜ in. (21.7 × 16.2 cm)
Musée Cognacq-Jay, Paris

Presumed Portrait of Mesdames Tallien and Récamier,
1795–1800
Oil on canvas
21¾ × 17½ in. (55.2 × 44.5 cm)
Musée des beaux-arts, Bordeaux

Young Woman and Child, 1799
Oil on canvas
25¼ × 21 in. (64.2 × 53.2 cm)
Musée des beaux-arts, Dijon

First Steps, or The Nursing Mother, ca. 1804
Oil on panel
24⅞ × 21⅛ in. (63 × 53.7 cm)
Collections Musée Jean-Honoré Fragonard, Grasse

Motherhood, 1815–20
Oil on canvas
24⅞ × 21 in. (63 × 53.2 cm)
Musée des beaux-arts, Lyon

The Drawing Lesson, or The Studio, ca. 1820
Oil on canvas
23⅜ × 19½ in. (60 × 49.7 cm)
Collections Musée Jean-Honoré Fragonard, Grasse

MARIE ÉLÉONORE GODEFROID (1778–1849)

Portrait of Jacques-Louis David (1748–1825), 1843/1848
Oil on canvas
24⅞ × 20½ in. (63 × 52.2 cm)
Musée national des châteaux de Versailles et de Trianon

ADRIENNE MARIE LOUISE GRANDPIERRE-DEVERZY
(1798–1869)

The Studio of Abel de Pujol, 1822
Oil on canvas
37⅞ × 50⅞ in. (96.2 × 129.2 cm)
Musée Marmottan Monet, Paris

The Studio of Abel de Pujol, 1836
Oil on canvas
37½ × 53⅛ in. (95 × 134.9 cm)
Musée des beaux-arts, Valenciennes

ANTOINE CÉCILE HORTENSE HAUDEBOURT-LESCOT
(1784–1845)

The Kissing of the Feet in St. Peter's, Rome, 1812
Oil on canvas
58⅜ × 77¼ in. (148.2 × 196.2 cm)
Château de Fontainebleau

The Miller, His Son, and the Ass, ca. 1820
Oil on canvas
16⅛ × 12⅞ in. (41 × 32.7 cm)
Musée Jean de La Fontaine, Château-Thierry

Self-Portrait, 1825
Oil on canvas
29⅛ × 23⅝ in. (74 × 60 cm)
Musée du Louvre, Département des peintures, Paris

Portrait of Claude, comte de Choiseul, 1835
Oil on canvas
28¾ × 22½ in. (73 × 57 cm)
Musée national des châteaux de Versailles et de Trianon

The Capture of Thionville, 1837
Oil on canvas
34¼ × 46 in. (87 × 117 cm)
Musée national des châteaux de Versailles et de Trianon

LOUISE MARIE JEANNE HERSENT (1784–1862)

The Good Mother, ca. 1815
Oil on canvas
25⅝ × 21⅜ in. (65.2 × 54.2 cm)
Château-Musée de Dieppe

ADÉLAÏDE LABILLE-GUIARD (1749–1803)

Portrait of the Actor Brizard in the Role of King Lear, 1783
Pastel on canvas
38⅝ × 31½ in. (98.2 × 80.2 cm)
Collection Théâtre national de l'Odéon, Paris

Portrait of Ducis, 1783
Pastel on canvas
39⅞ × 32 in. (101.2 × 81.2 cm)
Collections de la Comédie-Française, Paris

Portrait of a Woman, 1787
Oil on canvas
39¾ × 32⅛ in. (100.9 × 81.7 cm)
Musée des beaux-arts, Quimper

Portrait of Charles-Amédée-Philippe van Loo, 4th quarter
of 18th century
Oil on canvas
51¼ × 38⅝ in. (130.2 × 98.2 cm)
Musée national des châteaux de Versailles et de Trianon

JEANNE PHILIBERTE LEDOUX (1767–1840)

Portrait of a Young Girl, 1st half of 19th century
Oil on canvas
18⅛ × 15 in. (46 × 38.2 cm)
Musée des beaux-arts, Pau

MARIE VICTOIRE LEMOINE (1754–1820)

Portrait of the Artist, ca. 1780/1790
Oil on canvas
45⅛ × 34½ in. (114.7 × 87.5 cm)
Musée des beaux-arts, Orléans

HENRIETTE LORIMIER (1775–1854)

Portrait of Nicolas Lupot, 1805
Oil on canvas
23⅝ × 19½ in. (60 × 49.7 cm)
Musée de la lutherie et de l'archèterie française,
Mirecourt

Portrait of François-Charles-Hugues-Laurent Pouqueville (1770–1838), 1830
Oil on canvas
35⅞ × 29⅛ in. (91 × 74 cm)
Musée national des châteaux de Versailles et de Trianon

Portrait of Madame de Marjolin, née Duval, 2nd quarter of 19th century
Oil on canvas
22 × 18⅛ in. (56 × 46 cm) (unframed)
29⅝ × 25⅞ in. (75.3 × 65.7 cm) (framed)
Musée des beaux-arts, Grenoble

CATHERINE LUSURIER (1752–1781)

Portrait of Jean Le Rond d'Alembert, 1777
Oil on canvas
39 × 32 in. (99.2 × 81.2 cm)
Musée Carnavalet – Histoire de Paris

The Painter Germain-Jean Drouais at Age Fifteen, 1778
Oil on canvas
31½ × 25¼ in. (80 × 64 cm)
Musée du Louvre, Département des peintures, Paris

CONSTANCE MAYER (1775–1821)

The Dream of Happiness, 1st quarter of 19th century
Oil on canvas
52 × 72½ in. (132.2 × 184 cm)
Musée du Louvre, Département des peintures, Paris

ANGÉLIQUE MONGEZ (1776–1855)

Mars and Venus, 1841
Oil on canvas
8 ft. 1 in. × 9 ft. 10 in. (246.5 × 299.8 cm)
Musées d'Angers

EULALIE MORIN (1765–1837)

Portrait of Madame Récamier (1777–1849), 4th quarter of 18th century
Oil on canvas
45⅜ × 34⅜ in. (115.2 × 87.2 cm)
Musée national des châteaux de Versailles et de Trianon

ADÈLE ROMANY (1769–1846)

Portrait of the Artist's Father, 4th quarter of 18th century
Oil on canvas
23¼ × 19 in. (59 × 73.5 cm)
Musée national des châteaux de Versailles et de Trianon

Portrait of Mademoiselle Raucourt, of the Opéra-Comique, 1812
Oil on canvas
28¾ × 23⅝ in. (73 × 60 cm)
Collections de la Comédie-Française, Paris

SOPHIE RUDE (1797–1867)

Bernard Wolf (1778–1850), Author, Actor, and Director of the Théâtre de la Monnaie, Brussels, before 1823
Oil on canvas
49¼ × 33½ in. (125 × 85.2 cm)
Musée du Louvre, Département des peintures, Paris

LOUISE JOSÉPHINE SARAZIN DE BELMONT (1790–1870)

Marine Study, 1815/1850
Oil on canvas pasted on wood
5½ × 8⅜ in. (13.8 × 21.2 cm)
Musée des beaux-arts, Quimper

Marine Study, 1815/1850
Oil on canvas pasted on wood
5½ × 8½ in. (13.8 × 21.4 cm)
Musée des beaux-arts, Quimper

View of Saint-Pol-de-Léon, 1837
Oil on canvas
24½ × 35¾ in. (62 × 90.8 cm)
Musée des beaux-arts, Quimper

Naples, View from Fosilipo, 1842–59
Oil on canvas
54½ × 77½ in. (138.5 × 196.7 cm)
Musée des Augustins, Toulouse

EUGÉNIE SERVIÈRES (1784–1832)

Inês de Castro with Her Children at the Feet of Afonso IV,
King of Portugal, Seeking Clemency for Her Husband,
Don Pedro, 1335, 1822
Oil on canvas
44½ × 54¾ in. (113.2 × 139 cm)
Musée national des châteaux de Versailles et de Trianon

ARSÈNE TROUVÉ (act. 1830s)

Portrait of Jean-Baptiste Deburau, 1832
Oil on porcelain
10⅝ × 7⅜ in. (27 × 18.7 cm)
Musée Carnavalet–Histoire de Paris

NANINE VALLAIN (1767–1815)

Portrait of a Young Girl with a Lamb, 1788
Oil on canvas
39 × 31¾ in. (99.2 × 80.7 cm)
Musée Cognacq-Jay, Paris

ANNE VALLAYER-COSTER (1744–1818)

A Rooster and a White Chicken on a Stone Ledge, 1787
Oil on canvas
21⅜ × 25¼ in. (54.2 × 64.2 cm)
Musée de Tessé, Ville du Mans

Flowers in a Glass, end of 18th century
Oil on canvas
13 × 9½ in. (33.2 × 24 cm) (unframed)
Musée des beaux-arts, Carcassonne

MARIE THÉRÈSE VIEN (1728–1805)

Two Pigeons on a Tree Branch, 1762
Watercolor brush and pen and ink heightened with
white
12¼ × 14⅞ in. (31 × 37.7 cm)
Musée du Louvre, Département des arts graphiques,
Paris

ÉLISABETH LOUISE VIGÉE-LEBRUN (1755–1842)

Portrait of a Young Girl, 1775
Oil on canvas
30 × 24⅞ in. (76 × 63 cm) (unframed)
Musée des beaux-arts, Caen

Portrait of Joseph Vernet, 1778
Oil on canvas
36¼ × 28⅜ in. (92 × 72 cm)
Musée du Louvre, Département des peintures, Paris

Head of a Young Girl, n.d.
Charcoal on gray paper, heightened with white
11 × 8⅛ in. (28 × 20.7 cm)
Musée du Louvre, Département des arts graphiques,
Paris

Selected Bibliography

Compiled by Laura Auricchio and Jenny Florence

Allgemeines Künstlerlexikon: Die bildenden Künstler aller Zeiten und Völker. 69 vols. Munich, 1992–.

Arbaud, Léon. "Mademoiselle Godefroid." *Gazette des beaux-arts*, 2nd ser., 1 (1869), pp. 38–52, 512–22.

Ashmore, Helen. "Catherine Lusurier (1752–81): A Woman Painter in Eighteenth-Century Paris." *Apollo* 153, no. 471 (May 2011), pp. 34–40.

Auricchio, Laura. *Adélaïde Labille-Guiard: Artist in the Age of Revolution*. Los Angeles, 2009.

———. "Pahin de la Blancherie's Commercial Cabinet of Curiosity (1779–87)." *Eighteenth-Century Studies* 36, no. 1 (Fall 2002), pp. 47–61.

———. "Portraits of Impropriety: Adélaïde Labille-Guiard and the Careers of Professional Women Artists in Late Eighteenth-Century Paris." PhD diss., Columbia University, 2000.

———. "Self-Promotion in Adélaïde Labille-Guiard's 1785 *Self-Portrait with Two Students*." *The Art Bulletin* 89, no. 1 (March 2007), pp. 45–62.

Baillio, Joseph. "Une artiste méconnue, Rose Adélaïde Ducreux." *L'œil* 399 (October 1988), pp. 20–27.

———. *Elisabeth Louise Vigée Le Brun, 1755–1842*. Exh. cat. Fort Worth, 1982.

———. "Vie et œuvre de Marie Victoire Lemoine (1754–1820)." *Gazette des beaux-arts*, 6th ser., 127 (January 1996), pp. 125–64.

Ballot, Marie-Juliette. *Une élève de David, la comtesse Benoist, l'Émilie de Demoustier, 1768–1826*. Paris, 1914.

Barbotte, Juliette. "La dague de Félicie de Fauveau." *La revue du Louvre et des musées de France* 33, no. 2 (1983), pp. 122–25.

Batissier, Louis. "Mme Dehérain." *L'artiste*, ser. 2, 3, no. 1 (1839), pp. 72–73.

Bellier de la Chavignerie, Émile. *Dictionnaire général des artistes de l'école française depuis l'origine des arts du dessin jusqu'à nos jours: Architectes, peintres, sculpteurs, graveurs et lithographes*. 2 vols. Paris, 1882–85.

———. *Dictionnaire général des artistes de l'école française depuis l'origine des arts du dessin jusqu'à nos jours: Architectes, peintres, sculpteurs, graveurs et lithographes*. 2 vols. 1882–85. Reprint, Paris, 1997.

Bénézit, E. *Dictionary of Artists*. 14 vols. Paris, 2006.

———. *Dictionnaire critique et documentaire des peintres, sculpteurs, dessinateurs, et graveurs de tous les temps et de tous les pays par un groupe d'écrivains spécialistes français et étrangers*. New ed. 14 vols. Paris, 1999.

Blumenfeld, Carole. "Marguerite Gérard et la peinture de genre de la fin des années 1770 aux années 1820." PhD diss., Université de Lille 3, 2011.

———. "Marguerite Gérard et ses portraits de société." In *Marguerite Gérard: Artiste en 1789*, pp. 17–40.

Bordes, Philippe. *Jacques-Louis David: Empire to Exile*. Exh. cat. New Haven, 2005.

Bordes, Philippe and Régis Michel, eds. *Aux armes et aux arts!: Les arts de la Révolution 1789–1799*. Librairie du bicentenaire de la Révolution française. Paris, 1988.

Brem, Anne-Marie de. *Louis Hersent, 1777–1860: Peintre d'histoire et portraitiste*. Exh. cat. Paris, 1993.

Cameron, Vivian P. "Jeanne Marie Catherine Desmarquest." 2004 entry. In *Dictionary of Women in Pre-Revolutionary France*.

———. "Nanine Vallain." 2004 entry.
In *Dictionnaire des femmes de l'ancienne France*.

———. "Woman as Image and Image-Maker in Paris
during the French Revolution." PhD diss., Yale
University, 1983.

Chatelus, Jean. *Peindre à Paris au XVIIIe siècle*. Nîmes, 1991.

*Citizens and Kings: Portraits in the Age of Revolution,
1760–1830*. Exh. cat. London, 2007.

Constans, Claire. *Musée national du château de Versailles:
Les peintures*. Introduction by Jean-Pierre Babelon.
3 vols. Paris, 1995.

Denton, Margaret Fields. "A Woman's Place:
The Gendering of Genres in Post-Revolutionary
French Painting." *Art History* 21, no. 2 (June 1998),
pp. 219–46.

Dictionary of Women in Pre-Revolutionary France.
http://www.siefar.org/dictionnaire/en.

Dictionnaire des femmes de l'ancienne France.
http://www.siefar.org/dictionnaire/fr.

Diderot, Denis. *The Salon of 1765 and Notes on Painting*.
Vol. 1 of *Diderot on Art*. Edited and translated by
John Goodman. New Haven, 1995.

———. *The Salon of 1767*. Vol. 2 of *Diderot on Art*. Edited
and translated by John Goodman. New Haven, 1995.

Doy, Gen. "Hidden from Histories: Women History
Painters in Early Nineteenth-Century France."
In *Art and the Academy in the Nineteenth Century*,
edited by Rafael Cardoso Denis and Colin Trodd,
pp. 71–85. Manchester, 2000.

———. *Women and Visual Culture in Nineteenth-Century
France, 1800–1852*. London and New York, 1998.

Duncan, Carol. "Happy Mothers and Other New Ideas
in French Art." *The Art Bulletin* 55, no. 4 (December
1973), pp. 570–83.

Easterday, Anastasia. "'Labeur, Honneur, Douleur':
Sculptors Julie Charpentier, Félicie de Fauveau,
and Marie d'Orléans." *Woman's Art Journal* 18, no. 2
(Fall 1997-Winter 1998), pp. 11–16.

*Encyclopédie des gens du monde: Répertoire universel des
sciences, des lettres et des arts; Avec des notices sur les
principales familles historiques et sur les personnages
célèbres, morts et vivans*. Paris, 1840.

*Explication des ouvrages de peinture, sculpture, architecture
et gravure, des artistes vivans, exposés au Musée Napoléon,
le 15 septembre 1806*. Paris, 1806.

*Explication des ouvrages de peinture, sculpture, architecture
et gravure, des artistes vivans, exposés au Musée Napoléon,
le 14 octobre 1808, second anniversaire de la bataille d'Jéna.*
Paris, 1808.

*Explication des ouvrages de peinture, sculpture, architecture
et gravure, des artistes vivans, exposés au Musée Napoléon,
le 5 novembre 1810*. Paris, 1810.

*Explication des ouvrages de peinture, sculpture, gravure,
lithographie et architecture exposés au Musée royal,
le 1er mai 1831*. Paris, 1831.

*Explication des ouvrages de peinture, sculpture, architecture
et gravure, des artistes vivans, exposés au Musée royal
des arts, le 24 avril 1817*. Paris, 1817.

*Explication des ouvrages de peinture, sculpture, architecture,
gravure et lithographie des artistes vivants, exposés au
Palais national, le 26 décembre 1850*. Paris, 1850.

*Explication des ouvrages de peinture, sculpture, architecture
et gravure exposés au salon du Louvre*. Paris, 1793.

La femme artiste: D'Élisabeth Vigée-Lebrun à Rosa Bonheur.
Exh. cat. Mont-de-Marsan, 1981.

Fidière, Octave. *Les femmes artistes à l'Académie royale
de peinture et de sculpture*. Paris, 1885.

Fine, Amy M. "Césarine Davin-Mirvault: 'Portrait of
Bruni' and Other Works by a Student of David."
Woman's Art Journal 4, no. 1 (Spring-Summer 1983),
pp. 15–20.

Fourcaud, Louis de. *François Rude, sculpteur: Ses œuvres et son temps (1784–1855)*. Paris, 1904.

French Painting, 1774–1830: The Age of Revolution. Exh. cat. Detroit, 1975.

Gabet, Charles. *Dictionnaire des artistes de l'école française, au XIXᵉ siècle: Peinture, sculpture, architecture, gravure, dessin, lithographie et composition musicale*. Paris, 1831.

Gaze, Delia, ed. *Dictionary of Women Artists*. 2 vols. London, 1997.

Geiger, Monique. *Sophie Rude, peintre et femme de sculpteur: Une vie d'artiste au XIXᵉ siècle (Dijon–Bruxelles–Paris)*. Exh. cat. Dijon, 2004.

Godineau, Dominique. *The Women of Paris and Their French Revolution*. Translated by Katherine Streip. Studies on the History of Society and Culture 26. Berkeley, 1998.

Govier, Louis. "Bouliar, Marie-Geneviève." In Gaze, *Dictionary of Women Artists*, vol. 1, pp. 295–97.

———. "Contemplating Contradictions: Re-Viewing Marie-Geneviève Bouliar's *Aspasie*.' *Objet* 1 (1998–99), pp. 23–44.

Greer, Germaine. *The Obstacle Race: The Fortunes of Women Painters and Their Work*. New York, 2001.

Guffey, Elizabeth E. *Drawing an Elusive Line: The Art of Pierre-Paul Prud'hon*. Newark, DE, 2001.

Guiffrey, J. J. "Écoles de demoiselles dans les ateliers de David et de Suvée au Louvre." In *Nouvelles archives de l'art français*, pp. 394–401. Paris, 1874–75.

Hamy, Ernest Théodore. "Julie Charpentier, sculpteur et préparateur de zoologie (1770–1845)." *Bulletin du Muséum d'histoire naturelle* 5, no. 7 (November 28, 1899), pp. 329–34.

Harris, Ann Sutherland and Linda Nochlin. *Women Artists, 1550–1950*. Exh. cat. New York, 1976.

Havice, Christine. "In a Class by Herself: 19th Century Images of the Woman Artist as Student." *Woman's Art Journal* 2, no. 1 (Spring-Summer 1981), pp. 35–40.

Heim, Jean-François, Claire Béraud, and Philippe Heim. *Les salons de peinture de la Révolution française, 1789–1799*. Paris, 1989.

Heller, Nancy. *Women Artists: Works from the National Museum of Women in the Arts*. Washington, D.C., 2000.

Hyde, Melissa Lee. "Under the Sign of Minerva: Adélaïde Labille-Guiard's *Portrait of Madame Adélaïde*." In Hyde and Milam, *Women, Art and the Politics of Identity in Eighteenth-Century Europe*, pp. 139–63.

———. "Women and the Visual Arts in the Age of Marie-Antoinette." In Kahng, *Anne Vallayer-Coster*, pp. 75–93.

Hyde, Melissa Lee and Jennifer Milam, eds., *Women, Art and the Politics of Identity in Eighteenth-Century Europe*. Women and Gender in the Early Modern World. Aldershot, 2003.

Jackall, Yuriko. "Recovering the Work of Marie-Geneviève Bouliar (1763–1825): The Invention of Self in Revolutionary France." *Cahiers de l'histoire de l'art* 7 (2009), pp. 48–60.

Jal, Augustin. *Dictionnaire critique de biographie et d'histoire: Errata et supplément pour tous les dictionnaires historiques d'après des documents authentiques inédits*. Paris, 1867.

———. *Esquisses, croquis, pochades, ou, Tout ce qu'on voudra, sur le salon de 1827*. Paris, 1828.

———. *Salon de 1833: Les causeries du Louvre*. Paris, 1833.

Jeannerat, Carlo. "L'auteur du portrait de Vestris II, Adèle de Romance, et son mari, le miniaturiste François-Antoine Romany." *Bulletin de la Société de l'histoire de l'art français* (1923), pp. 52–63.

Jeffares, Neil. *Dictionary of Pastellists before 1800*. Online edition, updated May 18, 2010, http://www.pastellists.com.

Jouin, Henry. *Mademoiselle Marie-Geneviève Bouliard.* Paris, 1891.

Kahng, Eik et al. *Anne Vallayer-Coster, Painter to the Court of Marie-Antoinette.* Exh. cat. New Haven, 2002.

Lapauze, Henri, ed. *Procès-verbaux de la Commune générale des arts de peinture, sculpture, architecture et gravure de la Société populaire et républicaine des arts.* Paris, 1903.

Lemoine-Bouchard, Nathalie. *Les peintres en miniature actifs en France, 1650–1850.* Paris, 2008.

The Lure of Rome: Some Northern Artists in Italy in the Nineteenth Century. London, 1979.

Maestà di Roma: D'Ingres à Degas; Les artistes français à Rome. Milan, 2003.

Mainz, Valerie. "Charpentier, Constance." In Gaze, *Dictionary of Women Artists*, vol. 1, pp. 381–82.

Marguerite Gérard: Artiste en 1789, dans l'atelier de Fragonard. Exh. cat. Paris, 2009.

May, Gita. *Elisabeth Vigée Le Brun: The Odyssey of an Artist in an Age of Revolution.* New Haven, 2005.

Mirzoeff, Nicholas. "Revolution, Representation, Equality: Gender, Genre, and Emulation in the Académie Royale de Peinture et Sculpture, 1785–93." *Eighteenth-Century Studies* 31, no. 2 (Winter 1997–98), pp. 153–74.

Moisy, Pierre. "A Pupil of Greuze: Geneviève Brossard de Beaulieu." *Gazette des beaux-arts,* 6th pér., 32 (1947), pp. 177–84.

Naginski, Erika. "Fauveau's Dame Clémence, or Personifying Romanticism." In *Early Modern Visual Allegory: Embodying Meaning,* edited by Cristelle Baskins and Lisa Rosenthal, pp. 197–216. Aldershot, 2007.

Oppenheimer, Margaret A. "'The Charming Spectacle of a Cadaver': Anatomical and Life Study by Women Artists in Paris, 1775–1815." *Nineteenth-Century Art Worldwide,* Spring 2007. http://19thc-artworldwide .org/spring_07/articles/oppe.shtml.

———. "Three Newly Identified Paintings by Marie-Guillemine Benoist." *Metropolitan Museum Journal* 31 (1996), pp. 143–50.

———. "Women Artists in Paris, 1791–1814." PhD diss., New York University, 1996.

Oulmont, Charles. *Les femmes peintres du XVIIIe siècle.* Paris, 1928.

Paccoud, Stéphane and Sylvie Ramond, eds. *Juliette Récamier, muse et mécène.* Exh. cat. Paris, 2009.

Passez, Anne-Marie. *Adélaïde Labille-Guiard: Biographie et catalogue raisonné.* Paris, 1973.

Portalis, Roger. *Adélaïde Labille-Guiard, 1749–1803.* Paris, 1902.

Pupil, François. *Le style troubadour, ou, La nostalgie du bon vieux temps.* Nancy, 1985.

Pinette, Matthieu. *From the Sun King to the Royal Twilight: Painting in Eighteenth-Century France from the Musée de Picardie, Amiens.* Exh. cat. New York, 2000.

———. *Peintures françaises des XVIIe et XVIIIe siècles des musées d'Amiens.* Paris, 2006.

Roland Michel, Marianne. *Anne Vallayer-Coster (1744–1818).* Paris, 1970.

Sainte-Beuve, M.-E. "Une portraitiste du XVIIIe siècle Catherine Lusurier." *Gazette des beaux-arts,* 5th ser., 16, no. 779 (July-August 1927), pp. 80–86.

Salmon, Xavier. *Les pastels.* Paris, 1997.

Sanchez, Pierre. *Dictionnaire des artistes exposant dans les salons des XVII et XVIIIème siècles à Paris et en province, 1673–1800.* 3 vols. Dijon, 2004.

Sazerac, Hilaire Léon. *Lettres sur le salon de 1834.* Paris, 1834.

Schiff, Gert. "The Sculpture of the 'Style Troubadour.'" *Arts Magazine* 58, no. 10 (June 1984), pp. 102–10.

Schnapper, Antoine. "Portrait de Wolf, dit Bernard." In *1770–1830: Autour du néo-classicisme en Belgique*, edited by Denis Coekelberghs and Pierre Loze, p. 421, cat. no. 415. Exh. cat. Ixelles, 1985.

Schwab-Pourbaix, Clotilde. "Marie-Éléonore Godefroid et ses portraits conservés au Musée national des châteaux de Versailles et de Trianon." *La revue des musées de France* 58, no. 5 (December 2008), pp. 63–71.

Sheriff, Mary D. *The Exceptional Woman: Elisabeth Vigée-Lebrun and the Cultural Politics of Art*. Chicago, 1996.

———. "Gérard, Marguerite." In Gaze, *Dictionary of Women Artists*, vol. 1, pp. 580–82.

———. "Jacques-Louis David and the Ladies." In *Jacques-Louis David: New Perspectives*, edited by Dorothy Johnson, pp. 90–107. Newark, DE, 2006.

———. "Lemoine, Marie-Victoire." In Gaze, *Dictionary of Women Artists*, vol. 2, pp. 836–39.

———. *Moved by Love: Inspired Artists and Deviant Women in Eighteenth-Century France*. Chicago, 2004.

Taylor, Joshua C., ed. *Nineteenth-Century Theories of Art*. Berkeley, 1987.

Thieme, Ulrich and Felix Becker, eds. *Allgemeines Lexikon der bildenden Künstler von der Antike bis zur Gegenwart*. 37 vols. Leipzig, 1907–50.

Véron-Denise, Danièle and Vincent Droguet. *Peintures pour un château: Cinquante tableaux (XVIᵉ–XIXᵉ siècle) des collections du château de Fontainebleau*. Exh. cat. Paris, 1998.

Vidal, Mary. "The 'Other Atelier': Jacques-Louis David's Female Students." In Hyde and Milam, *Women, Art and the Politics of Identity in Eighteenth-Century Europe*, pp. 237–52.

Vigée-LeBrun, Élisabeth. *The Memoirs of Elisabeth Vigée-Le Brun*. Translated by Siân Evans. London, 1989.

———. *Souvenirs*. Edited by Claudine Herrmann. 2 vols. Paris, 1986.

Waller, Susan. *The Invention of the Model: Artists and Models in Paris, 1830–1870*. Aldershot, 2006.

Waresquiel, Emmanuel de. *Une femme en exil: Félicie de Fauveau, artiste, amoureuse et rebelle*. Paris, 2010.

Weston, Helen. "The Case for Constance Mayer." *Oxford Art Journal* 3, no. 1 (April 1980), pp. 14–19.

Wettlaufer, Alexandra K. "Dibutades and Her Daughters: The Female Artist in Postrevolutionary France." *Nineteenth-Century Studies* 18 (2004), pp. 9–38.

———. *Portraits of the Artist as a Young Woman: Painting and the Novel in France and Britain, 1800–1860*. Columbus, OH, 2011.

Wildenstein, Georges. "Un tableau attribué à David rendu à Mme Davin-Mirvault: 'Le portrait du violoniste Bruni' (Frick Collection)." *Gazette des beaux-arts*, 6th ser., 59 (February 1962), pp. 93–98.

Wintermute, Alan, ed. *1789: French Art during the Revolution*. Exh. cat. New York, 1989.

Yeldham, Charlotte. *Women Artists in Nineteenth-Century France and England*. 2 vols. New York, 1984.

Photograph Credits

Bridgeman-Giraudon/Art Resource, NY, Musée Fragonard, Grasse: pp. 26, 85

Angèle Dequier: p. 106

Lysiane Gauthier: p. 3

Marc Jenneteau: p. 65

C. Lancien, C. Loisel: p. 74

François Lauginie: p. 94

B. Legros: p. 89

Patrick Lorette: p. 18

Lyon/MBA (Alain Bassett): p. 42

Hugo Maertens: p. 60

Daniel Martin: p. 20

Metropolitan Museum of Art, New York/Art Resource, NY: p. 24

Pascual photographie: p. 58

Réunion des musées nationaux/Art Resource, NY: Château de Fontainebleau: p. 86 top (Jean-Pierre Lagiewski); Musée des beaux-arts, Nantes: p. 14 (Gérard Blot); Musée des beaux-arts, Valenciennes: p. 28 (René-Gabriel Ojeda); Musée Carnavalet – Histoire de Paris: p. 44 (Bulloz); Musée Cognacq-Jay, Paris: p. 80 (Bulloz); Musée du Louvre, Paris: pp. 8 (Gérard Blot), 21 (Thierry LeMage), 47 (Jean-Gilles Berizzi), 66, 77 (Daniel Arnaudet), 99 (Franck Raux), 100 (Daniel Arnaudet), 109 (Franck Raux), 121 (Thierry LeMage); Musée national du château de Compiègne: frontispiece, pp. 63, 136 (Michel Utardo); Musée national des châteaux de Versailles et de Trianon: pp. 11 (Gérard Blot), 12 (Daniel Arnaudet/Gérard Blot), 16 (Gérard Blot), 19 (Franck Raux), 25, 52, 71, 73, 79, 83, 105, 112, back endpaper (Gérard Blot); Palais des beaux-arts, Lille: p. 68

Roger-Viollet Agency, Paris: pp. 17, 35, 80, 115, 116

Martine Seyve: p. 123

C. Sinnig-Haas: p. 86 bottom

Vladimir Terebenin, Leonard Keifets, Yuri Molodkovets: p. 38 bottom

Illustrations

Page 2: Marguerite Gérard (1761 – 1837), *Young Woman and Child*, 1799 (detail). Oil on canvas. Musée des beaux-arts, Dijon

Page 3: Marguerite Gérard (1761 – 1837), *Presumed Portrait of Mesdames Tallien and Récamier*, 1795 – 1800 (detail). Oil on canvas. Musée des beaux-arts, Bordeaux

Page 136: Henriette Jacotte Cappelaere (act. 1846 – 59), *Ham, the Dog of Louis-Napoléon*, 1850 (detail). Oil on canvas. Musée national du château de Compiègne

Front endpaper: Jacques-François Blondel (1705 – 1774), *Elevation of the Colonnade and the Main Façade of the Louvre*, 1756 (detail). Print. Musée national des châteaux de Versailles et de Trianon. Réunion des musées nationaux/Art Resource, NY

Back endpaper: Anonymous, *View of the Parterre d'eau at Versailles*, 17th century (detail). Engraving. Musée national des châteaux de Versailles et de Trianon. Réunion des musées nationaux/Art Resource, NY

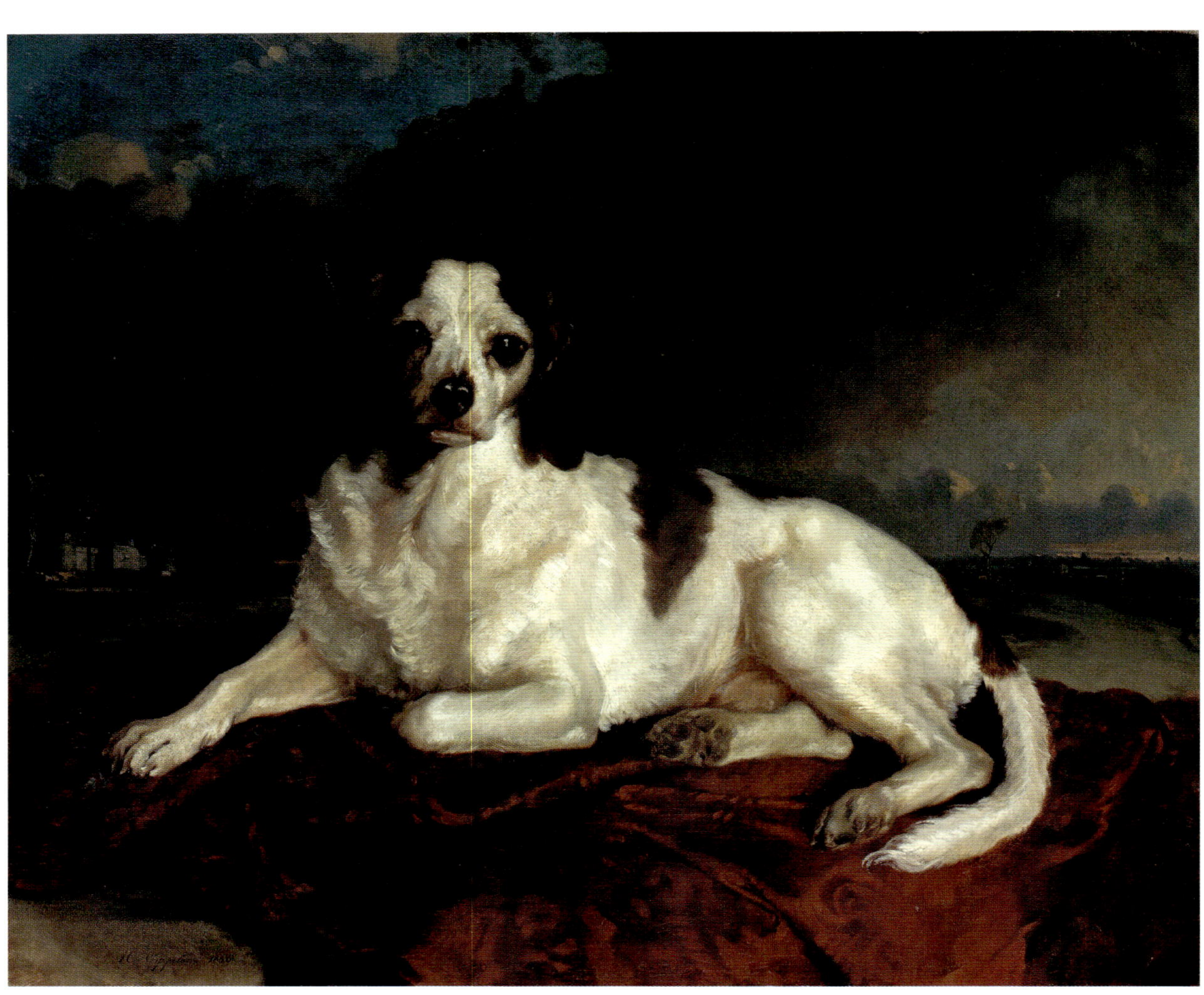

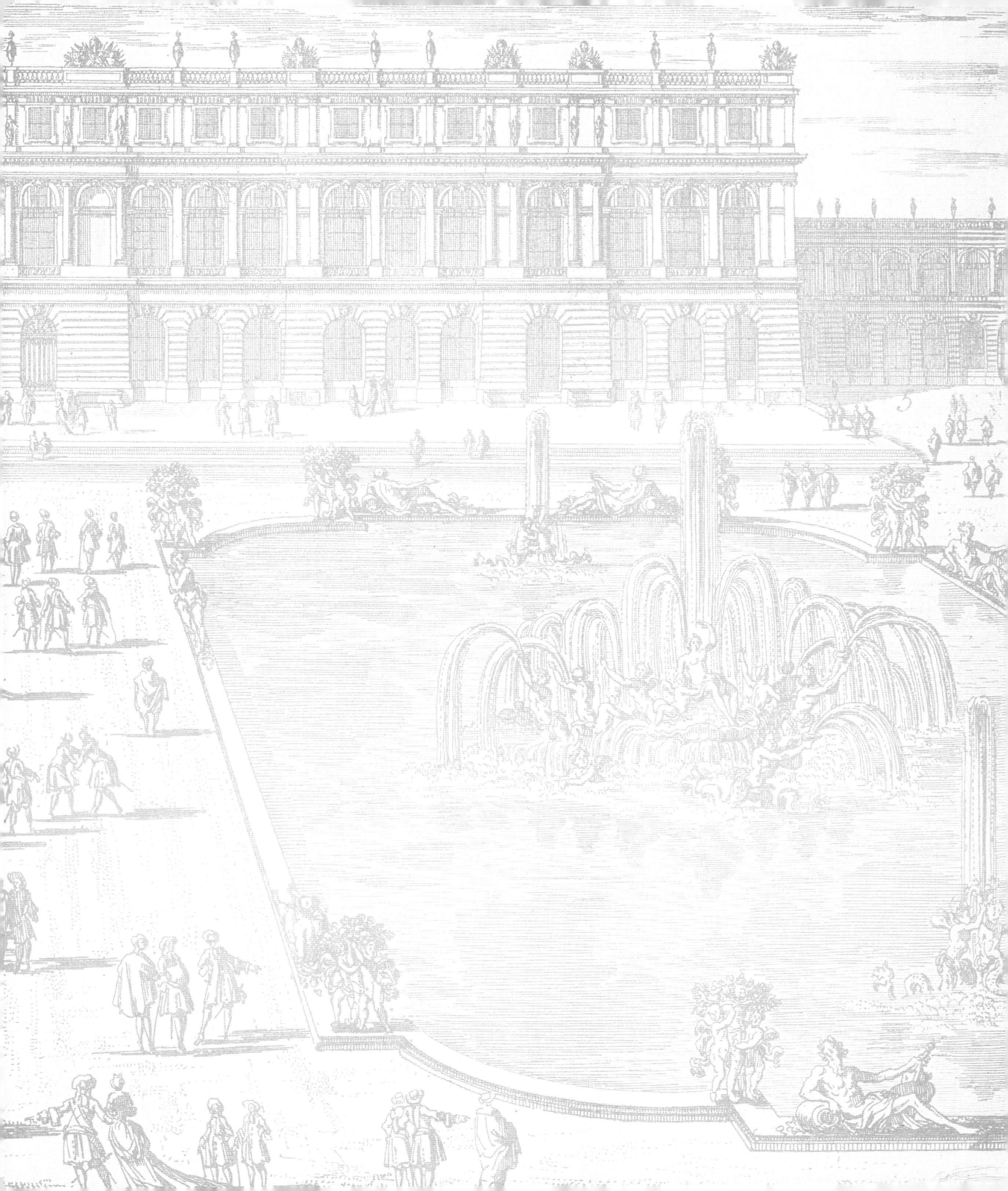

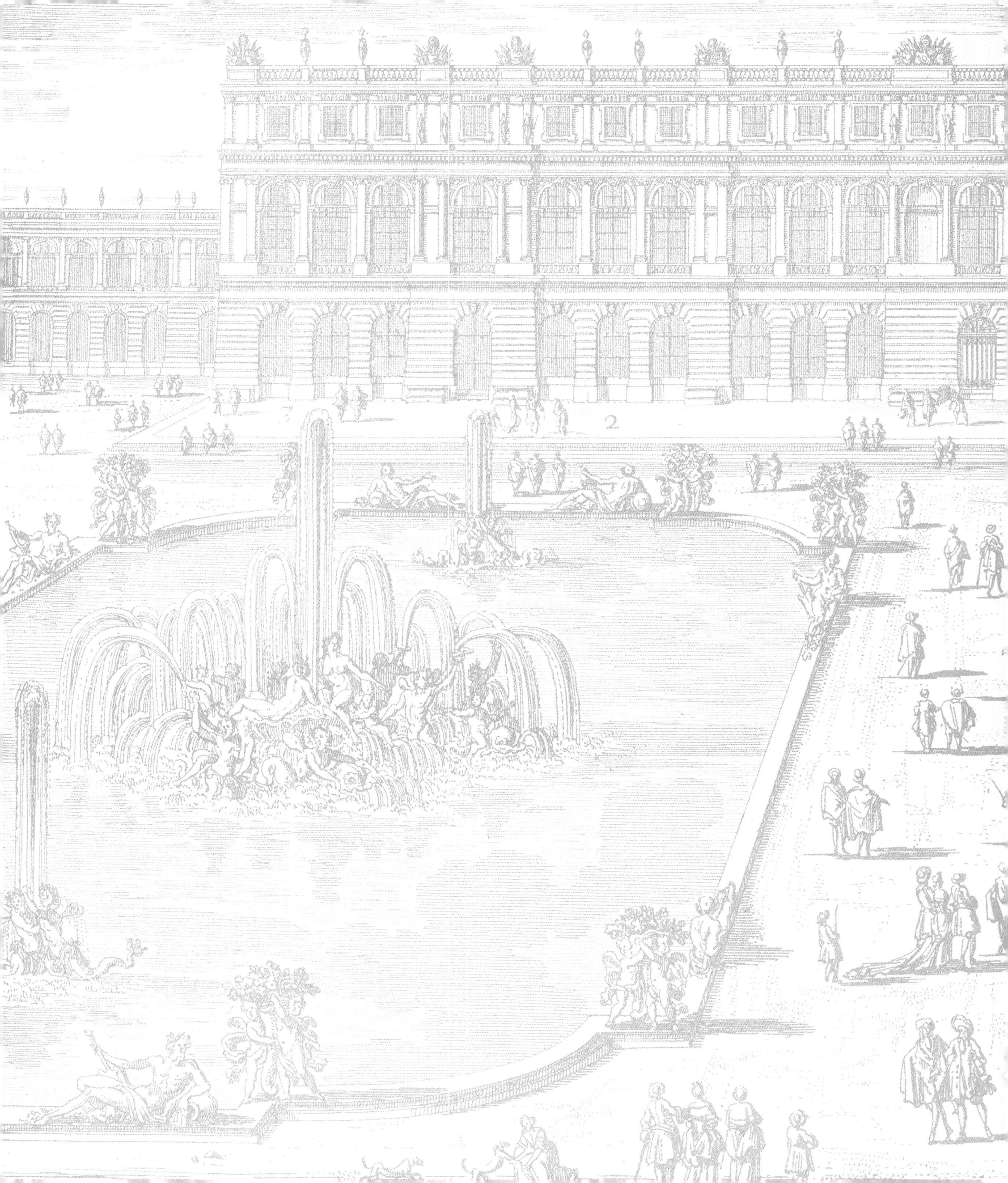
2